Retirement on the Rocks

Retirement on the Rocks

Why Americans Can't Get Ahead and How New Savings Policies Can Help

Christian E. Weller

RETIREMENT ON THE ROCKS
Copyright © Christian E. Weller 2016

All rights reserved. No reproduction, copy or transmission of this publication may be made without written permission. No portion of this publication may be reproduced, copied or transmitted save with written permission. In accordance with the provisions of the Copyright, Designs and Patents Act 1988, or under the terms of any licence permitting limited copying issued by the Copyright Licensing Agency, Saffron House, 6-10 Kirby Street, London EC1N 8TS.

Quotes leading each chapter taken from *Retirement Security 2015: Roadmap for Policy Makers: Americans' Views of the Retirement Crisis*. Biennial public opinion research conducted by the National Institute on Retirement Security and Greenwald & Associates, March 2015.

Any person who does any unauthorized act in relation to this publication may be liable to criminal prosecution and civil claims for damages.

First published 2016 by
PALGRAVE MACMILLAN

The author has asserted their right to be identified as the author of this work in accordance with the Copyright, Designs and Patents Act 1988.

Palgrave Macmillan in the UK is an imprint of Macmillan Publishers Limited, registered in England, company number 785998, of Houndmills, Basingstoke, Hampshire, RG21 6XS.

Palgrave Macmillan in the US is a division of Nature America, Inc., One New York Plaza, Suite 4500, New York, NY 10004-1562.

Palgrave Macmillan is the global academic imprint of the above companies and has companies and representatives throughout the world.

Hardback ISBN: 978–1–137–39562–7
E-PUB ISBN: 978–1–137–57515–9
E-PDF ISBN: 978–1–137–57514–2
DOI: 10.1057/9781137575142

Distribution in the UK, Europe and the rest of the world is by Palgrave Macmillan®, a division of Macmillan Publishers Limited, registered in England, company number 785998, of Houndmills, Basingstoke, Hampshire RG21 6XS.

Library of Congress Cataloging-in-Publication Data

Weller, Christian E., 1966–
    Retirement on the rocks : why Americans can't get ahead and how new savings policies can help / Christian E. Weller.
        pages cm
    Includes bibliographical references and index.
    ISBN 978–1–137–39562–7 (hardback : alk. paper)
        1. Retirement income—United States. 2. Pensions—United States. 3. Social security—United States. 4. Finance, Personal—United States. I. Title.

HD7125.W44 2015
332.024′0140973—dc23   2015021871

A catalogue record for the book is available from the British Library.

To Beth, Henry, and Georgina

CONTENTS

ILLUSTRATIONS

Figures

Tables

ACKNOWLEDGMENTS

I could have never completed this book without the help of many smart and dedicated people who inspired and guided me throughout. Particular thanks go to my wife, Beth Almeida, who encouraged me to pursue this project in the first place and who was always there for me and offered new insights when I came upon a seeming dead end, which got this book moving along again. I also owe a tremendous debt of gratitude to many experts in this field who graciously offered their insights, advice, and comments on the research that underlies this book as well as on specific chapters in it. My thanks go to Jennifer Erickson, Michael Ettlinger, Teresa Ghilarducci, Julia Gordon, Seth Hanlon, Shaun O'Brien, Heather MacIndoe, David Madland, Harry Stein, Alex Thornton, Joe Valenti, and Jeffrey Wenger. I am also very grateful to the University of Massachusetts Boston's leadership, specifically Chancellor Keith Motley, Provost Winston Langley, Dean Ira Jackson, and Professor Christine Brenner for their long-standing support to my research and this project, in particular. I am equally indebted to the support I have received from the Center for American Progress' leadership, particularly Carmel Martin, John Podesta, Neera Tanden, and Sarah Wartell, who always encouraged my work. My work on this book also greatly benefited from the enthusiasm and skills of my assistants, specifically Sara Bernardo, Jackie Odum, and Sam Ungar, as well as Michele Tolson who offered keen insights at every step along the way and who made sure the entire process went very smoothly with her sharp intellect, incredible organizational skills, and passion for people having a dignified retirement.

CHAPTER ONE

The Elusive Goal of a Secure Retirement

How would you personally define what a secure retirement means to you?[1]

"I think a pension, having a 401(k) and making sure your kids get to college." (White man, 37 years old)

"Being able to retire without seeking employment or additional income." (African American man, 63 years old)

Imagine you are on a sinking ship in a violent storm. Some passengers are outfitted with state-of-the-art survival suits and are directed to sturdy life rafts. But most passengers get tattered life vests and are told to sink or swim. Rather than reaching sunny shores, this latter group is treading water, fending for themselves. That is what retirement savings looks like for most households these days.

Savings is a key ingredient to making the American Dream a reality. Households need and want to save for a number of reasons, chief among them retirement and economic emergencies. But people also want to have savings for a down payment on a house, to start a business, and to pay for their children's education, for instance. Savings will allow people to pay their bills over time and to pursue their aspirations. Savings contribute to economic security for households, reduce demands on public safety nets during tough economic times, and strengthen economic growth. More savings is good not just for individual families but also for the nation as a whole.

Insufficient savings, on the other hand, can be devastating. A lack of emergency savings, for instance, can quickly push households into bankruptcy. The rise in personal stress associated with insufficient savings can lead to depression or divorce and even in extreme cases domestic violence.[2] Not having enough retirement savings can mean working longer in a physically demanding job in the face of debilitating medical problems or, if working is impossible, severely reducing one's spending on life's necessities.[3]

Saving enough for one's future is difficult for most people even in the best of times—when jobs are plentiful, wage growth is strong, and financial markets are stable. But in recent years, the task has only become harder. Long-term unemployment has been rising, wages have become more volatile, and boom-and-bust cycles in the stock and housing markets have become the norm, rather than the exception, over the past three decades. As a result, people have encountered mounting risks while trying to accomplish the already difficult task of saving for their future. The promise of a sunny retirement, in which people are in control of their economic destiny, is clearly out of reach, and instead households do whatever they can just to keep their heads above water.

This is not an accident but the result of fixable shortcomings in the way policy helps or does not help households to save. Just when risks have multiplied in the labor and financial markets, households increasingly have been left on their own to save more and to figure out how to manage these growing risks as best as they could.[4] Households increasingly had to save with do-it-yourself savings, such as 401(k) plans; Individual Retirement Accounts (IRAs) and housing as defined-benefit (DB) pensions have declined; and the value of Social Security's benefits has gradually decreased. At the same time, a patchwork of ineffective public policies around savings has eroded households' risk protections, making savings more and more exposed to the growing labor and financial market volatility. That is, risks and households' exposure to those risks have simultaneously increased.

This combination of growing economic risks and rising household risk exposure has had two adverse consequences. First, it has made it harder for many households to save, contributing to increasing wealth inequality. Put differently, the patchwork of US savings policies has worked well for a select few households but has left many more people without savings, and fails the majority of households in achieving their goals and ambitions.

Second, rising labor market and financial risk exposure in the face of growing labor and financial market risks has made Americans' savings more volatile. Many households fear losing their money when they need it most because of a stock or housing market crash, for instance, in the months before a planned retirement. This potential decimation of retirement savings is increasingly a very real possibility for American households.

The economic insecurity that people have lived through for the past three decades will shape their futures, too. Inadequate and more volatile savings are the twin legacies of public policies that failed to offer households meaningful protections for their savings in an increasingly insecure environment.

Without a serious rethinking of public policy to support broad-based savings, this lingering economic insecurity will rob millions of Americans of a dignified retirement, put them in serious economic harm when they experience unexpected economic emergencies, and require them to postpone homeownership and entrepreneurship, among other ambitions. Americans may be able to get by, but they will not be able to get ahead, when it comes to reaching a secure and meaningful retirement, never mind also achieving other goals. Rising wealth inequality and increasing wealth volatility means more widespread economic hardship for households, greater demand on government programs, and slower economic growth.[5]

One of the root causes of growing risk exposure is the widespread failure of savings policies in offering households meaningful risk protections for their savings. A serious rethinking of savings policies could address these shortcomings. The first step will be to understand the mechanisms by which household risk exposure has increased amid rising labor and financial market risks. Policy interventions can then address each of these mechanisms and help households gain more risk protections. This will increase savings and lower wealth uncertainty. And households will gain greater retirement income security as the primary result.

In chapters 2, 3, and 4, I offer a comprehensive, in-depth look at the combined effects of risk exposure in labor and financial markets on wealth inequality over the past three decades. I do not separate labor and financial markets in my discussion of household savings since both are integral to households' ability to build a secure future. My analysis of high-quality, nationally representative household data illustrates the linkages between risks and savings and demonstrates that risks have grown alongside risk exposure and wealth inequality. I also identify and analyze a number of key policy shortcomings in the patchwork of US savings policies in chapter 5 on Social Security; chapters 6, 7, and 8 on defined contribution (DC) retirement accounts; and chapters 9 and 10 on savings incentives and the complexities of tax-advantaged savings, which have made it increasingly difficult for households to gain meaningful risk protections with their savings. These analyses directly point to economic policy as the most relevant and most directly influential and, more importantly, changeable cause of rising wealth inequality. I discuss a range of policy solutions to address these failures in chapter 11, to assist policymakers in charting a course toward a more secure future for American families.

In this chapter, I offer some context for the issues discussed in the remainder of the book. I first discuss some of the key reasons for households to save, emphasizing that, while households save for many reasons, retirement requires the largest savings. I follow this discussion with an overview of savings instruments and a discussion of the general rationale for encouraging private savings outside of Social Security.

Reasons for Saving

Households save money for a number of reasons. First, they save for the possibility that their wages and salaries will decline or completely disappear and they will need to rely on income from their savings to pay their bills. Wages and salaries can decline, for example, when households experience an economic emergency, such as a prolonged illness, a spell of unemployment, divorce, or death of a family member. And when people retire, they typically no longer receive income from work, such as wages and salaries.[6]

Second, households save money because they often cannot get a loan for every purchase or investment they want to make. Even if they get a loan, personal savings are typically needed to supplement it. They need to put some of their own money down, for instance, when they buy a house. And they have to invest their own savings when starting or expanding a business.[7] People also often put money away to pay for their own and their children's education.

Third, households save for a number of idiosyncratic reasons. They may want to finance larger consumption in the future with the capital appreciation and interest earned on their savings. People often want to help out their aging parents and thus increase their spending to support them. Alternatively, some people want to save to leave something for their heirs or to donate to charity. Some people may simply like having lots of money for no other reason than to have it, just in case.

Middle-class households will typically need substantial amounts of savings to meet their goals. Retirement savings will by far make up the largest savings goal, although other motives such as having a down payment for a first home, paying for children's education, and having collateral for a new and expanding business can also require a lot of money. Fidelity Investments argues that "eight times ending salary" is a standard rule of thumb for households wanting to have an income in retirement equivalent to 85 percent of their preretirement earnings when they retire at 67 years.[8] According to Fidelity's calculations, somebody retiring at age 67 with final earnings of $73,640 would need to have saved $577,000—a ratio of savings-to-final earnings of 7.8—to have enough money, in combination with their Social Security benefits, to meet the 85 percent replacement income mark. This ratio increases to almost ten times the final earnings if a household wants to retire at age 65.[9] Suffice to say, people will need to save a lot of money both to cover their basic expenses when their primary income sources disappear and to allow them to achieve their future aspirations.

US public policy includes incentives for households wanting to save for most of the aforementioned reasons with the largest incentive going to long-term income security through retirement savings and housing. But while public policy is generally set up to help households achieve their goals, the effect is uneven. Current savings incentives work well for about one-third of households, completely leave out about one-fifth of households, and increasingly fail the remaining households in achieving their savings goals. And this situation has gotten worse. The need for better savings policies is large and growing, considering that, among other things, people can expect to live longer and spend more time in retirement in the future.

Forms of Household Savings

Households save for their future through a number of mechanisms, all of which are shaped by policy in one way or another. These savings mechanisms include Social Security; DB pensions; financial assets such as retirement savings accounts, mainly 401(k) plans and IRAs; and nonfinancial assets such as housing.

Savings are a store of future income. Households forego consumption today in exchange for income to pay for consumption in the future, for instance, during retirement. Because households cannot store all of the goods and services they will need in the future under a mattress or in a vault, they generally give money to an institution such as the government, a mutual fund, a bank, or an insurance company in exchange for a promise of future payments. Savings always boils down to exchanging a payment today for a promise tomorrow. This basic mechanism does not change with differences in the trustworthiness of the institution or the riskiness of the assets—stocks, bonds, real estate, and commodities, for example—that households invest in. The amount a saver will receive in the future can vary based on a number of key factors, but the basic premise—that savings are a promise of a certain payment in the future in exchange for a specific payment today—does not change.

Social Security, DB pensions, financial, and nonfinancial assets consequently are different forms of household savings—and most of them will go to pay for households' retirement.[10] Social Security, for instance, receives payroll taxes today in exchange for future retirement, disability, and survivorship benefits. DB pensions receive employer and employee contributions in exchange for future monthly retirement benefits or, in some instances, lump-sum payments. And households make contributions to financial assets, such as mutual funds in 401(k) plans and IRAs, and pay down their mortgages to save in housing hoping to draw down those assets when they need them.

Public policy plays a crucial role in shaping the exchange of a certain payment today for an uncertain promise of repayment in the future. Congress directly determines the taxes that Social Security receives and the benefits it will pay out. Federal policymakers also set the rules that govern private savings—DB pensions, financial assets, and nonfinancial assets—to make sure that those who receive people's money will actually honor their promises in the future. That is, public policy shapes how much risk protections households will have for their savings by influencing the amount people save as well as the uncertainty—riskiness—of the promise of future repayment.

Two potential problems with the role of public policy in household savings become readily apparent. First, politics can matter in shaping policy. Changes in the rules and regulations governing different forms of savings—Social Security, DB pensions, financial, and nonfinancial assets—then may not necessarily reflect responses to households' actual need for more or less risk protections. Policymakers, for instance, may decide to lower risk protections for households when economic risks increase, which is exactly what has happened over the last three decades.

Second, policy can become disjointed with various types of savings fragmented into separate savings mechanisms. Indeed, policy currently addresses savings in DB pensions separately from others, say, savings in housing. The resulting variety of savings incentives adds enormous complexity, making it difficult for households to save or to protect their savings against risks. Imagine again you are on a sinking ship and the only way to use a sturdy life raft to get to safety is to first assemble it from three different parts, using instruction manuals written in Hungarian. This is what saving for the long term looks like. As a result, many households give up saving or protecting their savings and leave a lot of their future economic security to chance.

Economic Risk Exposure with Different Forms of Savings

It is important to see the risk exposure arising from each savings mechanism to understand how severe the consequences of policy pitfalls—politicized and fragmented savings policies—can be.

Different forms of savings expose households to different levels of financial market risks. Social Security benefits, for instance, are not subject to financial market risks since benefits depend only on people's wages. Households can experience some limited risk exposure with DB pension benefits, if those risks increase the chance that a DB plan will be terminated. In comparison, other financial and nonfinancial assets, especially individualized savings in retirement accounts and housing, directly expose household savings to financial market risks. Households are likely to experience more risk exposure with individualized savings than with Social Security and DB pensions.

Individualized savings also exacerbate the negative effects of labor market risks—the chance of becoming and staying unemployed and of experiencing large earnings drops—on household wealth. People, for instance, cannot make contributions to an employer-sponsored retirement plan after they lose a job. Similarly, people often contribute less to their savings accounts when their earnings drop. Social Security benefits, in comparison, help counter these negative effects of labor market risks on household savings by offering higher benefits, relative to payroll tax payments, to lower than higher lifetime earners.

The balance in the past three decades has tilted toward individualized savings, such as retirement savings accounts and home equity, and away from Social Security and DB pensions. This has increased the possibility of greater labor and financial market risk exposure with savings. Social Security reform enacted in 1983 gradually increased the age at which people can receive full retirement benefits, from 65 to 67 years, starting with people born in 1960.[11] And private sector employers have shed DB pensions and increasingly offered retirement savings accounts, such as 401(k) plans, to their employees with uncertain benefits. The bottom line is that the potential for households to be exposed to these risks through their savings has increased over time, as individualized savings have become more pervasive.

The need for risk protections in household savings has also grown just as these protections have declined. Labor and financial markets, for instance, have become more volatile, requiring additional savings and other risk protections. The stock market, for instance, experienced two massive booms and busts in quick succession between the mid-1990s and 2009. The S&P 500 stock market index fell in inflation-adjusted terms by 42 percent from March 2008 to March 2009 alone, when it hit its lowest point during the Great Recession. And people live longer, which means they need not only more savings but also more assurances that their money will actually be there when they need it in during old age. The Census Bureau, for example, projects that the share of the population between the ages of 80 and 84 years will grow from 1.8 percent in 2012 to 3.2 percent in 2050 and the share of the population 85 years and older will grow from 1.9 percent in 2012 to 4.5 percent in 2050—faster than any other population segment.[12]

The Logic for Policy Interventions in Savings

Public policy urgently needs to address the growing gap between the increasing potential for risk exposure and the mounting need for risk protections to help households save enough for their future.

In principle, public policy should help households save for their future and protect household savings from unnecessary risks. Making sure that households have sufficient retirement savings from public and private sources will create long-term economic security for people since they can meet their current and future consumption goals. Sufficient and secure savings will also reduce the demand on public safety nets in the future since fewer households will be in danger of falling into poverty and experiencing material hardships. And economic growth will be stronger when households have enough savings to maintain their standard of living without having the need to cut their spending. It may be even stronger when households save enough to start and grow successful businesses in old age or switch to jobs and careers that better suit their skills later in life.

So making sure households have enough savings is clearly in the public interest. But households will generally not be able to save enough to meet all of their long-term needs, especially their retirement goals. Public policy needs to support households' savings through public savings and incentives and regulations for private savings.

Savings are an uncertain promise of future income, and institutions such as the government, DB pensions, banks, and insurance companies are better able to accept and manage this uncertainty due to their unique expertise and longer financial planning time horizons. Households that want to save enough money for their future goals need to make a series of complex decisions on when to start saving, how much to save, where to invest, how much to pay in fees, and when to make use of that money, while guessing on how long they will live (in the case of retirement). People really cannot know answers to all of these questions and thus either make blind financial decisions or rely on the expertise of private financial institutions for their savings.

But relying on private institutions can harm households wanting to save money since these institutions often operate with their own set of goals, such as rapidly growing short-term profits, that could compete with households' desires and needs for secure savings over the long term. For example, the recent financial crisis from 2007 to 2009 vividly illustrated that financial institutions can create excessive risk exposure for households since they can earn more money in the short term with higher risk investments.[13] Also financial institutions may limit options of low-cost, low-risk savings for some household groups, such as lower income households, if institutions see them as less profitable.

There are then three underlying principles that should guide policy intervention. First, policy needs to make it easy for households to save enough. After all, there is no "do over" if households reach retirement without enough savings. Second, policy needs to establish a balance between people's interest in building sufficient and secure savings and financial institutions' interest in wanting to be paid for their services, so that households can avoid excessive fees and risks. And third, policy needs to overcome market failures so that all households can build enough savings that are secure for the long term.

Offering Public and Private Savings

These policy principles explain why Social Security exists, for instance. It takes out the need to guess how much to save for basic retirement income, disability benefits, and survivorship benefits. Moreover, Social

Security reflects a trade-off. It offers a modest payroll tax, but its moderate benefit levels also require households to have additional savings to maintain their standard of living in retirement. Social Security covers all workers in the industries and occupations included in it, regardless of their income. But it pays relatively higher benefits to lower lifetime earners in proportion to their payroll tax payments compared with higher lifetime earners

The above policy principles also explain policy interventions in private savings. Policymakers, for instance, have established rules guiding the investments of DB pension funds, as well as employers' contributions to DB pensions, to discourage employers from putting their short-term corporate goals before the promises they made to their employees.[14] And policymakers have established rules that are meant to incentivize employers to offer retirement benefits to all of their employees, not just the well-paid ones. Moreover, policymakers have started to pay closer attention to risk exposure in 401(k) plans. They have especially encouraged auto-enrollment, whereby employees are automatically enrolled in a 401(k) plan and may opt out of its savings and investment options if they choose so. Auto-enrollment theoretically should increase savings and make it easier for households to balance between risky and non-risky investments.[15] That is, public policy encourages people to save, by striking a balance between private and public savings and by overcoming known market failures that create obstacles for savings for some household groups.

The policy rationales only suggest that the government should be active in encouraging sufficient and secure savings through public and private mechanisms. They do not say much about the balance between Social Security and private savings. Put differently, why should the government provide Social Security *and* support private savings rather than just offering Social Security, possibly at a much higher level? Why should the government offer incentives for private savings at all?[16]

Public savings such as Social Security can generally offer a strong, universal foundation by insuring risks that are otherwise impossible or very costly to insure. Social Security offers such basic insurance to households by providing some protections from the fallout of market, disability, and mortality.

But private savings can do a better job than Social Security in meeting some of households' goals.[17] A wide range of savings goals related to retirement and aging can vary with personal circumstances. These include financing a small business and supporting aging family members in addition to being able to maintain one's standard of living. Private savings mechanisms allow households to pursue and hopefully meet the savings goals that are best suited to their own needs and aspirations.

The United States, like other advanced economies, relies on a mix of public and private savings. Social Security constitutes a basic, universal savings program. However, it does not meet most households' complete savings needs in the case of retirement, disability, or a breadwinner's death.[18] Households often have to save substantial amounts outside of Social Security to meet their needs, and public policy has to support these savings.

The mix of private and public savings tends to reflect a country's values, social history, and politics. In the United States, this mix is tilted more toward private savings than public programs compared to other advanced economies.[19] This reflects the fact that US policy tends to put a heavy emphasis on personal responsibility while wanting to ensure that households have their basic needs covered.[20]

Because the mix of public and private savings is shaped by societal values and politics, this can also change over time. Specifically, the mix may need to shift toward public programs when support for private savings is regularly failing to generate sufficient and secure savings for most households. US savings policy indeed has not offered most households effective help to save enough for their future and protect their savings. These policy shortcomings have become more apparent over time. US savings policy will need to update Social Security and to vastly improve incentives for private savings to better offer real economic security amid high uncertainty in labor and financial markets.

Conclusion

American households have lived through successive tidal waves of economic risks and are now treading water with their savings. Job security and stable wages have diminished, while the stock and housing markets have become more volatile. The financial crisis of 2007 to 2009 alone was akin to a Category 5 hurricane for savings. The need for more risk protection via more savings and more secure savings in these uncertain times is clear.

But policy has made it harder for households to save more and to better protect their savings because of a growing emphasis on having households do much of what is necessary by themselves. The policy response has largely been similar to asking people to learn to swim while the boat is already going under in the storm.

In short, it will take a fundamental rethinking of our policy approach to help millions of Americans save more than they currently do for a sunny and comfortable future. I highlight the challenges to and the opportunities for building better life rafts—more and secure savings—for most people in the remainder of this book.

CHAPTER TWO

Americans' Growing Risk Exposure

How would you personally define what a secure retirement means to you?[1]

"Guarantees that what you put there will be there." (White man, 41 years old)

"As little debt as possible, don't have to live on a monthly budget but the main thing as little debt as possible." (White man, 34 years old)

"Job security while I am young." (White woman, 44 years old)

Saving enough money to pay for one's living expenses in retirement is daunting. But even if households save diligently, the money they put away may not be available when they need it because of a financial market crash just before retirement. Households typically want to invest their savings in something to earn a rate of return that will help pay for their retirement. Earning a rate of return generally comes with some financial risk—the possibility to lose part of the investment. People may invest their savings in stocks and hold a lot of money in housing, for instance, and stock and house prices may fall just before households need the money, leaving them with a lot less income to spend than anticipated. This is the essence of risk when it comes to savings. The question here is not whether taking risks is okay but what households can do to protect their savings from too much risk.

Other researchers have established that the chances of stock and housing market crashes have increased over time. Alongside this increasing up-and-down trend, household savings have also become increasingly volatile, experiencing larger up-and-down movements since the 1980s than before. This volatility stems in part from the aforementioned fact that price swings in stock and housing markets are greater than they were in the past. But, it also stems from households being more exposed to these market ups and downs, just as the stock and housing market boom–and–bust cycles took off. That is, risks and households' exposure to these risks have gone up simultaneously. As a result, swings in stock and house prices can do a lot more damage to household savings now than they could in the past.

That is not all. Labor market risks—the chance of being unemployed and having a substantial loss in one's earnings—have also increased over the past 30 years, according to a large body of research. Increasing labor market volatility can also threaten household savings when people lose their jobs, become unemployed, stay unemployed for long periods of time, and see sharp drops in their wages.

Growing economic risks and rising risk exposure put households in a bind. They need to save more for protection against labor and financial market risks, since exposure to these increasing risks poses a new cost to households. Savings become less stable and households cannot be sure their savings will be available when they need them. To offset this cost, households should theoretically save more. But, labor and financial market risk exposure have made it harder for households to save, leaving them financially less secure than without the increased risk exposure.

Households, for example, may find it harder to save now than in the past since their incomes have become less stable. And, rising risk exposure adds to the already increasing complexity of financial decisions that households have to make to protect their savings. It is a lot harder to navigate a boat through a Category 5 hurricane than through calm waters. Today there is an ever greater chance for people of making their own financial decisions and consequently their own mistakes with retirement savings and housing that can put large shares of these savings at risk. The analysis in this chapter shows that these dangers are real. The data show that households' exposure to financial market risks, in particular, has grown just as financial markets have become more unstable.

I start this chapter with a discussion of the literature on financial market risks, followed by a discussion of labor market risks, showing that both financial and labor market risks have increased since the early 1980s. I then distinguish households' risk *exposure* from market risks to show that households have become increasingly exposed to these risks as market risks have gone up. And, to conclude this chapter, I discuss the effects of rising risk exposure on household wealth amid an environment of high financial market risks.

Financial Market Risks

Household savings can fluctuate because prices of risky forms of savings, most notably stocks and housing, can experience large up-or-down movements.[2] And research has shown that stock and house prices have become more volatile since the 1980s,[3] increasing the chances of sale prices and returns being lower than expected.

Economists consider stocks and housing riskier types of savings than bonds and savings accounts, for instance. For some people, the notion of a house as a form of savings is an alien one, much less the characterization of it as risky investment. However, saving in housing, in particular, can be quite risky in ways that people may not always take into account. Households benefit from investing in stocks and housing, because of the potential future flows of income they may receive as owners. Income from stocks comes from the stockowner's claim on corporate income, in the form of dividends, and from capital gains when the stockowner sells stocks for more than the purchase price. Similarly, households receive income from owner-occupied housing in the form of saved rents, and they may be able to realize capital gains if they sell their house for a higher price than they paid for it. The valuations of stocks and housing, as well as the incomes earned on them, can unpredictably and wildly fluctuate over time. Compared to less risky investments, this raises the chance that households receive a lot less from their investments than they had expected.

There are some differences between stocks and housing, but both stocks and housing tend to be fairly volatile. Stock prices, for instance, fluctuate more than housing prices, making stocks riskier than housing in terms of unexpected changes in value. But, housing can be riskier than stocks, since housing is less liquid than stocks and people need to undertake greater efforts to turn their housing investments into cash than is the case for stocks. For instance, to liquidate part of their savings in housing, households have to actually get a home equity line of credit, which is often difficult when financial market risks materialize and housing markets are depressed.[4] Similarly, households' ability to sell their homes typically depends on local credit and labor market conditions.[5] Furthermore, households have to incur substantial transaction costs such as broker fees and sales taxes—typically around 10 percent of their home's value[6]—when they want to sell their houses to access their savings in housing. Housing is a substantially risky investment for households' savings,[7] in ways people often fail to appreciate.

Labor Market Risks

Households' savings also depend on the degree of risk in labor markets. Labor market risk refers to the chance that income from labor will fluctuate due to unemployment and sudden changes in wages and salaries.

In recent decades, labor market risks have increased alongside financial market risks.[8] The length of unemployment has trended upward since the 1980s,[9] and earnings have become more volatile, reflected in a growing chance of stagnant and even falling wages.[10] Both unemployment and drops in earnings can have adverse effects on savings. People are likely to save less when they are unemployed or when their earnings fall. Households may stop saving and they may even dip into their savings while they are unemployed, especially if they cannot cut their consumption enough to offset the drop in income.[11] They may even go so far as drawing down their accumulated savings. Households that experience a sharp drop in earnings even though they manage to remain employed may similarly reduce their savings or possibly draw down their savings to maintain their previous level of consumption.[12]

Rising Financial Market Risk Exposure

Economic theory posits that households would not necessarily become more vulnerable to financial market risks as stock and housing markets have become more volatile. In theory, people should reduce their exposure to financial market risks as these risks go up. This logic is akin to expecting that fishermen buy bigger boats with better safety gear if they plan on fishing further offshore in rougher seas. Greater risks should prompt people to seek more risk protections.

Risky Asset Concentration

Households can theoretically gain some protection from financial risk by diversifying their savings, thus spreading their risk exposure between risky and not-so-risky investments. Diversification is the opposite of concentrating of savings in risky assets—stocks and housing. I use risky asset concentration—the share of stocks and housing out of total household assets—as an indicator for diversification or, more accurately, the lack thereof.[13]

Diversifying savings and thus spreading the risk exposure offers some protection for savings against large price swings in stock and housing markets. Consider a simple illustrative example of two households with two different investment choices. Both households initially have $200,000 in savings. One allocates 80 percent—or $160,000—to stocks, while the other puts only 40 percent—or $80,000—in stocks. The rest of both households' money is invested in US treasuries, which are typically considered the safest investments. A drop in the stock market of 20 percent results in a loss of $32,000 to the first household, which is equal to 16 percent of its total savings. The same market drop leads to a loss of only $16,000 or only eight percent of the total to the second household. Spreading out assets between risky and nonrisky investments—diversification—lowers the household's risky asset concentration and its likelihood that a sharp market drop translates into massive wealth declines.[14]

There are some guidelines borne out of economic theory for households looking to diversifying their savings. Households looking to protect their savings through diversification should ideally invest, according to theory, so that the rates of return of different investments are uncorrelated with each other—that is, when one goes up or down, the other does not necessarily move in any particular direction.[15] Rates of return within one group of investments —stocks, bonds, or real estate—generally tend to be linked to each other because the market for each group of investments tends to be influenced by common factors. Monetary policy by the Federal Reserve can be such a common factor since lower interest rates make stocks and housing a more attractive investment than is the case with higher interest rates. Stock prices can also follow investment fads that drive up stock prices, for instance, regardless of whether companies' profits justify these prices.[16] This means that stock prices of one oil company, for instance, move closely with the stock prices of another oil company. That is, households looking to protect their savings should spread their savings across a number of unrelated investments.

The risk across different investment groups, though, could theoretically show some correlation. The price movements of stocks and bonds could in theory move together since lower stock prices often reflect a weakening economy that is about to go into or already going through a recession. A weaker economy could also go along with lower long-term interest rates on bonds. But, this correlation appears to be weak, especially over longer time periods.[17]

The ups and downs of prices on stocks and houses, though, tend to move in lock-step. Stock and house prices often fall when the economy turns sour and both rise when the economy improves.[18]

Prudently diversifying household savings as a protection against financial market risk suggests that households should move their savings away from risky investments such as stocks and houses into safer investments such as bonds and US treasuries, as financial market risks grow to maintain similar levels of risk protection.

Households may not have diversified their savings as financial market risks increased from the 1980s onward, though, for a number of reasons. As a result, risk exposure in fact increased alongside growing market risks.

Households may encounter psychological obstacles to changing their risky investments when financial market risks go up or down. For instance, they may be unable to fully process increasingly complex financial information in the face of wider market swings, especially if it pertains to outcomes that are a long way into the future such as the likelihood of a future stock or housing market crash. They may also be unable to stick to a financial plan because of other short-term influences on their lives such as worries about losing their job. And, they may exhibit a so-called status quo bias in financial decisions, which leads households to value their present situation more than may be prudent and inhibits necessary financial decisions. Finally, people may fall prey to financial herd behavior such as buying internet stocks in 1999 after they have already seen a sharp run-up in prices and had an increasing chance of a market downturn.[19] Households consequently may not regularly and systematically move out of risky investments when prices of stocks and housing rise; alternatively, they may not put more money into such risky investments when prices of stocks and housing fall.[20]

As a result of such obstacles, rapid changes in the prices of risky investments such as stocks may cause households to take on more risk than they had anticipated. Somebody who initially wanted to put half of their money into stocks and the other half into bonds may quickly find themselves with a larger stock investment than they had planned simply because stock prices have risen quickly (as they did during the stock market boom of the late 1990s) if they do not actively and frequently sell stocks and put the money back into bonds to maintain the preferred 50–50 split, a process called rebalancing.

The problem of too much financial market risk exposure may be worse than that. Households often change how much they save when their savings unexpectedly go up, for instance, because of a stock market boom. Such unexpected stock market gains could lead households to consume more and save less, which describes the so-called wealth effect.[21] That is, a stock market boom could lead to households cutting their savings and thus preventing them from building enough buffer against an inevitable stock market crash. They would consequently experience a lot of financial risk exposure unless they rebalance their investments in the middle of a stock market boom.[22]

Summary Data on Household Financial Risk Exposure

To investigate what has been actually unfolding vis-à-vis Americans' exposure to risks, I calculate financial and labor market risk exposure based on Federal Reserve data, specifically the triennial *Survey of Consumer Finances* (SCF). The SCF is a nationally representative household survey that contains detailed information on household finances, including all of their savings. The survey also includes information on other household characteristics such as age, race, ethnicity, education, and employment. And, it contains information on financial attitudes, including the length of household's financial planning horizon, and on financial behaviors, such as whether a household regularly saves. Complete data are available from 1989 to 2013, except for indicators on the length of unemployment, which exists only from 1995 to 2013. The SCF consequently allows researchers to study savings together with financial and labor market risk exposure.

Table 2.1 summarizes several financial and labor market risk exposure indicators from 1989 to 2013. I first present the median risky asset concentration—stocks and housing out of all savings—for households with any saving.[23] The data show the median risky asset concentration increasing from a low of 54.2 percent in 1989 to a high of 68.9 percent in 2004, before gradually declining again to 62.0 percent in 2013. This means households' risk exposure increased when stock and housing prices trended upward—the opposite of what should have happened according to theory.

Behavioral obstacles that impede households from better protecting their savings are the most likely explanation for rising risk exposure when the stock market was hot.[24] Other explanations such as investment savvy and easier access to credit do not hold water. Put differently,

Table 2.1   Financial and labor market risk exposure indicators (1989–2013)

Year	Median risky asset ratio	Median debt to asset ratio	Share of households with very high financial risk exposure	Share of households with high unemployment risk	Share of households with high earnings risk	Average length of unemployment (in weeks) for all households
1989	54.2%	24.6%	21.4%	17.7%	36.5%	n.a.
1992	57.6%	27.3%	23.1%	25.6%	63.7%	n.a.
1995	62.3%	31.4%	26.7%	13.3%	48.2%	n.a.
1998	64.4%	30.6%	26.1%	22.2%	41.1%	27.3
2001	67.7%	28.5%	26.5%	11.0%	69.5%	23.9
2004	68.9%	34.5%	30.7%	7.3%	39.7%	25.9
2007	68.2%	35.2%	29.1%	16.3%	50.0%	28.1
2010	64.4%	40.2%	30.1%	46.8%	51.3%	36.5
2013	62.0%	36.8%	26.9%	37.8%	49.9%	29.9

Notes: n.a. stands for not available. Risky asset concentration refers to the share of stocks and housing out of total household assets. Debt includes all household debt. A household is defined as having very high financial market risk exposure if its risky asset concentration is greater than 75 percent and its debt to asset ratio is larger than 25 percent. A household is considered having high unemployment risk exposure if it belongs to a group of households, defined by age, year, education, and race, that has an average unemployment rate in the top fourth of the distribution of all group-specific unemployment rates. A household is considered having high earnings risk if the relative standard error—standard error to average—of the group of households, defined by age, year, education, race, and earnings, that it belongs to falls into the top half of the relative standard error of earnings for its respective earnings percentile. Sample includes all nonretiree households. The length of unemployment is only calculated for nonretiree households with unemployed heads of households.

Source: Based on Board of Governors, Federal Reserve System, *Survey of Consumer Finances* (Washington, DC: BOG, various years).

although the risky asset concentration grew over the decades leading up to the Great Recession, this was not because the vast majority of households were skilled investors who completely anticipated the market boom and invested accordingly. Expecting households to be able to predict long-term market movements is unrealistic, considering that even financial experts are often unable to anticipate booms or busts. For instance, in the 2000s, many institutional investors, such as pension funds and mutual funds, did not predict or protect against the enormous losses from the housing market boom and bust.[25] In theory, households and professional investors should be able to predict that housing and stock prices would drop sharply after a period of growth, since stock and house price booms are followed by busts, which are then followed by booms.[26] Households that understood how these risky markets work and who have the means to diversify their portfolio should have regularly rebalanced their portfolio, but only a minority of investors actually did so during the boom years of the 1990s.[27]

Likewise, financial innovation and fewer credit constraints for households should have made it gradually easier for households to regain their optimal risky asset concentration after unexpected rises in the value of risky assets. It should have been particularly easy for households to diversify from risky housing assets as house prices rose, because mortgage and home equity markets were easing at the same time.

However, households generally did not take the available measures to rebalance their portfolios to counter increases in their risky asset concentration. Instead of reflecting widespread financial savvy and easier credit access among households, the risky asset concentration trend in the 1990s and 2000s likely reflected behavioral obstacles.[28] The bottom line then is that rising financial market risks have gone along with increasing risk exposure for most Americans.

Household Indebtedness

Indebtedness is also a key component to household risk exposure. A household's level of indebtedness can be measured using the ratio of debt to assets. High levels of debt relative to savings lead to higher risk exposure because gains and losses of savings are magnified.[29] A household with greater indebtedness faces a higher risk of losing significant shares of its wealth from comparatively much smaller drops in stock and housing prices.[30]

This discussion offers two important insights for using indebtedness as risk exposure measure. First, indebtedness is a separate risk exposure indicator than risky asset concentration and thus should be added to risky asset concentration to understand households' complete risk exposure. Second, indebtedness exposes households to risks in financial markets independent of the savings in which a household invests.

Table 2.1 shows the median ratio of debt to assets for households with any assets, highlighting the growing indebtedness of the typical household. The median ratio of debt to assets was 24.6 percent in 1989, before climbing to 40.2 percent in 2010. It then declined to 36.8 percent in 2013. That is, the typical household was still more indebted after several years of unprecedented debt declines in the wake of the Great Recession from 2007 to 2009 than it was at any point between 1989 and 2007.

Very High Financial Risk Exposure

Table 2.1 further presents a summary indicator of the share of households having very high financial risk exposure that combines data on households' risky asset concentration and their indebtedness. I specifically define households with very high risk exposure as those that have a risky asset concentration greater than 75 percent and a debt to asset ratio larger than 25 percent. In 1989, a little over one-fifth of households—21.4 percent to be exact—had very high risk exposure, compared to 30.1 percent immediately following the Great Recession in 2010 and 26.9 percent in 2013. It is notable that households still had a lot of financial market risk exposure in the years after the Great Recession, even though the value of stocks and houses fell (reducing concentrations in risky assets) and households lowered their indebtedness (either voluntarily by paying back their debt or involuntarily by being foreclosed on).

Increasing Labor Market Risk Exposure

Labor market risk exposure describes people's likelihood of involuntarily being out of a job and of possibly losing a share of their earnings, even when still employed. In order for the labor market discussion to mirror the financial market discussion, I distinguish between labor market risk exposure and actual labor market risk. Specifically, I differentiate between the possibility of experiencing unemployment and reduced earnings (labor market risk exposure) and actual unemployment and decreased earnings (actual labor market risks).

Labor market risk exposure is the chance of being unemployed and of seeing a drop in earnings. That requires defining unemployment risk and earnings risk for a group of households that have similar characteristics. The calculation of unemployment risk proceeds as follows. I calculate the unemployment rate for a group of households defined by age, race/ethnicity, and education in any given survey year. Age refers to five age groupings, starting with those younger than 30 years, followed by those between the ages of 30 and 39, 40 and 49, and so on, up to households 60 years and older. Race/ethnicity refers to a grouping of households into white non-Hispanic, and all others. And, education divides households by having at least a college degree and those without a college degree. That is, households fall into one of 20 groups for each survey year, and each group has a unique, corresponding unemployment rate. I define a household as having high unemployment risk if it belongs to a group that has an unemployment rate in the top 25 percent of all household groups across all nine years of data—1989 to 2013.

Table 2.1 shows the development of high unemployment risk over time. The chance of falling into a group with comparatively high unemployment bottomed out with 7.3 percent in 2004 and rose sharply to 46.8 percent by 2010, before falling again to 37.8 percent in 2013 (Table 2.1).

There is no clear trend in the probability of having high unemployment risk, which indicates that the unemployment risk has gone neither up nor down. But, that is somewhat misleading since the length of unemployment has gone up over time[31] as the truncated data from 1995 to 2013 in Table 2.1 show. Unemployment is always harmful to households' economic well-being, but this adverse effect increased over time as the length of unemployment also trended up.

I follow a similar procedure for defining high earnings risk as I do for high unemployment risk. I calculate the group-specific relative standard error—standard error to average—of real hourly earnings (in 2013 dollars) for households with positive real earnings in each group. I then define a household as having high earnings risk if it belongs to a household group with a relative standard error in the top half of all group-specific relative standard errors for its earnings quintile from 1989 to 2013. I separately calculate high earnings risk for the first fifth of earnings, the second fifth of earnings, and so on, to account for the fact that earnings dispersion and thus relative standard errors increase with earning levels.[32]

Table 2.1 summarizes the breakdown of the chance of high earnings risk by year. The chance of high earnings risk is relatively high from 2001 to 2013 with the exception of a relatively low chance of 39.7 percent in 2004. The chance of experiencing high earnings risk is generally greater in the period that starts with the recession in 2001 than in the earlier years, although there is no consistent upward trend.

To summarize, labor market risk exposure has been trending upward. At the same time, labor market risks—not just people's exposure to these risks—such as the length of unemployment and volatility of earnings for individual households have also grown.

Differences in Risk Exposure by
Demographic Characteristics

The combination of rising risks and increasing risk exposure in labor and financial markets translates into a persistence of economic insecurity into the future. Increasing financial market risk exposure makes wealth more volatile. Households may not have the savings they thought they had if risks materialize during stock and housing price crashes. The chance of more volatile wealth, though, is not equally distributed across households. Some groups of households face greater financial and labor market risks than others.

Table 2.2 summarizes labor and financial market risk exposure over time by race/ethnicity, income quintiles, education, and time period (early or later years). The data are split into observations for the early years (1989–1998) and for the later years (2001–2013) to make the summary manageable. The break between the early and later years coincides with substantial changes in the macro-economy. The years after 2000 are generally characterized by slower economic and job growth than the earlier years, as well as substantial stock and housing market swings that became more pronounced than in the earlier years.

Financial risk exposure varies by demographic characteristics in both periods. It is generally more pronounced among white households, households with incomes in the middle and fourth quintile, and households with at least a high school education than among communities of color, lower and higher income households, and households without a high school education (Table 2.2). Much of this difference generally results from substantially higher risky asset concentration than from higher indebtedness. Households of color, for instance, tend to have higher debt to asset ratios than white households, on average (Table 2.2), while whites have higher risky asset concentrations. While relative financial risk exposure varies between households with different demographic characteristics, one trend spans all the demographic groups: financial risk exposure consistently increased from earlier to later periods, because both risky asset concentration and indebtedness went up for most households (Table 2.2).

The picture of labor market risk exposure varies somewhat from trends in financial market risk exposure. White households, for instance, were less likely to experience high unemployment and high earnings risk exposure than was the case for households of color. There

Table 2.2 Financial and labor market risk exposure measures, by race, income, education, and time period

	Median risky asset ratio (%)		Median debt to asset ratio (%)		Share of households with very high financial risk exposure (%)		Share of households with high unemployment risk (%)		Share of households with high earnings risk (%)	
	1989–1998	2001–2013	1989–1998	2001–2013	1989–1998	2001–2013	1989–1998	2001–2013	1989–1998	2001–2013
Race/ethnicity										
White	63.4	69.4	29.3	32.2	26.7	30.1	10.6	12.4	40.4	41.8
Black	33.5	49.6	31.8	46.6	18.9	25.5	73.4	47.2	68.7	79.4
Hispanic	42.4	59.3	43.2	42.6	22.1	27.7	81.2	56.0	70.2	78.4
Other	52.9	59.1	23.9	31.6	20.9	27.7	61.4	35.7	70.0	78.4
Income quintile										
Bottom fifth	0.0	0.0	7.9	20.2	8.3	11.7	48.4	44.1	50.4	69.9
Second fifth	40.4	50.3	30.9	37.7	21.3	23.6	38.5	31.6	46.5	61.4
Middle fifth	62.4	73.1	40.1	47.7	29.3	36.6	28.4	22.7	45.1	54.9
Fourth fifth	71.2	76.5	38.6	42.3	36.6	40.9	21.6	17.2	49.4	50.9
Top fifth	65.3	69.7	24.6	24.4	27.2	29.6	10.9	9.1	48.3	36.4
Education										
Less than high school	65.5	68.6	13.3	22.8	17.9	20.8	48.9	40.8	50.1	69.4
High school	62.5	68.3	30.3	36.9	25.7	30.0	38.1	33.2	54.8	67.2
Some college	53.9	62.0	36.9	46.3	25.9	30.7	38.3	35.0	62.8	72.8
At least college	61.5	68.6	30.5	30.0	26.8	30.2	5.5	4.2	34.1	27.5

Notes: All variables refer to the head of household. Risky asset concentration refers to the share of stocks and housing out of total household debt. The median risky asset concentration and the debt to asset ratio are only calculated for households with savings. A household is defined as having very high financial market risk exposure if its risky asset concentration is greater than 75 percent and its debt to asset ratio is larger than 25 percent. A household is considered having high unemployment risk exposure if it belongs to a group of households, defined by age, year, education, and race, that has an average unemployment rate in the top fourth of the distribution of all group-specific unemployment rates. A household is considered having high earnings risk if the relative standard error to average—of the group of households, defined by age, year, education, race, and earnings, that it belongs to falls into the top half of the relative standard error of earnings for its respective earnings percentile. Sample includes all nonretiree households. Financial market risk indicators are calculated only for households with any assets. High earnings risk is calculated only for households in the labor force with positive earnings. And, high unemployment risk is calculated only for households in the labor force.

Source: Based on Board of Governors, Federal Reserve System, *Survey of Consumer Finances* (Washington, DC: BOG, various years).

are no clear systematic differences by income levels. But, households with some college education (but no degree) generally have higher unemployment risk and higher earnings risk than households with less and with more education (Table 2.2). Moreover, the chance of high earnings risk has typically increased over time, while the chance of high unemployment risk—based on the unemployment rate—has somewhat declined in many instances. The decrease in the unemployment risk, though, is misleading as the data in Table 2.1 suggest, since the length of unemployment has also gone up, even as the unemployment rates for all groups have trended downward. The bottom line is that economic risks generally have increased and that few households, particularly those with high income, have been protected from high and increasing levels of economic risks.

Conclusion

Prior research has established that financial and labor market risks have increased over the past 30 years. This analysis demonstrates that households' exposure to these risks has gone up right alongside. Economic insecurity has grown as a result.[33] It is no wonder, then, that Americans overwhelmingly feel that our nation is facing a retirement crisis.[34]

Absent a concerted effort by policymakers to right the ship, this economic insecurity can be expected to persist in the future, because labor and financial market risks reinforce each other. The transmission runs from labor market risk exposure to persistent financial market risk exposure and rising wealth inequality in society at large. The result then is that many households end up with less wealth and less predictable future wealth than they would have if risk exposure had not increased along with greater risks, as I will show in the next chapter.

CHAPTER THREE

More Risk, Greater Wealth Inequality

How would you personally define what a secure retirement means to you?[1]

"I don't believe in this world there is such a thing." (White woman, 67 years old)

"I would like to be able to make a decent income on savings and have it completely secured." (White woman, 74 years old)

The last three decades have been characterized by both rising wealth inequality and growing retirement income inadequacy, as a rising share of households is expected to be unable to maintain its standard of living in retirement. At the same time, labor market risks—longer spells of unemployment and less stable earnings—and financial market risks—larger boom-and-bust cycles in the stock and housing markets—have gone up, too. And, as established in chapter 2, households have become more exposed to the potential fallout from these market risks.

In this chapter, I comprehensively examine the data on the relationships between wealth inequality and labor and financial market risk exposure. The data show that growing risk exposure contributes to increasing wealth inequality, basically holding back savings for households that are exposed to high market risks. As a result, many households are increasingly ill-prepared for retirement, while they simultaneously face increasing uncertainty over whether their savings will actually be there when they need them, due to the unfortunate combination of increasing risks and rising risk exposure. Successive waves of labor and financial market risks have effectively sunk Americans' economic security and also prevented them from building sturdy financial life rafts for their future.

Wealth Inequality

The gap in wealth between rich households and households with fewer means has widened dramatically in recent years. Wealth means the difference between a household's savings and its debts, or what households can actually use to finance consumption in the future, after they pay off their debts. Households in the top fifth of the income distribution had 17 times the average wealth of households in the middle of the income distribution in 2013, up from a 7.1 in 1989 and a 9.1 in 1998 (Figure 3.1).[2] The gap in average wealth between the top fifth and the

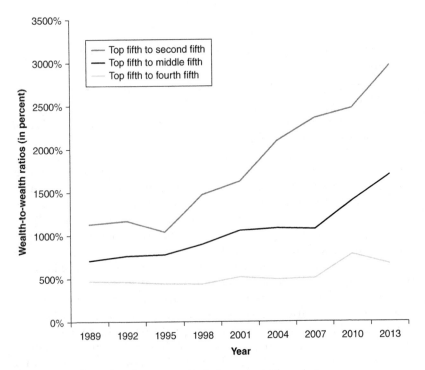

Figure 3.1 Select ratios of average wealth, by income quintiles and year.

Notes: All dollars are expressed in 2013 dollars. Wealth is the difference between household assets and household debt. Wealth includes all marketable wealth such as retirement savings accounts and owner-occupied housing, but it does not include the net present value of DB pension income that the household already receives or expects to receive in the future. Amounts in earlier years deflated using the research series for the Consumer Price Index for Urban Consumers (CPI-U-RS). Income distribution based on normal annual income. Sample includes only nonretired households older than 29 years and younger than 60 years.

Source: Based on Board of Governors, Federal Reserve System, *Survey of Consumer Finances* (Washington, DC: BOG, various years).

fourth and second-fifths of the income distribution has also increased over time.

The wealth gap has also increased for different groups of households as they got older. White wealth has pulled away from that of nonwhite Hispanics as they aged, for instance, as has the wealth of college-educated households from that of households without college degrees.[3] Table 3.1 shows that the wealth gap by race and ethnicity for households born between 1954 and 1963 increased during the 2001 recession and in the aftermath of the Great Recession. Whites had about four times the average wealth of nonwhites and Hispanics in 2013, up from less than three times in the years before the Great Recession in 2004 and 2007. In addition, the wealth gap by education grew almost continuously, such that households with at least a college degree in this group—born between 1954 and 1963—had about five times the wealth of households without a college degree in 2013, up from a ratio of 3.1 or less between 1989 and 1995 (Table 3.2).

Household wealth has become more unequally distributed no matter how we look at it. Later cohorts have seen greater wealth gaps than

Table 3.1 Average real wealth trends, by race, education, and year, holding birth cohorts constant

Year	White	Nonwhite, Hispanic	Ratio of whites to nonwhites or Hispanics	College degree	No college degree	Ratio of households with college degrees to those without
1989	$124,069	$26,275	472.2%	$172,394	$56,112	307.2%
1992	$134,723	$52,767	255.3%	$176,971	$74,882	236.3%
1995	$173,436	$50,147	345.9%	$232,922	$92,285	252.4%
1998	$312,406	$91,624	341.0%	$479,576	$144,042	332.9%
2001	$483,658	$110,490	437.7%	$702,566	$192,843	364.3%
2004	$603,105	$231,798	260.2%	$891,384	$229,341	388.7%
2007	$788,289	$321,721	245.0%	$1,256,147	$281,047	447.0%
2010	$772,082	$260,051	296.9%	$1,235,059	$235,158	525.2%
2013	$833,028	$209,484	397.7%	$1,285,718	$269,909	476.4%

Notes: All dollars are expressed in 2013 dollars. Wealth is the difference between household assets and household debt. Wealth includes all marketable wealth such as retirement savings accounts and owner-occupied housing, but it does not include the net present value of DB pension income that the household already receives or expects to receive in the future. Nominal dollar amounts are adjusted for inflation by the research series for the Consumer Price Index for Urban Consumers (CPI-U-RS). The sample includes households born between 1954 and 1963. They were between 26 and 35 years in 1989. The sample only includes non-retiree households. Sample sizes for Hispanics and households of other races/ethnicities are too small to generate reliable sample sizes. All nonwhite categories are hence combined. College degree includes only households with at least a college degree.

Table 3.2 Savings behavior and financial market risk exposure, by unemployment and earnings risk exposure level

Indicators of savings and financial risk exposure	Expected change, when labor market risk goes from low to high	Low unemployment risk	High unemployment risk	Low earnings risk	High earnings risk
Average chance of being a saver	Increase	48.9%	40.2%	54.1%	49.5%
Median ratio of nonretirement financial assets to income	Decrease	16.7%	4.5%	19.2%	9.2%
Median risky asset concentration	Decrease	66.3%	46.5%	70.0%	63.6%
Median debt to asset ratio	Decrease	29.1%	49.5%	29.3%	45.5%

Notes: Risky asset concentration refers to the share of stocks and housing out of total household assets. Debt includes all household debt. Households can self-identify as saving regularly, saving irregularly, or not saving. Long-term planners have a self-identified financial planning horizon of more than five years. A household is considered having high unemployment risk exposure if it belongs to a group of households, defined by age, year, education, and race, that has an average unemployment rate in the top fourth of the distribution of all group-specific unemployment rates. A household is considered having high earnings risk if the relative standard error—standard error to average—of the group of households, defined by age, year, education, race, and earnings, that it belongs to falls into the top half of the relative standard error of earnings for its respective earnings percentile. Sample includes all nonretiree households.

Source: Based on Board of Governors, Federal Reserve System, *Survey of Consumer Finances* (Washington, DC: BOG, various years).

was previously the case, and the wealth gap has also grown between particular household groups as they got older.

Wealth Inequality and Rising Risk Exposure

The growth in household risk exposure documented in chapter 2 has contributed to the increasingly unequal distribution of wealth among households. Households face several economic risks as they save for their future. Labor and financial market risks are especially important in this regard. Labor market risk refers to both unemployment risk—the probability of involuntarily being out of a job—and earnings risk—the instability of wages and salaries. Financial market risk, in comparison, refers to the chance of earning below-average rates of return because prices unexpectedly fall in the stock and housing markets. Households must manage their exposure to these economic risks to avoid the chance of losing more of their wealth than they had planned on.

But, households' exposure to labor and financial market risks has increased just as these risks have gone up, as I discussed in chapter 2. Labor market risk exposure and financial market risk exposure have grown over time and are especially pronounced among nonwhites and Hispanics, lower income households, and households with less education, as my discussion in chapter 2 shows. The same groups of households whose wealth has fallen behind that of whites, higher income households, and households with more education have also seen disproportionate increases in labor and financial market risk exposure.

How can rising risk exposure contribute to wealth inequality? High labor market risk exposure can impede savings for households that are at increased risk of losing their jobs. They simply stop saving or dramatically reduce their savings as they focus on the more immediate threat of becoming unemployed or seeing their wages being cut.

Such worries in turn can lead to increased financial market risk exposure over time. Following a spell of unemployment or a drop in earnings, households could end up with fewer savings and higher risk in their savings as they concentrate more on their current jobs than managing the complex financial decisions necessary to protect their savings in retirement accounts and housing, for instance. Labor market risk exposure contributes to the growing wealth gap and increasing uncertainty in savings.[4]

Linkages between Labor and Financial Market Risk Exposure

Greater labor and financial market risk exposure contributes to rising wealth inequality, such that households with high risk exposure end up with less wealth over time than is the case for households with low risk exposure. Very briefly, the logic and data I present on the links between risk exposure and wealth inequality below tell the following story. People are generally unable to directly protect themselves from high labor market risk exposure. In theory, people should then offset high labor market risk exposure, if they experience it, by lowering their financial market risk exposure. But, this is not the case, as the data show, and instead they encounter both high labor market risk exposure and unchanged financial risk exposure. This combination of labor and financial market risk exposure impedes saving and can lead

to substantial wealth loss, when financial markets go through boom
and bust cycles. Households with high labor market risk exposure ultimately end up with a lot less wealth than households without such
risk exposure because of fewer risk protections, even though they have
more risk exposure. This establishes the link between risk exposure
and wealth inequality.

I begin my discussion on risk exposure and wealth inequality with
considerations related to labor market risk exposure. Households
often have only limited control over labor market risk exposure.
Diversification is, in theory, an important risk management tool, but
households generally cannot easily diversify their labor market risk
exposure. Diversifying in this case would mean holding multiple jobs
that are economically unrelated to each other. Workers develop skills
that make them especially well suited to some jobs and industries and
not others. In addition, institutional factors, like job-related health
insurance benefits, encourage full-time jobs, making it difficult for
workers to hold multiple part-time jobs as a strategy to diversify their
labor income. These limits to households diversifying their labor market income mean that rising labor market risks more or less directly
translate into rising labor market risk exposure. People will quickly feel
more economically insecure if something goes wrong in their industry
and/or in their occupation.

Households have to find other ways to protect their economic security against labor market risk. Specifically, greater labor market risk
exposure theoretically should lead households to quickly reduce their
financial market risk exposure, so that they can at least protect their
savings, even if they cannot do much to protect their income right now.
Households, after all, want to protect their total economic security in
the present and in the future. To counteract increased labor market risk
exposure, households could quickly take a number of steps—investing
more in emergency savings (nonretirement financial assets),[5] shifting to
less risky investments, and reducing debt to asset ratios.[6]

This view of households behaving optimally and cutting their financial risk exposure when their labor market risk exposure goes up tends
to ignore real-life complications to households wanting to protect their
savings from risk, though. Households may systematically find it difficult to concentrate on the long term and change their savings behavior
accordingly, because they are stressed about losing their job or experiencing a wage cut in the here and now. Similarly, households may face
increasingly complex financial decisions in managing their financial
risk exposure during times of increased labor market risk, due to the

growing reliance on individualized savings, such as individual savings accounts and housing. This complexity already makes it hard to make optimal decisions to protect savings such as retirement savings from more financial market risks,[7] but it quickly becomes very cumbersome when households have to make such decisions across several different forms of savings such as housing and nonretirement savings, too. And, households may not be able to save more as a means to counteract higher labor market risk exposure, even if they wanted to, because they may experience a simultaneous decline in employer benefits, such as access to 401(k) plans, which are an important conduit for more savings. Moreover, even if households can figure out what the theoretically optimal decisions to protect their savings are, they may not be able to act on those decisions. An overreliance on employer-sponsored savings vehicles, like 401(k) plans, for instance, means that many key decisions are made by employers and not employees, even though the risks of investment losses are all borne by the employees. The bottom line is that households with high labor market risk exposure may not save more and may not be able to reduce their financial market risk exposure in short order.

Table 3.2 summarizes some data on the link between labor and financial market risk exposure for the period from 1989 to 2013.[8] The table shows savings behavior, nonretirement financial assets, and financial market risk exposure both by type and level of labor market risk exposure. The logic I discussed above suggests that households theoretically should respond to higher labor market risk exposure by saving more, especially by increasing emergency savings (nonretirement financial assets) and by decreasing their risky asset concentration and debt to asset ratios. However, as I also described above, households can encounter systematic and substantial real-life barriers that interfere with their ability to respond to increased labor market risk exposure optimally.

Households can experience unemployment and earnings risk exposure as two distinct labor market risks. Table 3.2 consequently divides all households into those with high and those with low unemployment risk and again into those with high and those with low earnings risk. Households have high unemployment risk exposure if they belong to a household group, defined by age, year, race, and education, that has an average unemployment rate in the top fourth of all group-specific unemployment rates. Households have high earnings risk exposure if they belong to a household group, defined by age, year, race, education, and earnings quintile, that has an average relative standard deviation of the real hourly earnings in the upper half of its respective earnings quintile over the period from 1989 to 2013.[9]

Table 3.2 shows four indicators for emergency savings and risk exposure summarized by the two labor market risk exposure measures. The four indicators include the average probability of being a saver, the median ratio of nonretirement financial assets to income, the median share of stocks and housing out of all savings, and the median ratio of debt to assets. The median is the value of a variable, in this case the debt to asset ratio, that divides a group of households exactly in half. Half of all households have more debt relative to assets and the other half has less. Again, we theoretically should see households being more likely to save, having more emergency savings, having a lower risky asset concentration, and owing less debt when they experience more labor market risk exposure.

But, that is clearly not what is happening. Table 3.2 shows no consistent link between higher labor market risk exposure and lower financial market risk exposure.[10] Households that experience high unemployment risk, for instance, have lower risky asset concentrations and thus lower financial market risk exposure than is the case for households with low unemployment risk, just as theory predicts. However, households with high unemployment risk also have more debt relative to their total savings and thus higher financial market risk exposure than is the case for households with low unemployment risk (Table 3.2). Similarly, households with high earnings risk have a lower risky asset concentration but also have a higher debt to asset ratio than households with low earnings risk.

While no contemporaneous link between higher labor market risk exposure and lower financial market risk exposure is evident, increased labor market risk exposure is clearly associated with fewer, not more, savings (Table 3.2). Households with high unemployment and high earnings risk exposure are actually less likely to be savers and have lower median nonretirement financial assets to income ratios than is the case for households with low unemployment and low earnings risk exposure (Table 3.2), suggesting that high labor market risk exposure does not go along with more savings.

Moreover, regardless of whether households face high or low labor market risk exposure, they appear to experience comparable financial market risk exposure. My calculations show that households with high unemployment risk have a 27.4 percent chance of having very high financial market risk exposure, compared to a 25.5 percent chance for households with low unemployment risk.[11] And, households with high earnings risk have a 31.2 percent chance of very high financial market risk exposure compared to a 29.8 percent chance for households with low earnings risk. That is, households with high labor market risk exposure tend to have similar financial market risk exposure as households with low labor market risk exposure. The implication then is that households appear to encounter systematic and substantial real-life obstacles to savings and risk protections, such that large numbers of households end up with high risk exposure on multiple fronts when they experience labor market risk exposure at a time of increasing labor and financial market risks. That is, households are indeed getting caught in a Category 5 hurricane without better protections.

Delayed Effect of Labor Market Risk Exposure on Financial Market Risk Exposure

The impact of labor market risk exposure on savings and financial market risk exposure may linger for a while, as the primary obstacles to saving more and reducing risk exposure—both behavioral and policy-related—are unlikely to disappear.

I now calculate what happens to financial market risk exposure after households experience either high earnings risk or high unemployment risk. This calculation requires some additional explanation. I use the Federal Reserve System's *SCF*, which has detailed information on household finances and labor market circumstances. But, it is a cross-sectional data set that does not follow the same households over time. To address this shortcoming, I calculate averages for household groups, defined by birth date, race, education, and year, so that I can follow similar groups of households over time. This approach is also called a synthetic cohort approach.[12]

This approach allows me to define earnings risk somewhat differently than before. I refer to this as slow earnings growth, rather than high earnings risk, to distinguish from the earlier risk measure. My previous calculations used household-level data, which allowed for a nuanced discussion of risk exposure by household characteristics, but which prevented comparisons over time. I earlier calculated earnings risk as the volatility of wages and salaries in any given year as an approximation of the chance that earnings fall. I now define earnings risks as actually having low earnings growth from one survey year to the next survey year—over a three-year period. A group of households

Table 3.3 Lagged effect of labor market risk exposure on financial market risk exposure

Labor market risk indicator and number of lags	Average chance of being a saver	Median risky asset concentration	Median debt to asset ratio	Share of households with very high financial risk exposure
High unemployment risk				
No lag	40.7%	48.2%	1256.0%	23.5%
Three-year lag	40.5%	46.2%	700.4%	21.6%
Six-year lag	39.7%	48.4%	643.7%	20.6%
Nine-year lag	41.0%	50.5%	579.7%	23.0%
High earnings risk				
Three-year lag	45.4%	55.7%	308.0%	23.2%
Six-year lag	46.3%	55.4%	392.4%	22.9%
Nine-year lag	45.0%	56.5%	249.1%	22.8%
Lagged three times	45.8%	56.6%	331.7%	23.3%

Notes: Sample includes all nonretiree households. Calculations are only done for households in the labor force. Calculations reflect synthetic cohort defined by birth date, race, education, and year. High unemployment risk is defined by group-specific unemployment rates that fall into the top fourth of unemployment rate. High earnings risk is defined by three-year real hourly earnings growth rates that fall into the bottom third of earnings growth rates.

Source: Based on Board of Governors, Federal Reserve System, *Survey of Consumer Finances* (Washington, DC: BOG, various years).

has low earnings growth if the growth of its real hourly earnings during a three-year period falls into the bottom third of all group-specific three-year earnings growth rates. This calculation, though, necessarily eliminates 1989 as an observation year, since we are measuring year-over-year changes.

Table 3.3 shows financial risk exposure in the years after a household experiences low earnings growth and high unemployment risk. The table specifically shows the median risky asset concentration, the median indebtedness, and the average share of households with very high financial risk exposure—at least 75 percent risky asset concentration and 25 percent debt to asset ratio—during the same year and three, six, and nine years after the same group of households experienced low earnings growth and high unemployment risk.

The data show again no systematic increase in savings behavior and no systematic decrease in financial risk exposure after households experience high labor market risk exposure (Table 3.3). The average share of savers after high unemployment risk was about 41 percent and the average share of savers after low earnings growth was about 46 percent, but there is no discernible trend in either case toward increasing savings behavior after households experienced high labor market risk exposure. And, the share of households with very high financial risk exposure falls from 23.5 percent in the year when households experience high unemployment risk to 21.6 percent three years later and to 20.6 percent six years later, but rises to 23.0 percent nine years later (Table 3.3). This is largely a result of declining indebtedness, as households save more when they age, while the risky asset concentration slightly increases over time, as this particular cohort invested increasingly in stocks and housing during the boom years (Table 3.3). After households experience high earnings risk, the share of households with very high financial risk exposure remains basically stable with about 23 percent, and neither indebtedness nor risky asset concentration showed any meaningful trends (Table 3.3). Again, there is little evidence that households systematically adjust their savings behavior and financial risk exposure after experiencing high labor market risk exposure. Put differently, even considering longer-term effects, households have been caught in the perfect storm of rising labor and financial market risks without added protections.

The persistence of financial market risk exposure after households experience high labor market risk exposure likely reflects systematic behavioral obstacles to managing risk exposure in complex individual savings.[13] After all, the importance of other explanations such as high transaction costs and persistent liquidity constraints to diversify risky assets has somewhat declined over time as credit market competition has increased, interest rates and some fees have declined, and credit market access has grown.[14] That should have made it easier for households to manage their financial risk exposure over time and thus helped households to better respond to high labor market risk exposure. Lower liquidity constraints, for instance, theoretically should have made it easier for households to reallocate their risky and illiquid housing assets and reduce debt. Households, though, increasingly borrowed to finance consumption such as college education and health care when debt became more easily available.[15] The actual use of debt further supports the notion that households faced substantial obstacles to reduce their risk exposure when labor market risks increased. The facts that households' savings did not go up and, more importantly, that their risk exposure did not decline suggest that people systematically encounter problems in protecting their savings from too much risk. This is especially troublesome, when labor and financial markets become riskier, as have been the case for the past 30 years.

Long-Term Effect of Labor Market Risk
Exposure on Wealth Inequality

Financial market risk exposure and thus persistent savings uncertainty is only one long-term consequence of rising labor market risk exposure. Households with high labor market risk exposure also tend to accumulate fewer savings over time than households with less labor market risk exposure.

I show the link between labor market risk exposure and wealth inequality graphically in Figure 3.2. This figure reports the wealth-to-income ratio for near-retiree households between the ages of 50 and 59 years in 2013 (i.e., those within 10–15 years of reaching a typical retirement age), broken down by how many cumulative episodes of high unemployment or high earnings risk they experienced between 1992 and 2013.[16]

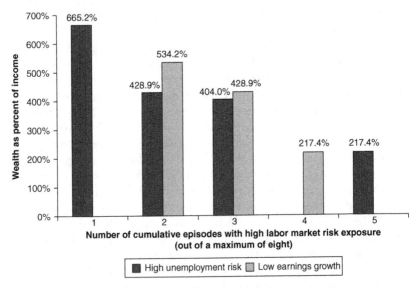

Figure 3.2   Median wealth-to-income ratios for near-retiree households in 2013 by number of cumulative high labor market risk exposure episodes (out of a maximum of eight).

Notes: Sample includes households between the ages of 50 and 59 in 2013. Calculations are only done for households in the labor force. Calculations reflect synthetic cohort defined by birth date, race, education, and year. High unemployment risk is defined by group-specific unemployment rates that fall into the top fourth of unemployment rate. High earnings risk is defined by three-year real hourly earnings growth rates that fall into the bottom third of earnings growth rates.

Source: Based on Board of Governors, Federal Reserve System, *Survey of Consumer Finances* (Washington, DC: BOG, various years).

Households experienced between one and five cumulative episodes characterized by high labor market risk exposure. Specifically, households experienced one, two, three, or five cumulative episodes with high unemployment risk and experienced two, three, or four cumulative episodes with low earnings growth (Figure 3.2).

Figure 3.2 indicates that groups of households that have experienced more frequent episodes of high labor market risk exposure ended up with substantially lower wealth-to-income ratios in 2013. Near-retirees in 2013 who had two episodes of high unemployment risk, for instance, had a median wealth-to-income ratio of 428.9 percent, compared to only 217.4 percent for those who experienced five such episodes. Near-retirees with two episodes of low earnings growth had a median wealth-to-income ratio of 534.2 percent, compared to 217.4 percent for those who experienced four such episodes (Figure 3.2). The wealth-to-income ratio drops by 111.9 percentage points for each additional episode between one and five episodes of high unemployment risk. And, it decreases by 158.4 percentage points between one and three episodes of high earnings risks (Figure 3.2). Put differently, each episode of high labor market risk lowers wealth for the typical household near retirement by more than one year's worth of income. Households with high risk exposure, who arguably need more protections to enjoy a secure retirement, actually end up with fewer savings and less security over time.

This parallel between higher labor market risk exposure and lower wealth–income ratios illustrates the connection between high labor market risk exposure and increased wealth inequality. Households with high labor market risk exposure in the past, which theoretically should have saved more money to protect against future labor market uncertainty than households with less labor market risk exposure, in fact ended up with less wealth relative to income.

Conclusion

The growing risk exposure households have experienced over the past three decades has contributed to increasingly unstable savings and rising wealth inequality. Labor market risk exposure in the present, in particular, translates into less wealth in the future as households near retirement. This link between high labor market risk exposure and growing wealth inequality likely reflects systematic behavioral obstacles—an inability to quickly execute increasingly complex financial decisions in a more and more volatile world. Households consequently have saved less (rather than more) and maintained (rather than reduced) their financial risk exposure, even as they were exposed to an environment marked by high labor market risks. Today's economic insecurity will linger long into the future and substantially reduce the chances of a secure and desired retirement.

CHAPTER FOUR

The Looming Retirement Shipwreck

How would you personally define what a secure retirement means to you?[1]

"Live at the same standard while I worked and not have to take another job." (White man, 69 years old)

"Not living under a bridge." (White man, 66 years old)

Some households have experienced sharp wealth gains, and many others have seen no or only small wealth increases over the past few decades as rising household risk exposure has impeded savings. But, this growing wealth gap by itself does not tell the whole story. Wealth is a store of future income that people can rely on when they no longer have income from work, for instance, when they retire. Rising wealth inequality then means that a growing share of households will likely not be able to maintain their standard of living in retirement and hence will have to make substantial spending cuts or significantly delay retirement.

Everyone envisions and designs their transition into retirement somewhat differently.[2] But everyone wants to stay economically in control of their lives after retirement. People also often want to remain productive as they age, for instance, by continuing to work with more flexible schedules, by volunteering, and even by starting their own businesses.[3] Remaining productive in these ways, though, requires a lot of savings in addition to Social Security. Older households also want to be sure that they can pay their bills before pursuing their aspirations and goals in retirement.[4]

Researchers have long studied people's ability to maintain their standard of living in retirement. The exact findings of these studies differ, but three common themes stand out. First, a large share of households will not be able to maintain their standard of living in retirement. Second, communities of color, households with less education, single women, and lower income households are more likely to face economic difficulties in old age than is the case for whites, single men, households with more education, and higher income households. And third, the share of households that are expected to encounter significant economic problems in retirement has been growing for the past three decades, which has led researchers to warn about the looming retirement crisis.[5]

This chapter summarizes the research on retirement income adequacy as one of the most meaningful real-life reflections of wealth inequality. I first discuss standard definitions of retirement income adequacy and then highlight findings on retirement income adequacy.[6]

Defining Retirement Income Adequacy

Researchers interested in understanding whether households are on track to save enough for retirement ultimately want to link individual savings in the present to the income people will need in the future. Two broad approaches to retirement income adequacy exist, reflecting separate notions of retirement needs, although they arrive at similar conclusions.[7]

One approach tries to capture people's ability to pay for basic living expenses. This measure implicitly reflects the value-based principle that all retirees should have enough money available to pay for life's basic necessities. It estimates whether households' projected future retirement income from Social Security, DB pensions, and private savings (including housing) will be greater than the federal poverty line or a multiple of it, such as twice the poverty line.[8] The poverty line often serves as a proxy for the bare minimum income needed to survive in retirement.[9] In 2010, for instance, 12.1 percent of households aged between 47 and 64 years were expected to have retirement income that was below the poverty line.[10]

Another approach attempts to measure whether or not people will have the resources to sustain their quality of life postretirement. This retirement income adequacy approach defines adequacy as a minimum retirement income relative to people's preretirement earnings.[11]

A household is then adequately prepared for retirement if their expected retirement income is greater than a minimum share, such as 75 percent of household's earnings, before they retired.[12]

This ratio of retirement income to preretirement earnings is also known as the replacement rate. It measures the share of preretirement earnings a household can replace with the income it can expect to receive from Social Security, DB pensions, and private savings. Defining retirement income adequacy as a minimum replacement rate explicitly states that retirees should be able to maintain their standard of living in retirement.

These two retirement income adequacy measures are complementary in informing public policy. The first, value-based measure, tells policymakers which households are likely to fall short of being able to pay for basic necessities in retirement; it can, therefore, help policymakers design targeted public programs to help people cover those basic costs. Medicare and Medicaid, among other public programs, are rooted in this approach.

The second relative income measure tells policymakers which households will likely have to cut their typical consumption in retirement. It thus tells policymakers where to target policy interventions that can boost savings. Employment-based retirement benefits, such as DB pensions and 401(k) plans, are anchored in this approach, since they tie savings to earnings.

Importantly, Social Security's retirement benefits present a combination of the two approaches by giving relatively generous benefits to people with relatively low earnings and by tying retirement benefits to people's lifetime earnings.

The replacement rate approach will generally suggest that households will need more savings to maintain their standard of living in retirement than to just cover basic necessities. I consequently focus the rest of this chapter on the evidence related to replacement rates.

Evidence on Retirement Income Preparedness

The evidence on retirement income adequacy generally shows that a large share of households, especially among communities of color, single women, and households with less education, is ill-prepared to maintain their standard of living in retirement. And the share has grown over long periods of time, according to most studies that provide longer-term views.[13]

A study of the trends in wealth-to-income ratios for households over time offers some approximation of whether households have become increasingly better prepared for retirement. Wealth is the store of future income that households can draw upon when their income shrinks due to retirement or other circumstances.[14] Therefore, researchers typically report wealth relative to income to capture trends of average economic security over time.[15] This ratio gives a sense of whether savings have at least kept pace with current income and thus with households' current purchasing power.

Importantly, the wealth-to-income ratio should have gone up over time for a number of reasons. Newer retirees have faced rising costs that prior cohorts did not have to bear, and households need to have additional savings to pay for these additional retirement costs. These include longer life expectancies and more time spent in retirement, the declining growth of Social Security benefits (due to rising retirement age), and increasing labor and financial market risk exposure. Risk exposure is a cost to household because it increases the chance of losing a substantial amount of money, and households would need to build up additional savings as a protection against this potential loss.

Figure 4.1 shows the median wealth-to-income ratios for four different age groups among nonretirees older than 30 years from 1989 to 2013. The median is the midpoint of all available wealth-to-income ratios, so that half of all households in any age group have less wealth and the other half have more wealth. Wealth-to-income ratios sharply dropped after the Great Recession, after they had remained relatively stable in the 1990s and increased somewhat in the 2000s. There is no clear and consistent upward shift in wealth, which we should have expected to see if households saved more for retirement while simultaneously addressing rising costs associated with retirement savings.

These trends are especially troublesome since the wealth-to-income ratio should have also risen, more or less automatically in these data, because more people save with 401(k) plans and IRAs nowadays than in the past. These savings are included in household wealth, while future benefits from DB pensions are not.[16] Wealth-to-income ratios should have gone up in the data simply because defined contribution (DC) accounts have become more widespread. There is little evidence that retirement preparedness has improved for typical households. We should in fact see stable and possibly falling retirement income adequacy rather than improving retirement preparedness over time, judging from

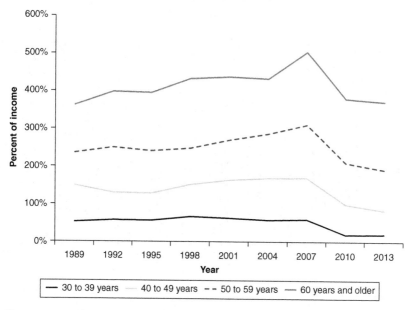

Figure 4.1 Median wealth-to-income ratios, by age group and year.

Notes: All figures are in percentage. The sample includes only households under the age of 60, with the heads of households indicating that they are not yet retired.

Source: Based on Board of Governors, Federal Reserve System, *Survey of Consumer Finances* (Washington, DC: BOG, various years).

the wealth-to-income ratios. And, that is exactly what the existing research shows, as I discuss below.

Most Households Are at Risk of Having to Cut on Their Living Expenses in Retirement

I summarize the data from the Center for Retirement Research at Boston College (CRR), specifically their National Retirement Risk Index (NRRI) as an indicator of retirement income preparedness.[17] This index offers reliable comparisons over time, is based on very detailed wealth and income calculations for each household, and generally errs on the side of overstating retirement preparedness when making methodological decisions.[18] For instance, CRR assumes that households will liquidate all of their savings held in their house by taking out a reverse mortgage to pay for all types of consumption, including nonhousing

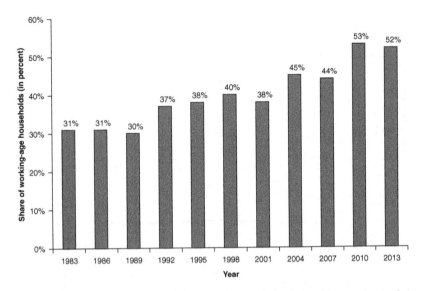

Figure 4.2   Share of working-age households at risk of not being able to maintain their standard of living in retirement, by year.

Notes: All data are in percentage, showing the share of households, not yet retired and younger than 65 years, who are expected to be unable to maintain their standard of living in retirement.

Source: Alicia Munnell, Wenliang Hu, and Anthony Webb, "NRRI Update Shows Half Still Falling Short" (Boston: Center for Retirement Research at Boston College, 2014).

consumption. This likely overstates the actual retirement income for many households that do not liquidate their home equity.

The NRRI then measures the share of working-age households that have not yet reached the full retirement age and that are at risk of being unable to maintain their standard of living in retirement based on their expected income from Social Security, DB pensions, and individual savings, including 401(k) plans, IRAs, and housing.

Figure 4.2 summarizes the NRRI from 1983 to 2013. The data show a trend toward a growing share of working-age households that are inadequately prepared for retirement. An estimated 52 percent of working-age households were at risk of not being able to maintain their standard of living in retirement in 2013, up from 31 percent in 1983. That is, the share of households that are inadequately prepared for retirement is large and increasing, according to this measure.

Importantly, the NRRI shows shortfalls that are below those recorded by other researchers. A report by the National Institute on

Retirement Security (NIRS), for instance, finds that 65 percent of households fell short of their savings targets in 2010 using savings levels recommended by the financial service industry and the same data as the NRRI.[19] The NRRI, in comparison, finds that in 2010 only 53 percent of working-age households were at risk of not being able to maintain their standard of living in retirement.[20]

Even studies that find lower shares of households inadequately prepared for retirement than is the case for the NRRI have found evidence of increasing retirement income inadequacy. A widely cited and comparatively optimistic assessment of retirement income adequacy by researchers at the University of Wisconsin in 2006 found that those born between 1931 and 1941, based on data from the University of Michigan's Health and Retirement Study, had only a 16 percent chance of falling below their optimal savings target.[21] An update of this research, though, coauthored by William Gale from the Brookings Institution in 2009—before the full effect of the Great Recession was felt—found that 26 percent of households were inadequately prepared for retirement.[22] And similarly, studies that break down data by age find that younger generations are less prepared for retirement than older cohorts.[23]

The overwhelming evidence suggests that a substantial share of households are already inadequately prepared for retirement, and the problem of households being inadequately prepared for retirement has been getting worse.

Retirement Income Adequacy by Demographics

The estimates for the share of households that are inadequately prepared for retirement vary with household characteristics. The respective shares tend to be greater among communities of color, single women, and those with lower education than among white households, single men, and households with higher education.

Few researchers provide consistent breakdowns of retirement income adequacy by household characteristics. New York University Professor Edward Wolff offers such breakdowns for households aged between 47 and 64 years in his research on wealth inequality.[24] This research shows that 51 percent of households in this age group in 2010 were unable to replace 75 percent of their preretirement income in retirement.[25] The relevant share for non-Hispanic whites is 45 percent, compared with 60 percent for African Americans and Hispanics. Also

59 percent of single women can expect to have to cut on their living expenses once they retire, while this applies to only 51 percent
of single men, based on 2010 data. Finally, households with less than
12 years of schooling—those without a high school diploma or General
Educational Development—have an estimated 61 percent chance of
falling short of maintaining their standard of living in retirement, while
only 43 percent of households with 16 or more years of schooling—
those with at least a college degree—may have to cut on consumption
in retirement.[26]

Risk Exposure Not Systematically Included in
Retirement Income Adequacy Research

The question of whether people will have enough money for retirement is straightforward enough, but it is also very broad, leading to a
multitude of approaches and research findings. These variations depend
on a number of methodological issues, which I discuss in the appendix
in more detail.

Most important for the discussion of this book is the treatment of
households' exposure to financial and labor market risks in retirement
income adequacy studies. Studies on retirement income adequacy
generally relate household savings—future expected income—to
preretirement income. Although different types of savings expose
households to different levels of financial market risks, these studies
make no distinction between expected Social Security income, DB
benefits, and income from financial (e.g., 401(k) plans) and nonfinancial savings (e.g., housing). Since risk exposure is a cost to households,
savings that expose them to more risks and offer fewer protections
consequently are less valuable as sources of future income. Dollar for
dollar, Social Security income, for instance, is more valuable to households than 401(k) savings because it does not expose them to financial
market risks.

Households' financial risk exposure has increased over time, which
is not captured in retirement income adequacy studies. Accounting for
the growing risk exposure in household savings would consequently
show an even more quickly worsening trend toward retirement income
adequacy than the existing studies do.[27] Such an adjustment could
also show wider gaps in retirement preparedness by demographics since
the household groups that are least likely to be adequately prepared
for retirement—single women, households with little education, and

communities of color—tend to be also the household groups with the largest financial market risk exposure, especially debt.

The growing labor market uncertainty is similarly not captured by most retirement adequacy studies. An increasing uncertainty of future earnings—labor market risk—should theoretically lead households to want to save more and seek out safer investments with their savings. Inversely, a given amount of savings will provide less retirement security in a more uncertain world since households need to set aside more money for unexpected labor market emergencies—unemployment and wage declines. Rising labor market risks then translate into less retirement income adequacy, all else equal. Only a few studies explicitly model earnings uncertainty and show that a growing share of households is inadequately prepared for retirement.[28]

Conclusion

A large and growing share of households has fallen behind in preparing for retirement as wealth inequality has grown. Rising and widespread wealth inequality means that a growing share of households in an aging society will likely have to make substantial and painful cuts to their living standard in retirement and thus have to rely on public assistance or help from family members as they get older. And these possibilities could become even greater when financial market risks materialize—stock and housing markets crash—as was the case from 2007 to 2009 since households are increasingly exposed to such risks. Households' growing risk exposure, amid increasingly turbulent labor and financial markets, has left many households with a sinking feeling of a retirement.

Appendix

Most retirement income adequacy studies differ on three methodological choices: target replacement, projections of future retirement
income, and calculations of preretirement income. I briefly discuss
what these methodological choices can mean for researchers' conclusions on the level of retirement income adequacy. Researchers typically
do not change methodologies from one study to the next, so that trends
in retirement income adequacy do not tend to be influenced by these
choices. And, as I discuss in the main text, researchers across the board
have concluded that retirement income inadequacy has become a growing problem. As for the main three methodological choices, retirement
income adequacy is greater if the target replacement rate is lower and
the assumed cuts to consumption in retirement are smaller if all savings, including housing, are available to pay for retirees' spending and
if preretirement income is lower. The biggest differences and debates
center on future consumption patterns of retirees and thus the correct
replacement rate, followed by considerations of how much retirement
income individual savings will provide.

Target Replacement Rates

Researchers use a wide range of target replacement rates.[29] It can range
from as low as 70 percent to as high as 85 percent.[30] NIRS used a
replacement rate of 85 percent in its study and found that 65 percent
of households were inadequately prepared for retirement in 2010.[31]
CRR, in comparison, uses a varying replacement rate that averages to
73 percent for all working-age households in the NRRI. The NRRI's
target replacement rate is higher for lower income households and single earners have to account for fixed costs in retirement, particularly
health-care costs.[32] NIRS has found that 53 percent of households were
inadequately prepared for retirement in 2010. A widely cited study
by researchers at the Urban Institute concludes that between 34 and
43 percent of households in the early 2000s could expect to have less
than 75 percent of their preretirement earnings in retirement.[33] The
Retirement Security Projection Model from EBRI models replacement rates of 50, 70, and 90 percent.[34]

Differences in target replacement rates often reflect differences in researchers' assumptions about whether or not households will maintain or reduce their spending as they get older. Most studies assume that people will cut their spending to some degree, as reflected in target replacement rates of less than 100 percent for households to reach what is considered adequate retirement income. But some studies also assume that households gradually decrease their consumption as the share of widows and widowers among retirees increases. The assumption here is that smaller households will cut consumption, even if they live in the same house as before, for instance. The rate at which consumption is expected to decline explains a large share of the difference in retirement adequacy findings.[35]

It is important to note that researchers acknowledge that households change their consumption behavior when they retire. However, this consumption behavior could change in a number of different ways. People may replace less costly consumption in certain areas, such as eating at home, with more costly consumption, such as eating out. They may lower clothing consumption and increase health-care consumption, which generally has seen faster price increases than other consumption. That is, it is unclear whether households actually do and can lower their spending in retirement, and this question is still an unresolved empirical issue.[36] Assuming that households on average reduce their spending when, for instance, children move out or spouses die leads researchers to overstate retirement income adequacy.

Projecting Future Sources and Levels of Retirement Income

Estimating future retirement income also leads to some differences in the conclusions on retirement income adequacy. Researchers generally assume that future retirement income will come from Social Security, DB pensions, and from liquidating all private savings—retirement accounts, nonretirement accounts, and, in some instances, home equity. Projecting the future amount households will have available in accounts, such as 401(k) plans and IRAs, creates some of the largest differences in projecting future retirement income. That is, researchers typically project future Social Security and DB pension benefits in comparable ways, but differ in their approaches to projecting private savings.

Future Social Security benefits will depend on how much a household earned during their careers. Researchers use some variation of a statistical method known as regression analysis to forecast households' earnings into the future up to an assumed retirement age, generally the age at which households can receive full benefits from Social Security.[37] Researchers can then estimate the future Social Security benefits a household can expect based on the established Social Security benefit formula. Calculating future DB pension benefits also depends on people's earnings with a particular employer prior to retiring. Researchers then can also estimate future DB pension benefits, as long as they have sufficient information on the details of a particular DB pension plan.[38] The calculations, then, show the future income retirees can expect from Social Security and DB pensions with only small methodological variations.

However, calculating how much retirement income households can expect from their private savings is subject to some debate. There is some difference of opinion, for instance, over whether or not housing should be part of retirement income adequacy calculations. Categorizing housing similar to other savings that are accessed to pay for everyday expenses, like food and health care, likely overstates future retirement income. In reality, most people do not use housing in this way and primarily benefit from it by living in their home, rent free. Few people actually free up home equity for spending by taking reverse mortgages. The inclusion of housing in calculations of expected retirement income assumes that retirees will indeed take reverse mortgages, which probably exaggerates future retirement income.[39] For example, one study finds that 84 percent of households meet their wealth target when all housing wealth is considered. However, the percentage of households meeting their wealth target drops to 61 percent when only half of a household's housing wealth is counted as available for retirement consumption.[40]

Even greater variation in retirement income adequacy projections arises due to differences in how researchers calculate the future amount households may have saved in their 401(k) plans and IRAs. Some use balances in 401(k) plans and IRAs, just as they generally do with other household savings such as nonretirement assets.[41] However, this does not take into account people earning returns on their savings, saving more, and paying down debt, likely understating future savings available to pay for retirement.[42]

Alternatively, researchers can make some projections on how savings balances will grow in the future, based on their assumptions about future savings rates and future rates of return on both current and future account balances.[43] But if savings rates or rates of return on savings decline over time, this may cause researchers to overstate the amount households will have available in their 401(k) plans and IRAs when they retire.

Current retirement savings projections are based on the most recent rates of return, from the early 1980s to 2010. This may overstate projections of what people will have in their accounts at retirement, since these rates tend to be fairly high due to considerable stock market booms. Similarly, people may not save at the same rate as they did in the past, which may cause overstated predicted future savings. Realistically, households may lower their future savings rates if retirement account contribution by employers declines. Indeed, there is some evidence on declining contributions from employers to the retirement plans they sponsor. Recent projections of 401(k) plan and IRA account balances likely overstate future savings.

This is especially true for younger households that are still decades away from retirement and for whom small variations in savings rates make substantial differences in projected retirement income adequacy. In 2006, the CRR estimated that just a three percent decline in the share of pay contributed to 401(k) plans and IRAs would increase the percentage of Generation Xers who may be at risk of being unable to maintain their standard of living in retirement from 49 to 57 percent. For early Baby Boomers, comparatively, the same savings rate decline would only raise the share of households at risk of not being able to maintain their standard of living in retirement from 43 to 47 percent.[44]

Retirement income adequacy depends also on how households will convert their savings into retirement income. Researchers commonly assume that retirees will annuitize all of their assets, converting them into lifetime streams of income.[45] In reality, though, few households annuitize their savings, and it is more common to self-manage retirement asset withdrawal. Some researchers consequently assume that households will withdraw from their assets at rates based on maximum life expectancies as insurance against running out of money in retirement.[46] Under the two scenarios—full annuitization and self-management—the same initial retirement assets can be expected to lead to about one-fifth less monthly retirement income for those who self-manage withdrawals compared to those who annuitize.[47] This difference in expected monthly income exists because under annuitization, retirees share the risk of outliving their savings with each other and monthly payments are determined based on average life expectancy. On the other hand, those who self-manage retirement asset withdrawal need to plan for the possibility that they may live longer than average. Therefore, they need to calculate their monthly withdrawals based on the maximum possible life expectancy to avoid outliving their money. The same savings at retirement can have different implications for retirement income, depending on whether they are expected to annuitize or self-manage withdrawals.

Calculating Income and Consumption Growth before Retirement

Finally, retirement income adequacy studies also vary on how they handle preretirement income. Researchers typically average preretirement income over a certain period of time. This period of time can be relatively short, encompassing only the final few years of a person's career, or it can be rather long, encompassing people's entire careers. Final earnings will be higher than average lifetime incomes, since incomes tend to go up over a person's career.[48]

The average income before retirement further increases with two additional key variables. First, preretirement income is greater if researchers include all forms of income such as capital gains, interest and dividend income, business income, among others, in their income calculations.[49] Using only wage and salary earnings likely understates the amount the average household regularly lives on and the amount households will need to replace in retirement to maintain their standard of living.[50] Second, preretirement income is adjusted for either inflation or wage growth prior to retirement to make income during those years comparable with each other. Wage-adjusting preretirement income implies that retirees should benefit from the average productivity gains during their careers when they retire.[51] Adjusting preretirement income just for inflation and not just wage growth, which is faster than price increases, does not make this assumption. Correcting all preretirement income just for inflation implicitly assumes, for instance, that the living standards 40 years before retirement are as good a comparison point for retiree living standards as the ones recorded just one year before retirement. Since wages typically rise faster than inflation, wage adjustments are greater than price adjustments. Greater preretirement adjustments, though, increase all recorded incomes before retirement and hence raise households' average preretirement incomes and thus the savings necessary to maintain their standard of living in retirement.[52]

Social Security: The Leaky Lifeboat

How would you personally define what a secure retirement means to you?[1]

"A financially secure retirement would mean that there would not be any surprises with Medicare or Social Security." (White woman, 66 years old)

Households have had a hard time saving enough for their future amid growing economic insecurity. Labor and financial markets have become more volatile over the past three decades, and households' exposure to these risks has increased. This combination of rising risks and falling protections has contributed to increasing wealth inequality as especially households with high risk exposure have seen smaller savings gains than their counterparts.

Risk protections can come from Social Security and household savings. Public policy needs to set the parameters for Americans to find the right balance between too much and too little economic risk exposure in their savings. The balance has shifted toward more risk exposure over the past three decades, just as labor and financial market risks have grown, in part because policy has weakened Social Security's risk protections.

Social Security benefits are part of household savings for virtually all households. They offer substantial risk protections to households since these benefits do not depend on financial market risk and they partially counter the effects of high labor market risks on households' future income. Yet, a closer look at enacted and proposed changes to Social Security shows how policy has already weakened and could further weaken this basic, universal protection against too much household risk exposure.

I discuss enacted and possible future changes to Social Security that have already eroded or could erode households' risk protections in the future, just when households need those protections since labor and financial market volatility is high.

I consider five key Social Security policy issues in this chapter that illustrate the growing tension between the rising need for and the declining value of Social Security's benefits amid rising risks. First, rising inequality following increasing labor market risks has increased Social Security's financial shortfall. Social Security pays progressive benefits—lower wage earners receive relatively higher benefits than higher wage earners; and it imposes regressive taxes—lower wage earners pay a larger share of their wages in Social Security taxes than higher wage earners. Rising earnings inequality has created a widening gap between tax revenue and promised benefits, and this widening gap has worsened Social Security's financial outlook.

Second, Social Security pays a spousal benefit for spouses who have much lower lifetime earnings than their partners. The design of this benefit, which harkens back to the days when single-earner couples were the norm, creates an inequity between single-earner couples and dual-earner couples, where both spouses have substantial earnings throughout their career. The surviving spouse of dual-earner couple will receive a relatively lower survivorship benefit than the surviving spouse of a single-earner couple. But dual-earner couples have become more common over time, in part because families' need for additional earnings increased amid rising labor market risks. The result is that dual-earner couples have somewhat weaker retirement income protections than single-earner couples, even though part of the reason for both spouses working is the need for more incomes.

Third, policymakers established a special minimum benefit in 1972, but they designed it in such a way that its value has been gradually eroding ever since.[2] A key protection from the longer term consequences of growing labor market risk simultaneously became more important and weaker.

Fourth, Social Security reforms enacted in 1983 also set in motion an increase in the age at which workers can receive full Social Security benefits, from 65 years to eventually 67 years for people born after 1959.[3] The first cohorts of workers retiring with a full-benefit retirement age of 67 years will also have experienced greater labor and financial market risks than prior cohorts. A range of Social Security reform proposals advocate even further increases in the full-benefit age beyond 67 years, although labor and financial market risks remain high. This across-the-board benefit cut has lowered Social Security's insurance value for those who especially needed its protections.

Social Security's insurance value has fallen due to the rising full-benefit age, even if we consider that people on average live longer now than in the past. That is, some households can on average expect to receive permanently lower benefits for a longer time. But this only holds for higher income earners, as life expectancy for lower income earners has not moved much or even fallen.[4] Lower income earners who disproportionately depend on Social Security benefits in part because of greater risk exposure during their working years have to make do with permanently lower benefits for similar or shorter periods of time than in the past if they want to retire before the full retirement age.

Fifth, Social Security serves as a key counterweight to rising financial market risk exposure, too. Neither its revenue nor its benefits depend on financial market performances. Proposals to direct some portion of the Social Security payroll tax into individual investment accounts would change that, though. Workers would then face financial market risk exposure with part of their Social Security savings.

I briefly discuss these five points. My discussion highlights the rising tension between the growing need for Social Security benefits and the gradually falling value of these benefits for many families. It also provides some background on public opinion polls to show that policy considerations at the end of the book are, at least in part, anchored in people's anxieties about their future, not just in the economics of household savings.[5]

Social Security's Universal, Yet Basic Retirement Benefits

Social Security is a public insurance program that applies to almost all workers. All private sector employees, the self-employed, and public sector employees in most states are covered by Social Security. There are 14 states, including Alaska, California, and Massachusetts, where the majority of public sector workers are exempt from Social Security and instead pay into a state retirement system.[6] But many of these public sector workers will also work part of their careers in jobs, either in other states or in the private sector, that are covered by Social Security, so that Social Security is close to a universal insurance program. By

Table 5.1 Number of beneficiaries and average monthly benefit, by benefit type (August 2014)

Type of benefit	Number of beneficiaries (in millions)	Average monthly benefit
Total Social Security	58.6	$1,191
Retirement benefits	47.7	$1,235
Retired workers	41.6	$1,256
Spouses of retired workers	2.3	$657
Children of retired workers	0.6	$634
Survivor benefits	6.1	$1,088
Children of deceased workers	1.9	$815
Widowed mothers and fathers	0.1	$922
Nondisabled widow(er)s	3.8	$1,251
Disabled widow(er)s	0.3	$713
Disability benefits	10.9	$1,001
Disabled workers	9	$1,145
Spouses of disabled workers	0.2	$310
Children of disabled workers	1.8	$342

Source: Social Security Administration, "Monthly Statistical Snapshot" (Washington, DC: SSA, August 2014).

2013, 87 percent of all American workers had already worked long enough that they could expect to receive some Social Security retirement benefits in the future.[7]

Social Security's official name—Old-Age and Survivors Insurance and Disability Insurance—is a mouthful, but describes the breadth of its insurance protections. Retirement benefits have been part of the program for more than 80 years, but other parts of the program are younger. Policymakers added, for instance, survivorship benefits in 1939 for surviving family members when the primary breadwinner dies and created a disability insurance program in 1956 for workers and their families when the main earner becomes disabled.

While the program offers a broad range of benefits, the benefit levels tend to be modest. The average retirement benefit for a retired worker, for example, amounted to only $1,302 in August 2014, while other benefits were, on average, lower than that (Table 5.1).[8]

Calculating Social Security Benefits

A little background on how Social Security currently operates is necessary to understand the five linkages between rising risk exposure and

Social Security's present and future benefits. This section first discusses how Social Security calculates benefits and then describes where Social Security receives its income to pay for these benefits.

Social Security benefits are tied to workers' wages and salaries such that absolute benefits increase with earnings; they are progressive such that lower income earners receive relatively more in benefits than higher income earners; and they are primarily paid for with payroll taxes imposed on current wages and salaries.

The Social Security Administration bases its benefit calculations on the Average Indexed Monthly Earnings (AIME). This is an average of a worker's 35 years of highest earnings. Earnings in past years are increased by the average wage growth that has occurred since then, which makes earnings in earlier years comparable to earnings in later years. A worker who earned money subject to Social Security taxes for less than 35 years has the missing years recorded as years of zero earnings. Somebody who has earned a wage and paid Social Security taxes for 31 years, for instance, then has four years of no or zero earnings, which lowers her AIME. Importantly, only the highest 35 years of a worker's wages and salaries subject to Social Security taxation form the basis for the calculation of Social Security benefits.

Social Security then uses the AIME to calculate people's monthly benefits using a progressive benefit formula such that higher AIMEs result in higher benefits, but the increases in benefits become smaller as the AIME gets larger. Workers in 2014 could expect to receive 90 percent or $0.90 for each dollar of the first $816 of their AIME as benefits, 32 percent or $0.32 for each dollar over $816 but below $4,917, and 15 percent or $0.15 for each dollar over $4,917. The AIME is potentially split into three different amounts, each multiplied by a different and progressively smaller percentage and then added together to arrive at a person's Primary Insurance Amount (PIA)—this is the amount a single beneficiary will receive upon retirement at the full-retirement benefit age, for example

The PIA also forms the basis for other relevant retirement calculations to determine the benefits for eligible dependents. Spouses,[9] even former ones, children, and dependent parents can qualify for an additional benefit that depends on the primary beneficiary's PIA, if they do not have any or only low PIAs themselves. Take, for instance, the case of a married couple. The couple will receive the higher amount of either the sum of both spouses' PIAs or 150 percent of the higher earning spouse's PIA. That is, there is a spousal benefit equal to half of the higher earning spouse's benefit. This spousal benefit often applies if one spouse took long periods out of the labor market for caregiving responsibilities.

Social Security also offers survivorship benefits, which are most relevant for widows or widowers (Table 5.1), but can also apply to surviving children.[10] A surviving spouse, mostly widows since women tend to have greater life expectancies than men, will receive 100 percent of her husband's PIA if she is receiving spousal benefits.[11] Otherwise, widows or widowers will receive their own benefit, but lose the deceased spouse's benefit.

Early retirement benefits are also calculated based on the PIA. Traditionally, workers could receive their full PIA if they waited until age 65 years—ultimately to 67 years, when all changes are I place—to receive full retirement benefits. They could, however, receive benefits as early as age 62 years, but they would then have to accept permanently lower Social Security benefits for the rest of their lives. The PIA's reduction was 20 percent when the full-benefit age was 65 and a worker retired at age 62. And the PIA reduction at age 62 will be equal to 30 percent when the full-benefit age has gone up to 67.[12] A higher full-benefit age lowers either the monthly benefit amount or the time that workers can expect to receive benefits.

Paying for Social Security Benefits

How are Social Security benefits paid for? Social Security's primary source of income is payroll tax revenue. Most employers and employees each pay 6.2 percent of wages and salaries to Social Security.[13],[14] Wages and salaries above an annual cap are not subject to taxation so that there is an annual maximum. This maximum amount of wages and salaries subject to taxation—$118,500 in 2015—annually increases with the average wage.[15] Social Security's tax revenue then equals the product of 12.4 percent (from the 6.2 percent contributions each from the employers and employees) times the earnings up to the cap for all people participating in Social Security.

Social Security receives additional income from its trust funds. This is particularly important since total payroll tax revenue has been falling short of benefits since 2009, after Social Security had received more tax revenues than it paid out in benefits every year after 1983.[16] The additional tax revenue in excess of benefit payments since 1983 was invested in government bonds held in Social Security's trust funds.[17] The interest Social Security earns on its trust funds helps to cover the difference between payroll tax revenue and benefit payments so that Social Security can fully pay all promised benefits.[18] The 2014 Social Security Trustees report projected that the program can continue to cover the expected shortfall between benefits and tax revenue with its interest earnings through 2019.[19] Social Security will then have to start selling government bonds from the trust funds to cover the difference between benefit payments and payroll taxes. The 2014 Trustees Report estimated that Social Security will eventually run out of government bonds to sell in 2033.[20] The tax revenue will only cover 77 percent of Social Security's promised benefits, once Social Security has sold all of the government bonds in the trust funds.[21]

Policy Implications of the Way Social Security Works

We can now revisit the five linkages—rising earnings inequality, survivorship inequities, special minimum benefit, higher full-benefit age, and individual account investments—between rising risk exposure and Social Security policy.

First, increasing earnings inequality puts a strain on Social Security because it raises the growth of future benefits, relative to Social Security's tax revenue, and because it reduces the amount of earnings that are subject to Social Security taxation and thus reduces the Social Security tax revenue.

Social Security benefits are designed akin to insurance benefits, so that those with lower lifetime earnings receive relatively higher benefits, compared to the taxes they paid, than those with higher lifetime earnings. Consider the Social Security Administration's hypothetical examples of lifetime low-wage and medium-wage earners in 2013 to illustrate this point. A low-wage earner earned $21,074 in 2013, while a medium-wage earner had $46,832 that year—a difference of 122.2 percent. The difference in the amount of annual payroll taxes between these two workers is also 122.2 percent or $3,194 (0.124×($46,832−$21,074)). If this difference in earnings had been in place over an entire career, lifetime low-wage earners would have received an annual Social Security benefit equal to $11,626 (in 2013 dollars) if they had retired at age 66 in 2014, and medium-wage earners would have received $19,151. This is a difference of only 64.7 percent, well below the earnings and payroll tax increase of 122.2 percent.

The hypothetical benefits would have been equal to about 55 percent of average wage-adjusted lifetime earnings for low-wage earners and to roughly 41 percent for medium-wage earners.[22] Benefits go up with earnings, but the rate of increase slows as lifetime earnings increase. Now remember that rising earnings inequality has resulted in a growing share of workers with low wages over time.[23] This growing group of workers not only pays less in taxes than it would have paid with higher wages, but these workers can also expect relatively higher benefits than would have been the case with higher wages. Growing earnings inequality has reduced tax revenues for Social Security more than it has slowed the increase in future benefits, due to the way Social Security benefits are calculated.

Increasing earnings inequality in the United States has also meant that top earners have seen above-average wage increases.

The result has been that a growing share of earnings has moved above the maximum taxable earnings—the cap, above which earnings are no longer subject to Social Security taxes. In 1983, following the last major Social Security reform, 10.0 percent of earnings were above the cap and 6.3 percent of tax payers had earnings above the cap. By 2011, the share of earnings above the cap had increased to 16.5 percent, while the share of tax payers with earnings above the cap fell to 6.2 percent.[24] The bottom line is that growing earnings inequality resulting from top earners pulling away from the middle has directly translated into a shrinking tax base for Social Security.

The shrinking tax base has directly worsened Social Security's expected future shortfall. Several colleagues and I estimate that faster wage growth in line with productivity growth between 1983 and 2015 would have reduced Social Security's shortfall by 6.8 percent in 2015. And we estimate that the shortfall in 2015 would have been 10.1 percent smaller if Social Security's tax base had stayed constant at 90 percent of earnings.[25]

Second, Social Security survivorship benefits can differ for widowed spouses, depending on the preretirement earnings of a married couple, and thus create an inequity between surviving spouses. Surviving spouses of couples where each spouse received their own retirement benefit will receive a smaller share of the couple's combined retirement benefits than surviving spouses of couples where one spouse received spousal benefits (equal to half of the main breadwinner's retirement benefit).

This inequity is best explained with a comparative example. Consider two married couples. One couple had one main breadwinning spouse during their working years and hence receives 150 percent of this spouse's PIA, which in this example is equal to $20,000 per year, so that the couple receives $30,000 in annual benefits. The second couple had two earners with identical earnings during their working years and each beneficiary receives $15,000, totaling $30,000 in annual benefits for this couple. When a spouse dies in the first instance, the spousal benefit—50 percent of the PIA or $10,000—goes away. When a spouse dies in the second case, that spouse's PIA or $15,000 entirely disappears. The surviving spouse of a single-earner couple receives two-thirds of the couple's total benefit, whereas the surviving spouse of a dual-earner couple receives less than two-thirds, exactly one-half of the couple's combined benefit.

Importantly, the surviving spouse of a dual-earner couple will always receive less than two-thirds of the couple's combined benefit since the existence of two separate benefits means that each spouse's own benefit is greater than 50 percent of the other spouse's benefit. Social Security's benefit structure provides relatively greater income security to single-earner married couples than to dual-earner married couples. This inequity then partly undermines couple's goal to gain more economic security as the number of dual-earner couples has, in part, increased to stabilize family incomes.

Third, Social Security is a crucial income benefit, but it does not necessarily keep people out of poverty, even if they worked all their lives at relatively low wages. The AIME for low-income earners can be relatively low, leading to comparatively low benefits that may fall below the poverty line. Social Security currently offers a backstop through a supplemental minimum benefit that has been in place since 1972.[26] Its value increases with inflation each year, while all other benefits increase with wages. The value of this minimum benefit has been gradually eroding over time, since wages tend to rise faster than inflation. An ever smaller share of low-income earners hence benefits from this minimum benefit.[27] That is, policy has failed to strengthen the income floor for low-wage workers at a time when the need for this added protection has particularly increased due to growing labor market risks for lower wage workers.

Fifth, diverting part of Social Security taxes intended for retirement savings into individual investment accounts—often referred to as Social Security privatization—would increase the financial market exposure for families. Social Security privatization refers to the diversion of some share of payroll taxes in individual accounts. Most recently and most prominently, President George W. Bush proposed such a move in 2005, although a number of policymakers and think-tank experts have subsequently offered their own privatization proposals.

Importantly, privatization would expose workers to more financial risks than is currently the case in Social Security through two different channels.[28] Workers would have to first invest some of their Social Security taxes themselves in financial instruments such as mutual funds and, depending on the specific privatization proposal, they would have to convert part of their savings into lifetime streams of income upon retirement. Both the investment during workers' careers and the conversion into lifetime streams of income expose workers to novel financial market risks, to which they were not exposed before in Social Security.

The value of financial market instruments—stocks, bonds, and mutual funds—can vary widely during a worker's career and often stay up or down for long periods of time. The value of workers' individual accounts depends on their financial acumen and on sheer luck, specifically whether one is lucky to live through a prolonged up ("bull") market or unlucky to live through an extended slump ("bear") market.[29] Put differently, workers can follow all the right advice on financial investments and still come up short simply because they lost in the "intergenerational lottery."

Building up money in an individual account is just the first step. Workers will also have to convert the money into streams of income when they retire. Some privatization proposals, such as the one made by President George W. Bush, envision that workers convert a minimum amount of their savings into lifetime streams of income, typically by buying an annuity from a life insurance company. The monthly income—annuity—that a fixed amount of savings can purchase varies, however, with interest changes. Buying an annuity means handing over a large check to a life insurance company in exchange for a promise of a lifetime monthly income. The life insurance company then needs to spread out the invested amount plus any expected interest earned on that investment over the average remaining life expectancy for a worker. That means higher interest rates turn into higher monthly incomes and lower interest rates turn into lower monthly incomes simply because the life insurance company can expect more or less additional money to pay out as lifetime incomes. Workers retiring when interest rates are high once again win relative to those who happen to retire when interest rates are low—yet another "intergenerational lottery."

Many workers, though, may not purchase annuities or at least will not use all of their savings for an annuity. They instead may try to manage the withdrawals from their savings accounts during retirement on their own. Those households remain exposed to financial market risks with their savings.

Workers' retirement security from savings in individual accounts depends in part on timing—whether they worked and retired during an up or a down market. And in the case of down market, there is often no possibility for individuals to recover all of the money they lost since it would require delayed retirement and continued work.

Public Opinion Polls Mirror Rising Anxieties

The discussion over the rising tension between the growing need for Social Security's insurance protections and the gradually weakening of said insurance values is not just an issue of economics but also reflects public concerns. Public opinion polls on Social Security show widespread concern over people's retirement outlook.[30] But survey respondents typically value Social Security as a basic benefit, feel strongly about its progressive benefit structure, and tend to oppose further increases in the full-benefit age as well as privatizing Social Security. People appear to look for policies to strengthen Social Security's value at a time of rising risk exposure and a lack of policy assistance in building meaningful risk protections.

Most workers are not very confident they will have the resources to retire comfortably. Only 18 percent of workers in 2014 felt very confident they will be able to live comfortably in retirement. In comparison, more than 40 percent had no confidence they will live comfortably in retirement.[31]

And this number overstates confidence among low-income and middle-income workers.[32] Only seven percent of households with incomes less than $35,000 in 2014 and only 11 percent of households with incomes between $35,000 and $74,999 were very confident in their ability to live comfortably through retirement, compared to 36 percent of households making $75,000 or more in 2014.

Moreover, the trend lines in Figure 5.1 show that, generally, confidence has not risen over time. Retirement confidence remained relatively stable from 1993 to 2007, sharply dropping throughout the Great Recession of 2007 to 2009 and its aftermath. It has only started to recover somewhat in 2014.

Amid consistent worries about retirement preparedness, a majority of Americans expect to rely on Social Security as a crucial report of retirement income. In an annual 2014 Gallup poll, 31 percent of

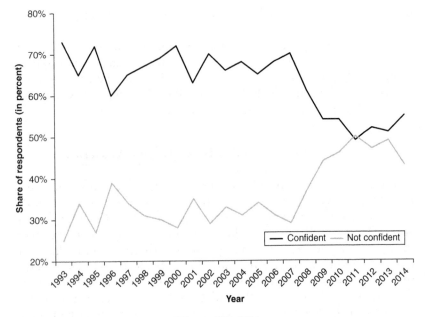

Figure 5.1 Workers' retirement confidence, 1993–2014.

Notes: I combine responses to simplify the graph without loss of information. "Confident" includes those survey respondents who indicated that they were very confident and those who said they were somewhat confident. "Not confident" combines respondents who were not too confident and those who were not confident at all.

Source: Employee Benefits Research Institute (EBRI), "Retirement Confidence Survey" (Washington, DC: EBRI, various years), accessed April 30, 2014, http://www.ebri.org/surveys/rcs/

respondents said they expected to rely on Social Security as a major source of their retirement income, 51 percent as a minor source, and only 16 percent indicated they did not expect Social Security to be a source of future retirement income for them.[33]

The number of people expecting to rely on Social Security has gradually increased. The share of Americans expecting to rely on Social Security as a major source of income hit a low point with 25 percent in 2004 and 2006—years before the Great Recession started—before climbing to its highest level of 31 percent in 2013 and 2014.[34]

But Americans are doubtful about Social Security's future, especially its ability to pay full promised benefits. Gallup, for instance, reports that a full 60 percent of respondents—the highest dating back to 1989—in a July 2010 poll indicated they did not think Social Security could pay full benefits when they will retire.[35] And in a 2009 poll by ABC News and *The Washington Post*, 23 percent of respondents were not so confident and 38 percent were not confident at all that Social Security could pay full benefits through retirement.[36] Other polls, not cited here, typically show widespread worry about Social Security's long-term ability to pay for full benefits. That is, Americans are worried about Social Security's insurance value beyond the ongoing and proposed erosion of Social Security's insurance value.

But survey respondents' fear that Social Security will not be able to help to generate a secure retirement is also reflected in their preferences for reforms of Social Security. This sheds some light on four of the five policy issues—rising inequality, minimum benefits, higher full-benefit age, and privatization—and leaves reforms to survivorship benefits as a generally unexplored topic.[37]

Polling data generally indicate a desire to strengthen Social Security's benefits. A 2014 survey by the National Academy for Social Insurance, for example, found that 72 percent of respondents agreed that "[t]o provide a more secure retirement for working Americans, we should consider increasing Social Security benefits."[38] And 53 percent agreed strongly with the statement that "we need to reform Social Security and protect it to ensure that it's a safety net the American people can count on," and another 10 percent agreed, but not strongly, in a November 2008 poll by Democracy Corps and the Campaign for America's Future.[39] The polling data hence indicate public support for maintaining and possibly improving Social Security benefits for workers who have generally had the largest labor market risk exposure in recent decades.

Surveys further show that people typically prefer to strengthen Social Security largely by making the program more progressive by introducing a minimum benefit and by eliminating or raising the cap on earnings. The National Academy of Social Insurance's 2014 survey found that 71 percent of respondents supported a package of reform that would create a minimum benefit, raise the annual cost of living adjustment, eliminate the cap, and raise the payroll tax rate.[40] Gallup asked about a small number of reforms in 2010 and 67 percent thought that requiring higher income earners to pay taxes on all of their earnings—eliminating the cap—was a good idea. These numbers are similar to the ones Gallup recorded five years earlier in 2005.[41] Similarly, a 2005 survey by *The Washington Post*, Kaiser Family Foundation, and Harvard University found majority support for alternate wordings about benefit cuts for the wealthy. These included 60 percent support for "reducing the rate of growth in benefits for wealthy retirees only" and 54 percent support for "cutting guaranteed benefits for wealthy retirees only."[42] A 2005 poll by CBS News and *The New York Times* similarly found that 63 percent of respondents favored raising the cap on earnings subject to Social Security taxes.[43] Additionally, AARP found in a poll on Social Security reform options conducted in 2007 that raising the cap enjoys the largest support, with 71 percent of respondents favoring this idea among a range of other proposals, far ahead of the 59 percent of respondents who favored increasing the payroll tax, the second most popular reform option in this poll.[44] And, there appears to be direct support for Social Security's progressive benefit formula. A Bloomberg National poll in 20013 found that 59 percent of respondents favored "creating a sliding scale for Social Security so that poorer people get more benefits and wealthy people get fewer benefits."[45]

Taken together, these polling data suggest that most Americans support strengthening Social Security's insurance value for low-income and middle-income beneficiaries, possibly by creating a stronger minimum benefit. A 2013 poll by the National Academy of Social Insurance found that 57 percent of respondents favored creating a new special minimum benefit, while only 13 percent opposed this proposed benefit increase.[46]

Benefit reductions and tax increases on a broader scale garner significantly less support. This is true for increases in the full-benefit age, which are generally unpopular. Gallup found in 2005 and 2010 that 63 percent of respondents thought that raising the full-benefit age was a bad idea.[47] AARP also found that only 33 percent of respondents in 2007 favored raising the retirement age.[48] And only 31 percent favored a higher full-benefit age when asked in the 2005 *Washington Post*, Kaiser Family Foundation, and Harvard University poll, "If it were necessary to keep the Social Security program paying benefits as it does now, would you favor or oppose raising the age at which a person can retire and receive full Social Security benefits?"[49] And merely 19 percent answered favorably to the question "Would you favor or oppose raising the age at which a person can retire and receive Social Security benefits?" in a February 2005 CBS News and *New York Times* poll.[50] And only 28 percent of respondents in a 2013 National Academy of Social Insurance poll favored gradually raising the full-benefit age to 70.[51]

And finally, Americans generally are skeptical of privatization. Privatization gathered a lot of interest in 2004/5 when President George W. Bush laid out a specific proposal. Gallup conducted a series of polls during the 2004/5 debate over Social Security privatization.[52] About half of all respondents—48 percent—initially opposed the idea of allowing part of Social Security taxes to be invested in stocks or bonds in December 2004, while 48 percent supported the idea. The share opposed to diverting money to financial investments slowly increased as the debate went on and people learned more about the proposal, so that by June 2005 more than half—53 percent—of all respondents opposed the proposal, while 44 percent supported the idea. The bottom line is that Americans view privatization with some skepticism and their concerns seem to increase as they learn more about the details of the relevant proposals.

Conclusion

This chapter links rising market risks and growing risk exposure to the changing role Social Security has played as an insurance against market risks. This discussion shows that there already is a growing tension between rising risk exposure and declining risk protection due to past policy decisions. A number of policy proposals, especially those suggesting a higher full-benefit age and allowing individuals to divert part of their Social Security payroll tax into individual accounts, could further increase this tension.

Public opinion data show that people are generally anxious in part because of this tension and often prefer easing the tension by strengthening Social Security's retirement income insurance value. However, strengthening the value of Social Security as a key protection from increasing risk exposure in an era of high labor and financial market risks will require reversing the course that has dominated Social Security policy for the past three decades.

CHAPTER SIX

Sink-or-Swim Retirement Plans

How would you personally define what a secure retirement means to you?[1]

"I would say not a 401K because they are too unstable. I would say just a pension from a work group from a union or a union retirement that is the security that is given to us. It is what makes me feel secure in my life to guarantee that I have a retirement to fall back on." (White man, 54 years old)

"I think it's helpful and I like a 401(k) plan to have secured income in retirement." (African American woman, 25 years old)

People's exposure to both labor and financial market risks has increased since the 1980s, while labor and financial markets have also become more unstable. The combination of growing risk exposure and rising risks has contributed to increasing wealth inequality, as households with high risk exposure have experienced lower wealth gains over time than households without high risk exposure. In this chapter, I focus on some of the mechanics of rising financial risk exposure with individualized savings, such as retirement savings accounts and housing.

Financial risk exposure depends on having some private savings outside of Social Security. People can be exposed to financial market risks with their savings by investing in stocks and housing and by going into debt, since indebtedness exacerbates the impact of rises and falls in the value of stocks and housing.[2]

Savings come in different forms with different risk exposure implications, and retirement is the primary reason for people to save for the future. Retirement savings include Social Security, DB pensions, and private savings—namely defined contribution (DC) plans such as 401(k) plans, which are offered by employers to their employees, and IRAs, which people can invest in on their own—and other types of savings such as housing.

Some refer to the combination of these three future income sources as the three-legged stool. Others prefer to call it three layers of retirement income, as Social Security covers a much larger share of the population than either DB pensions or private savings do.

Neither analogy, though, captures the large-scale changes that have occurred in how Americans save for their retirement. DB pensions have become less prevalent since the early 1980s, while DC savings plans have become increasingly popular. Falling DB pension coverage and rising DC plan coverage alone mean that a growing share of American workers has potentially become exposed to key financial market risks. This rising financial risk exposure with retirement savings is further exacerbated by households saving in housing, which remains a large and crucial form of savings for many households.[3]

I briefly summarize the economic debate on the growing risk exposure with household savings in this chapter. I first present how the neoclassical economic perspective on exposing more workers to greater financial risks with their savings, for instance, through DC plans, has changed over time. I then discuss the exposure to financial market risk in DC plans and housing and how this potential for household risk exposure compares to that in DB pensions.

The shift toward individualized savings and away from pooled savings, such as DB pensions, has not only increased the potential for more financial risk exposure but also raised the actual financial risk exposure of households. This has happened at a time when financial markets have become more volatile, and the possibility of massive savings losses has gone up, too. First, policy has moved toward encouraging more potential risk exposure by encouraging the rise of DC accounts and fostering financial policy changes that have increased access to homeownership and savings in housing. Second, financial risk exposure has indeed increased. This follows in large part because households have fewer risk protections in DC savings plans than in DB pensions and they have systematically encountered obstacles to building meaningful risk protections with individualized savings. Third, the financial risk exposure of households without DB pensions has risen faster than that of households with DB pensions. This goes counter to what we theoretically should have expected, if households acted completely rationally. Those households without some measure of financial market risk protection, for instance, from a DB pension, would have gradually reduced their risk exposure as financial risks increased. Financial risks indeed increased and financial risk exposure also rose especially among households that had no access to the risk protections offered by DB pensions. The disproportionate increase in risk exposure among households without DB pensions suggests that households on average are currently not well equipped to handle the rising risk exposure amid massive market swings with individualized forms of savings. The bottom line then is that policy has moved households toward more risk exposure without offering meaningful risk protections for their savings at a time when labor and financial market risks have increased.

The Economic Logic of Changing Potential Individual Risk Exposure

Economic risk refers to the uncertainty of savings. Potential savings gains and losses depend significantly on movements in key financial markets for stocks and housing—actual risks—and on individuals' ability to maneuver those markets by changing their risk exposure to fit their preferences and needs.

People can encounter financial market risk while they save for retirement and in retirement as well. Households could lower their financial market risk exposure in retirement by investing in annuities that pay lifetime streams of income upon retirement. But, households do not either use the financial tools available or have the necessary resources to invest in annuities. People who do not purchase annuities will have to manage their own finances through retirement, which can leave them exposed to financial market risks.

Historically, workers who had savings specifically intended for retirement had those savings in the form of DB pensions, in addition to the equity in their home. DB pension benefits limit households' financial market risk exposure since benefits typically do not directly depend on financial market swings, since households cannot influence their risk exposure, and since DB pensions generally pay annuities and thus limit retirees' financial market risk exposure. This does not mean that DB pensions are risk-free since employers can go bankrupt and beneficiaries will receive less in benefits than they had expected. But this employer default risk is limited since private DB pensions are government-insured up to specific limits and public DB pensions have implicit backing from federal, state, and local governments.

Over time, DB plans have become less common and DC accounts have gained in prominence. Additionally, a growing number of households have gained access to home equity as a key form of savings. The potential for households' financial risk exposure consequently has changed and, in fact, has increased over time.

The underlying policy changes—discussed in more detail below—that ultimately resulted in increased individual risk exposure followed to some degree the logic of neoclassical microeconomic theory, whereby households optimally save for their future and optimally allocate their savings in full knowledge of the associated risks. Importantly, this theoretical framework emphasizes the value of individual decisions and choices above many other considerations since individuals are supposedly rational and can, on average, make optimal decisions based on their complete knowledge of complex financial savings vehicles. Moreover, individuals do not like risk; they are risk-averse. Greater risk exposure hence poses an increased cost to individuals. Individuals who act rationally would theoretically save more to compensate for this added cost and reduce their risk exposure.[4] Saving more and lowering risk exposure are in theory two sides of the same coin. Households will need to save more to meet their savings goals when they reduce their risk exposure since lower risk exposure should in theory go along with lower expected returns and thus lower savings over time. The implication then is that households will save more money if individual risk protections, such as Social Security benefits, lost insurance value over time, which has indeed happened. This argument also implies that moving from DB pensions to individual savings accounts with greater individual risk exposure, such as 401(k) and IRAs, would equally lead to more savings.

More recent theoretical and empirical developments in economics have identified a different and more complex story about households' savings in the face of risk exposure. It turns out that, despite what neoclassical microeconomic theory argues, individuals may not always be good at making the requisite choices to optimally manage their savings for long-term goals. They may have access to all of the relevant information, but they may encounter psychological obstacles such as processing a lot of complex information in quick order and when trying to figure out multiple things at once to optimally manage their risk exposure. Many households will take on too much risk exposure with their savings amid rising risks and they may not increase their savings at all in response to greater risk exposure, even though the theory of rational optimization suggests that they should.

Research done in the field of behavioral economics has shown that the logic of households optimally managing their risk exposure across all of their savings has its limits, since it makes behavioral assumptions about household decisions that may systematically not apply.[5] People may not fully understand complex risks, may not completely understand how to protect themselves from these risks, and may not act upon this knowledge, even if they have it, for instance, because the costs to making these decisions of higher savings occur today, while the benefits of higher retirement income occur much further in the future. Households may not save enough to fully compensate for the added risk exposure and institute enough risk protections for their savings. Greater risk exposure as a result of an increased emphasis on individual forms of savings consequently occurred without sufficient savings gains.[6] On the contrary, greater risk exposure appears to have actually reduced savings for those households with high risk exposure.

Policy Changes Increase Households' Financial Risk Exposure

The changes in the way people save have come in large part as a result of a series of policy changes, reflecting a growing emphasis on individual savings and individual choices in savings and thus household risk exposure in retirement savings. There has been an increasing acceptance on the part of policymakers to let households handle more of their own finances, including the commensurate increase in financial risk exposure over the past 30 years.[7] Neoclassical economic theory said that not only would this be okay but that it could potentially reverse the baffling decline in the U.S. saving rate that had occurred in the 1980s.[8] Four primary policy changes stand out in this regard, although these have not been the only ones that led to an increasing emphasis of individual savings over forms of pooled savings such as DB pensions and Social Security.

First, Congress slowed the growth of Social Security benefits with its comprehensive reform in 1983, which scheduled a gradual increase in the full-benefit retirement age from 65 to 67 years, starting with those beneficiaries born in 1938. That is, people born in 1938 turned 65 in 2003 and were the first cohort to see a full-benefit retirement age above age 65. Beneficiaries could still retire as early as age 62, but they would have to accept larger, permanent cuts in their retirement benefits than was the case for previous generations.[9] A minimum

20-year preparation period between enacting legislation to raise the full-benefit age and the actual increase in the full-benefit age supposedly gave households sufficient time to save more money to compensate for Social Security's slowly declining insurance value. This same 20-year period, though, marked a sharp decline in the U.S. personal saving rate,[10] putting some doubt on the overall logic that households can adequately prepare for the increase in financial risk exposure—a point I will return to below.

Second, the decline in DB pension coverage has followed in part changes in DB pension funding rules,[11] although the stated goal of new funding rules was to strengthen DB pensions, not to weaken them. Employers have partly moved away from DB pensions because of policies that have increased the volatility and thus lowered the predictability of the contributions they have to make to their DB pensions. The government prescribes through the tax code how employers with DB pensions need to calculate how much money they owe their current and former employees for their future pensions. The Pension Protection Act of 2006 (PPA) ultimately legislated changes to this calculation that had long been debated. PPA's new rules increased employers' uncertainty over how much they will have to pay for their DB pension plans each year.[12,13] The uncertainty associated with DB pension funding rules, even before PPA codified this volatility, has proved to be a powerful new disincentive for employers to offer DB pensions.

Third, DC plans became increasingly popular as retirement savings plans after Congress enacted changes in the tax code in the late 1970s that gave rise to 401(k) plans. The Revenue Act of 1978 added section 401(k) to the tax code—hence the moniker 401(k) plans—which sanctions cash or deferred arrangements, formalizes their design, and provides for regular guidance. Employers began to add a lot of 401(k) plans after 1981 when the Internal Revenue Service formally clarified the rules for these retirement savings plans.[14] The number of 401(k) plans, for instance, grew from 30,000 in 1985 to 417,000 in 2005 and the number of active participants increased from ten million to 47 million during the same time.[15] The growth of DC plans has meant that a rising number of private sector workers could potentially become exposed to financial risks, as I discuss in more detail below.

Fourth, the rise of the U.S. mortgage market with greater access to mortgages and lower costs of borrowing started in the 1970s and 1980s, following several key legislative changes. The early 1970s saw the creation of the Federal Home Loan Mortgage Corporation, also known as Freddie Mac. This was the federal government's second purchaser of home mortgages after the Federal National Mortgage Association (Fannie Mae), which had been around since 1938. More capacity to offer mortgages and at favorable terms meant that more potential home buyers could get mortgages at lower interest rates than was previously the case.[16] This mortgage creation capacity further accelerated with Freddie Mac selling mortgage-backed securities—bundles of mortgages to back up bond issuances—in 1971 and Fannie Mae starting to do so in 1981.[17] Further, the Tax Reform Act of 1986 also phased out the tax deductibility of most nonmortgage interest payments, leading to a shift of consumer debt toward mortgages, which included home equity lines.[18] More people became homeowners and the typical homeowner owed a larger share of their home's value to the bank as a result of the mortgage market trends that followed the legislative changes. More people got the possibility to save for their future through housing, while many homeowners also became increasingly exposed to housing market risk due to higher indebtedness.

A myriad of large-scale policy changes led to a growing emphasis of individual savings DC retirement accounts and housing over pooled DB pensions and Social Security. These changes meant that households potentially faced more financial risk exposure than before, in part because the possibility for risk exposure is inherent in individual accounts. As households increasingly saved for their retirement in individual accounts, they had to make more and more complex financial decisions on their own and ultimately ended up with greater financial risk exposure. The bottom line is that policymakers pushed households to make more choices on their own, for which they were ill-equipped, and the result has been increasing wealth inequality and growing economic insecurity. As ordinary Americans have been treading water, the attitude from policymakers has been the equivalent to "take some swimming lessons," leaving people to sink or swim.

Financial Risk Exposure with Different Savings Forms

Households are generally not exposed to financial market risk with DB pensions. This follows from the basic way all DB pension plans operate. Employers and occasionally employees, especially in the public sector, contribute part of workers' earnings to a pension fund. These contributions are then pooled and professionally managed by in-house or hired investment managers. This reduces investment risk since investment managers are less likely than individuals to make common investment mistakes such as not rebalancing their portfolio when market prices changes and overemphasizing employer stock or cash in their portfolio.

A traditional DB pension fund then pays out a regular benefit to beneficiaries when they retire.[19] The fund will typically draw on its own assets to pay benefits, which allows the pension fund to keep investing all remaining assets. This means that a DB pension fund can generally ride out a bad market since most of the money stays with the fund and can be invested for the long haul. This process is called self-annuitization—DB pension funds manage their own assets to pay benefits to their beneficiaries. This also means that DB pension plans can smooth out the peaks and valleys in financial markets for their beneficiaries, because they can expect to be investing money for several decades. Being able to smooth out market fluctuations over long periods of time is necessary to reduce financial risk exposure since financial markets, especially the stock market, tend to move up and down in long waves.[20]

Self-annuitization, like annuitization through life insurance companies, also reduces financial market risk exposure in retirement. The beneficiary will receive a guaranteed monthly benefit for the rest of their lives and thus theoretically cannot outlive their retirement savings and is no longer exposed to financial market risks in retirement.[21]

So, DB pension plans typically reduce households' financial market risk exposure. This is not to say that households cannot experience risk exposure with DB pensions. DB pensions, especially those of the so–called cash balance type, which refers to the way benefits are calculated, increasingly offer beneficiaries the option of a lump sum.[22] Beneficiaries can then take their benefits as one lump–sum payment when they leave an employer or when they retire, rather than receiving monthly lifetime payments. Taking lump-sum payments from a DB pension turns a pooled form of investment into individual savings and exposes households to financial market risks akin to those in DC accounts since people now need to manage their own finances rather than leaving the money in a DB pension fund.

People are exposed to more financial risks in DC plans than is typically the case with DB pensions, but the level of financial risk exposure can vary with DC plan designs. DC plans are often called "do-it-yourself" retirement savings plans because most DC plans require the participant to decide on how much and where to invest their money. That is, DC plans expose households to large financial market risks if they save too little and invest with too much risk.

The designs of DC plans can increase these risks. Many participants find DC plan features, including the investment options available to them, so confusing that they save less money than they otherwise would.[23] Once people save in a DC plan, they need to invest their money. This can lead to large risk exposure and it can cause households to experience unacceptably large losses.

Consider the following example to see how households could unwittingly end with too much risk exposure. People may initially decide to put half of their money in stocks and half their money in bonds, reflecting their own risk tolerance. But then the stock market rallies and stock prices rise faster than bond prices, requiring that DC plan participants actively reinvest their stock market gains into bonds to maintain their preferred balance between stocks and bonds. This rarely happens as households generally do not actively change the way their savings are invested when stock prices move up or down.[24] Households may end up owning more stocks in their portfolio than they are comfortable with if there is a stock price boom.

DC plan designs have gradually changed to help people lower their risk exposure. Many of the new design features basically switched the default option—what happens when the participant does not make a decision—from avoidance to participation. A growing number of DC plans now automatically enroll participants with a minimum default contribution rate, for example, three percent of pay.[25] Some plans even automatically increase the contribution rate every year, for example, from three to four percent at the participant's first work anniversary, then to five percent at the second anniversary, and so on, up to a preset maximum contribution rate. The participant then has the option not to participate in a DC plan but needs to make an active choice not to do so. Similarly, DC plans can and do now offer default investments other than cash such as mixed investments that include interest-bearing bonds.[26] And DC plan participants increasingly have the option of investing in so-called model portfolios, which automatically rebalance their assets to keep the share of stocks constant to match the participants' initial target, for instance, at 60 percent.[27] The default in this case switches to active rebalancing, which helps participants avoid too much or too little risk taking. DC plan participants can reduce their investment risk exposure by saving more and avoiding common investment mistakes such as not rebalancing their portfolio if they take advantage of the increasingly common default options. That is, they can often reduce financial risk exposure by doing nothing, as long as their employers offer them these choices.

It is, however, difficult for households to avoid all financial market risk exposure with DC plans. It takes active decisions, a high level of financial sophistication, and possibly a fair amount of money to reduce the exposure to market risk. Market risk exposure follows from large long-term swings in stock and housing markets. Stock market swings are akin to winning or losing the generational lottery because stock market swings can take more than a generation to come full-circle.[28] One generation of workers will likely see above-average stock and housing market gains, while the next one will see below-average stock market gains. DB pension plans can smooth out these market swings because they can expect to "live" longer than one generation, while DC plans by definition only exist for one generation. And that generation is either a winner or a loser of the generational lottery.

The goal then is to shift market risk from households with a DC plan to institutions that can expect to be around for a long time. These institutions are typically financial service companies that offer some type of long-term insurance product that offers an explicit minimum guaranteed rate of return and reduces households' exposure to long-term market swings.

The exact insurance product will depend on what type of guarantee people are looking for and which bank or insurance company offers the desired product. Insurance companies already offer insurance that guarantees a minimum rate of return over long periods of time.[29] The alternative approach is to use a number of sophisticated financial hedging products such as options and futures and other hedging strategies such as short-selling—betting that a stock will fall in value. Such products exist, often combined under the heading of an absolute return fund, but they require that DC plan participants actively seek out those products; know the risks, costs, and benefits associated with them; and are willing to pay often substantial amounts of money for the protection these lower-risk financial products offer.

It equally takes effort and money to eliminate financial market risk exposure in retirement. Life insurance annuities are the typical insurance product that DC plan participants can use to protect against longevity risk. Few DC plans—less than a quarter—offer annuities to their participants, leaving participants to find such insurance products on their own.[30] This search often leads them to an insurance broker, who charges a fee for selling an annuity. The typical annuity costs between five and seven percent to the total amount spent on an annuity, substantially lowering the retirement income participants receive.[31] Moreover, the most common annuity product is an immediate annuity that pays a fixed monthly income to the beneficiary, but this monthly benefit does not increase with inflation.[32] Beneficiaries consequently have to manage the income they receive from all of their other sources to protect against financial market risk exposure in retirement, even if they make the effort and spend the time to buy a typical life insurance annuity.

The bottom line is that households have the opportunity to reduce their risk exposure in DC plans. But acquiring those risk protections in DC plans requires individual initiative, effort, and, in several instances, substantial costs.

Risk Exposure in Housing

Housing constitutes a risky asset akin to stocks. Savings in housing again expose households to financial market risks, somewhat similar to the risk exposure associated with savings held in stocks.

First, housing market swings tend to be smaller and shorter than stock market swings. But indebtedness can exacerbate housing market swings in both directions—up or down. But in the end, households care more about the downside risk since they tend to be risk-averse and they increasingly worry about the downside risk as they near retirement since they have less time left to recover from a market downturn. And mortgage debt access has increased, so that the chance of a substantial loss has grown over time, at least through the Great Recession of 2007 to 2009. The bottom line is that housing market risk exposure has become more severe over time.

Second, the chance of substantial financial market risk exposure that exists with housing is further exacerbated by the need for individual choices to manage such risk exposure. Homeowners often underestimate the riskiness of their asset.[33] They do not, for instance, rebalance their entire portfolio in response to housing market swings, for instance, by taking out a home equity line when house prices appreciate to invest in safer financial assets such as bonds.[34] Households instead have used home equity lines during the housing market upswings in the 1990s and 2000s to pay for necessary consumption such as health care and education.[35] The result has been increasing indebtedness rather than more diversified portfolios, highlighting the pitfalls of risk exposure in owner-occupied housing.

Third, households can experience risk exposure long into their retirement with housing, as they do with financial savings. Households, for instance, could run out of resources to maintain their residences. They may need to access their savings tied up in their house to pay their bills by taking out a reverse mortgage, but those financial products tend to be expensive and rarely used.[36] Therefore, risk exposure associated with housing persists for many households well into retirement.

The bottom line is that financial risk exposure in savings tied up in housing has grown over time, exacerbating the shift toward greater financial risk exposure in retirement savings vehicles.

Very High Risk Exposure Especially Increases for Households without DB Pensions

A few numbers may help to illustrate the link between increasingly individualized savings and rising risk exposure. I define a household as having very high financial risk exposure if its risky asset concentration—stocks and housing out of total savings—is greater than 75 percent and its debt to assets ratio is greater than 25 percent.

The change in the way people save for retirement from DB pensions to individual savings should have meant that we would see less risk exposure or at least a slowdown in the growth of financial risk exposure. This follows from the economic argument that households are risk-averse and that DB pensions offer financial market risk protections that DC plans do not. Households, if they indeed saved in the way neoclassical economic theory predicted, should manage their individual savings more conservatively without DB pensions than with DB pensions.

This implies three things. First, overall household financial market risk exposure should have declined as traditional risk protection in the way of DB pensions has decreased. But household financial risk exposure has increased, not declined. Second, households without DB pensions should have less risk exposure than households with DB pensions. And third, the gap in financial risk exposure between households without and those with DB pensions should have at least stayed stable or even widened—those without DB pensions having ever less risk exposure than those with DB pensions. The implication of a stable or widening risk exposure gap—those with DC plans should become more conservative over time—follows from the lack of financial market risk protections in retirement with individualized savings amid increasing longevity. Households without DB pensions increasingly need to become more financially conservative and reduce their risk exposure as they near retirement since their money needs to last longer than in the past.

Figure 6.1 shows my summary financial risk exposure measure—share of households with very high risk exposure—for households 50 years and older by plan coverage—with DB pensions, with DC plans but no DB pension, and without any retirement plan at all. I only focus on older households since they are more likely to have savings and hence financial risk exposure than younger households. The data show that the financial risk exposure of all older households, regardless of plan coverage, has grown over time. The data show that for much of the past few decades—from 1995 to 2010, to be exact—the risk exposure differed very little by plan coverage. That is, those with lesser risk protections from a DB pensions were almost as likely as those with DB pensions to have a very high risk exposure (Figure 6.1). The risk exposure gap initially narrowed from 1989 to 1995, then remained relatively

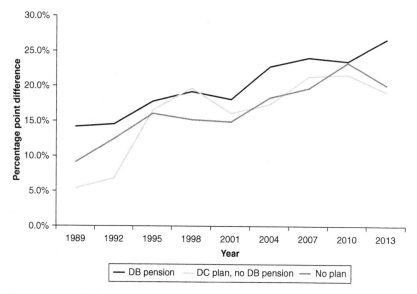

Figure 6.1 High financial market risk exposure, by type of retirement plan coverage and year.

Notes: A household has very high financial risk exposure if it has a risky asset concentration—stocks and housing out of total assets—that is greater than 75 percent and debt to assets ratio that is greater than 25 percent. Older households are those older than 49 years and younger households are those between 25 and 50 years.

Source: Based on Board of Governors, Federal Reserve System, *Survey of Consumer Finances* (Washington, DC: BOG, various years).

Table 6.1 Financial risk exposure measures, by type of retirement plan coverage and year

	1989	1992	1995	1998	2001	2004	2007	2010	2013
Median share of stocks out of financial assets									
No plan	**20.7%**	**24.2%**	**35.0%**	**46.3%**	**46.2%**	46.4%	48.3%	**38.5%**	53.9%
DB pension	34.1%	36.7%	37.7%	47.0%	51.7%	**46.3%**	48.0%	40.1%	**40.8%**
DC plan and no DB pension	27.8%	33.8%	36.8%	48.4%	47.4%	48.2%	**47.0%**	41.9%	42.7%
Median share of stocks and housing out of total assets									
No plan	55.2%	65.1%	79.9%	**61.9%**	**57.9%**	69.1%	**57.0%**	69.7%	**52.0%**
DB pension	64.1%	63.1%	**58.0%**	69.9%	72.2%	70.5%	72.9%	66.1%	68.6%
DC plan and no DB pension	**50.7%**	**51.0%**	66.8%	66.3%	64.9%	**65.6%**	66.1%	**60.2%**	64.5%
Median debt to assets ratio									
No plan	16.1%	20.8%	23.2%	33.1%	34.8%	41.7%	35.7%	54.8%	50.9%
DB pension	12.3%	18.6%	17.8%	20.9%	20.3%	22.8%	22.8%	25.1%	28.5%
DC plan and no DB pension	**8.2%**	**13.1%**	**14.5%**	**17.1%**	**15.5%**	**18.0%**	**19.8%**	**24.5%**	**20.6%**

Notes: All figures are in percentage. The lowest figures for each risk category in any given year are in bold. Calculations are only done for households 50 years and older, who are not retired. "DB pension" refers to households that have DB pension benefits from a past or current job. "DC plan" refers to households having 401(k) plans and IRAs. The median share of stocks out of financial assets is only calculated for households that have any direct or indirect stock investments. The median share of stocks and housing out of total assets is only calculated for households with any assets. And the median debt to assets ratio is only calculated for households with any debt. That is, the three risk exposure measures are not directly comparable with each other since they all refer to different subsamples of older nonretired households.

constant during the years of stock and housing market booms before widening again in the aftermath of the Great Recession. Put differently, there is no indication that those with fewer risk protections from DB pensions actually became more financially conservative during a time of increasing economic risks and growing longevity.

The trends in household shares with very high risk exposure do not depend on one single risk exposure measure, but rather reflect differences and trends in both risky asset concentration and indebtedness.

Table 6.1 summarizes the two risk exposure measures—risky assets out of all assets and debt to assets ratio—by plan coverage and year. Households' exposure to stock and housing markets does not materially differ by plan coverage. No group of older households—divided by retirement plan coverage—has systematically held more or less risky assets than the other two groups. Not having the risk protections from a DB pension does not make households more financially conservative in the way they allocate their money.

Households do differ in their indebtedness by retirement plan coverage. Households with DC plans have always had less debt than households with DB pensions. But the gap between the two groups has shrunk over time, at least through 2010, with households with DC plans becoming more quickly indebted than households with DB pensions (Table 6.1). This again contradicts economy theory, which predicts that households with lesser risk protections from DB pension should have more slowly increased their financial market risk exposure.

Conclusion

Public policy in the United States has increasingly emphasized individual forms of savings—DC retirement plans such as 401(k) plans and housing—and put a lower priority on pooled savings arrangements such as DB pensions and Social Security. The result has been a growing financial risk exposure for households as they need to manage more of their finances on their own and often fail to make optimal and very complex financial decisions amid growing economic uncertainty. Households can avoid some financial market risk exposure with a significant effort and substantial amounts of money. But in the end, households will face greater financial risk exposure than in the past either way. Either they cannot exert the effort and spend the money to reduce their risk exposure, or the available risk protections are not up to the task of protecting households from the growing risk exposure.

Financial risk exposure then has increased at exactly the same time that financial risks—stock and housing market ups and downs—have also grown.

Two points are worth emphasizing with respect to households' growing financial risk exposure. First, Americans are increasingly struggling to maneuver through the rougher waters of labor and financial markets. People frequently fail to lower their financial risk exposure when they experience high labor market risk exposure. The combination of high labor market risk exposure and rising financial market risk exposure has made many households increasingly economically vulnerable. They are less likely to pay their bills in an emergency and in retirement, for instance. The discussion over household risk exposure is not just a textbook discussion of academic value, but it impacts people's lives in direct and harmful ways.

Second, financial service companies can reap large rewards, at least for a while, from the policy push toward greater risk exposure. Investments in DC plans come with greater fees than investments in DB pensions, in part because banks need to manage funds across a large number of small accounts. And more stock investments that could lead to greater household risk exposure typically generate more fees than other financial investments in DC plans. And households seeking to gain meaningful risk protections against financial market risk will have to pay substantial fees for novel investment products and annuities from insurance companies. That is, addressing the growing household risk exposure can be good business for those who know how to chart a course through the stormy waters.

CHAPTER SEVEN

A Perfect Storm: Labor and Financial Market Risks Feed on Each Other

How would you personally define what a secure retirement means to you?[1]

"You do the best you can and then surrender the rest to God." (White woman, 54 years old)

"Having a diversified portfolio to have enough money to live on." (White man, 66 years old)

Saving money for the future, especially for retirement, has gone along with an increasing financial risk exposure for Americans largely because of a growing emphasis on individual savings, especially in retirement savings accounts and home equity, than has been the case in the past.

The growing reliance on individual savings contributes to rising wealth inequality. Underlying this link between individual savings and wealth inequality is a negative and increasingly tight interaction between labor market risks and people's savings that does not exist to the same degree in pooled savings, such as DB pensions. Individual retirement savings, in particular, transfer labor market risk into savings. Households that experience labor market risk—unemployment spells and earnings decreases—end up saving less in these individual accounts and in home equity than they would have otherwise. Such individual savings build a connection between economic insecurity in the present and economic insecurity in the future.

The longer term link between labor market risk exposure and household wealth means that households that face greater chances of being unemployed and experience slow earnings growth tend to end up with substantially less wealth as they near retirement than households that do not experience high labor market risk exposure. This chapter now focuses on the more short-term link between labor market risks and savings, allowing me to highlight some of the mechanics by which labor market declines adversely interact with individualized savings and ultimately contribute to rising wealth inequality. People with a lot of labor market risk exposure end up with fewer savings than those with less labor market risk exposure. Understanding how labor market risks increasingly connect to savings also sheds some light on how policy could weaken this link in the future and hence strengthen households' risk protections and help them build more economic security.

Labor and Financial Market Patterns

The link between labor market risk exposure and ultimately below-average savings also arises over the course of a business cycle.[2] A business cycle consists of an expansion and contraction, or recession, of the economy. Economic growth tends to be above average during an expansion and falls below average, possibly even turning negative, during a recession. The labor and financial markets move with the business cycle such that, during an economic expansion, unemployment falls, compensation—wages and benefits—increases, and stock and housing prices rise. The opposite is true during a recession, when unemployment rises, compensation falls, and the stock and housing prices plummet.

Figure 7.1 shows two key indicators—the unemployment rate as a measure of labor market risk and the value of the stock market as a proxy for financial market risk—since the end of the business cycle in November 1982. The two indicators have moved in opposite directions during that time. When stock prices went down, unemployment went up. Similarly, during times of rising stock prices, unemployment fell. And, these co-movements between unemployment and stock market coincide with the business cycle since the 1980s, but to a lesser degree during the time before the 1980s.

During the time since the 1980s, the emphasis on individualized savings over pooled forms of savings such as DB pensions started to grow. The link between labor and financial market risks and the potentially harmful effects of labor market risks on savings has become especially pronounced just as household savings became increasingly exposed to financial market risks. That is, households felt the pain of a worsening

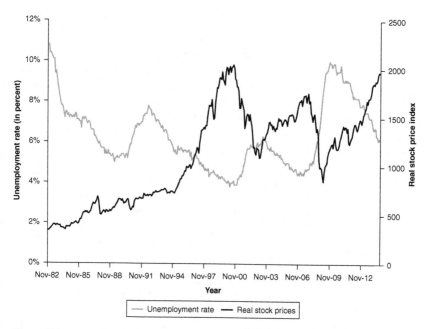

Figure 7.1 Unemployment rates and real stock prices in the 1980s.

Notes: Recessions occurred from July 1990 to March 1991, from March 2001 to November 2001, and from December 2007 to June 2009. The last recession is also referred to as the Great Recession.

Sources: Bureau of Labor Statistics, "Current Population Survey" (Washington, DC: BLS, 2014), accessed November 6, 2014, http://www.bls.gov/data/#unemployment, for the unemployment rate, and Robert Shiller, "Irrational Exuberance—IrrationalExuberance.com" (New Haven, CT: Yale University, 2014), accessed November 6, 2014, http://www.irrationalexuberance.com, for the real S&P composite index. Business cycle dates are provided by the National Bureau of Economic Research (NBER), "Business Cycle Dates" (Cambridge, MA: NBER, 2014) accessed November 6, 2014, http://www.nber.org/cycles.html.

economy during a recession more acutely since the 1980s since their jobs and their savings were more intricately linked than before.

The Typical Sequence of Labor and Financial Market Changes

The co-movements between labor markets and stock and housing markets during the business cycle are not perfectly in sync. Some things happen earlier, while others happen later.

As a rule of thumb, the sequence goes something like this during an expansion. The stock market, which tends to be a forward-looking economic indicator, starts to recover before the economy enters an expansion. Housing prices, in comparison, tend to move more closely with the business cycle since they directly depend on people's incomes, which depend on the state of the economy. House prices hence recover at about the same time as the economy enters an expansion.[3] Finally, employment typically has a delayed reaction to an economic expansion such that unemployment falls once the economy is already in a recovery, especially since the 1990s, when economic recoveries coincided with lackluster labor market growth. That is, people do not get their jobs back until the economy is well into its expansion and stock prices and, to a lesser degree, house prices have already risen for some time.

The picture changes when it comes to a recession.[4] Stock and housing prices tend to decline before the economy enters a recession.[5] The unemployment rate, in comparison, moves more closely with the business cycle in recessions, often rising as the economy starts to fail, rather than having a delayed reaction as is the case in expansions. And employers start to cut compensation early during a recession, again not waiting for the economy to suffer through parts of a recession before lowering their workers' pay. That is, people are out of a job and experience wage cuts by the time stock and housing prices fall.

Labor Market Realities Worsen Savings Outcomes Further

Fluctuations in unemployment—losing and gaining jobs—create several links to lower savings over the business cycle. The adverse effects of unemployment associated with a recession tend to be more pronounced and long-lasting than the corresponding positive effects associated with an economic expansion. This is a well-known phenomenon called labor market hysteresis, whereby unemployment falls more slowly after a recession than it increased at the start of the recession. I hence focus on the impact of rising unemployment on household savings, especially individualized savings such as retirement accounts in this discussion.

Using individualized forms of retirement savings often depends on working for an employer. Employers, for one, sponsor tax-advantaged retirement savings accounts, which help many workers to save if they have access to such savings accounts at work. It is possible to save in other nonemployer-dependent retirement savings accounts, such as IRAs, but fewer workers take advantage of that than save in employer-based savings plans, such as 401(k) plans. For instance, 79 percent of workers whose employers sponsored a retirement plan had a retirement savings account in 2013. However, only 42 percent of all workers, including those whose employers did not sponsor a retirement plan, had a retirement savings account.[6]

It is not just retirement savings that depend on working for an employer, but also saving in housing often depends on having a comparatively well-paying job. Getting a new mortgage as well as paying for and refinancing an existing mortgage often depend on having steady income from an employer. Losing a job then limits households' ability to save money with their home. Unemployed workers cannot get a new mortgage to buy a house, cannot make their payments, and may lose their home even if they have equity in their house, and they frequently cannot refinance to lower their mortgage payments.[7] Unemployment closes the door to having access to individualized savings, such that the economic pain from job loss in the present can translate into foregone savings and less wealth over time.

Limited ability to save with individualized savings during an unemployment spell is not the only way unemployment can hurt household savings. Households with unemployed workers have less income during unemployment, even if they still have opportunities to save in tax-advantaged savings vehicles. One spouse may still be employed and have a 401(k) plan, while the other was laid off. Cuts to earnings will likely result in fewer savings because households need to keep paying their bills. Most households will be less likely to save when a family member is unemployed than when all are employed.[8]

Even workers who still have a job during a recession can be impacted and save less. Employers cut back on offering retirement savings plans in the first place during recessions.[9] This is especially true in the private sector, where employers quickly try to save money on compensation by cutting benefits. The share of private sector workers working for an employer with a retirement plan fell in 1991, after 2000, and after 2007, as the economy went through a recession in 1991, 2001, and in 2008 and 2009 (Figure 7.2). Employers increased access again once the recovery started in 1992, but kept cutting access in the years after 2001 and 2009, even though the economy and, more importantly, corporate profits recovered once the recession was over.[10] The share of private sector wage and salary workers working for an employer with a retirement plan stood at a low of 48.5 percent in 2012, well below the already low 52.7 percent in 2007, just before the Great Recession started.[11]

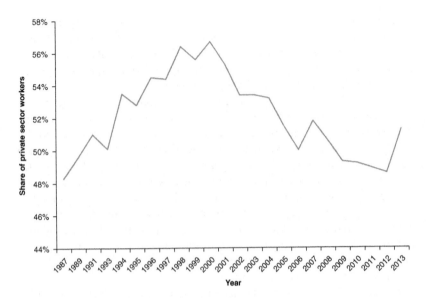

Figure 7.2 Private sector workers with employer-sponsored retirement plan at work, select years from 1987 to 2013.

Notes: Data refer to the share of private sector workers aged between 21 and 64 who worked for an employer that sponsored a retirement plan. Retirement plans refer to either DB pensions or DC account plans.

Source: David Copeland, "Employment-Based Plan Participation: Geographic Differences and Trends, 2013," EBRI Issue Brief No. 405 (Washington, DC: Employee Benefits Research Institute, 2014), accessed March 25, 2015, http://www.ebri.org/publications/ib/index.cfm?fa=ibDisp&content_id=5451

Furthermore, the tax code offers larger rewards to higher income earners. A drop in income due to unemployment hence lowers the tax incentives people receive to save money. The loss of savings incentives could lower household savings even further.[12] This adverse effect of fewer incentives on household savings may be especially pronounced among lower income households who may even become ineligible for some savings incentives, such as the Saver's Credit, as their incomes are too low to qualify for this nonrefundable federal savings match.[13] With a nonrefundable tax credit, people receive the full credit only if they paid federal income taxes of at least the same amount. Otherwise, they only receive the amount they paid in income taxes, or they get no credit if they paid no income taxes. Low-income people often pay a range of federal taxes, especially Social Security and Medicare taxes, but only limited amounts of federal income taxes and thus do not always qualify for nonrefundable credits such as the Saver's Credit.

The Impact of Labor and Financial Market Co-movements on Rates of Return

All of this timing, or co-movement, between labor and financial markets matters for savings outcomes beyond just putting away less money during tough economic times. The co-movement basically means that it becomes likely that households will buy high and sell low, thus costing them money in the form of foregoing savings, as they experience swings of unemployment coincident with the ups and downs of the economy. That is, households could have had more savings by the time they retired if cyclical timing of labor and financial markets had not worked against them.

Here is how the argument of buying high goes. Stock and house prices are lowest when households can least afford to buy, because of job losses and cuts in compensation. Households often wait until the labor market recovers and they again have secure jobs to buy stocks and houses. But by then, prices will have already risen. People buy more stocks and houses when prices are no longer at their lowest point. The flipside of such purchases above their lowest price is that the rate of return households can expect on their savings is lower than it would have been if they had bought at the bottom of the market.

What about selling low? Households face economic hardships from job losses and compensation cuts just when prices are falling. They increasingly dip into their savings by prematurely withdrawing money from retirement savings accounts,[14] by taking out loans from 401(k) plans,[15] and by falling behind on mortgage payments.[16] Households are essentially locking in their financial losses, again reducing the rate of return on their savings over their careers due to the pain they feel in the labor market during an economic downturn.

Labor Market Risks by Demographic Characteristics

One key point on the link between labor markets and household savings is that the increasing reliance on individual savings in retirement accounts and housing can contribute to wealth inequality. Households that experience more labor market risks will end up with fewer savings because of the cyclical co-movements between labor and financial markets than is the case for people who do not experience labor market risk exposure.

But importantly, some household groups tend to experience systematically worse labor market risk exposure, than is the case for others.

In particular, communities of color, low-income households, and households with little formal education tend to fare worse in the labor market than whites, higher income households, and households with more education.[17] These groups of households with higher labor market risk exposure will likely face worse savings outcomes—lower rates of return for each dollar they invest—simply because they face more pressure from the labor market to buy high and sell low.[18]

The adverse link between labor market risk and wealth inequality over the business cycle is especially pronounced for communities of color.[19] The labor market experience of some communities of color tends to be systematically different than that of whites, even after accounting for key variables such as education.[20] African Americans, for example, tend to have unemployment rates that are twice as high as those of whites and tend to experience longer spells of unemployment, a phenomenon occasionally referred to as last-hired-first-fired.[21] That is, the link between labor and financial market risks is potentially more severe for some communities, most notably African Americans, Latinos, some subpopulations of Asian Americans, as well as Native Americans, than it is for whites.[22]

Households that already face substantial hurdles to saving enough for their future economic security have to contend with added risks that do not apply to the same degree to their counterparts. The differential degree to which communities of color, lower income households, and households with little education experience the link between labor and financial market risks hence contributes in part to wealth inequality by race and ethnicity, income, and education.[23]

Some Illustrative Examples of the Impact of Labor and Financial Market Risk Linkage on Savings

This discussion so far on the way labor and financial market risks interact may become clearer with some illustrative examples to show the impact of these co-movements on total savings over a career.[24]

The baseline example is somebody who has been fully employed and saving for 35 years from July 1979 to June 2014. The hypothetical savings rate is a constant 10 percent of earnings.[25] Earnings follow a standard age–earnings profile that first rises and then flattens out as people get older.[26] Given the constant savings rate, savings also first rise and then flatten out. And this hypothetical worker invests money in a balanced investment portfolio with a constant 60 percent allocated to stocks, 20 percent to treasury bonds, and 20 percent to corporate bonds.[27] All earnings of the portfolio are reinvested while maintaining the 60–20–20 split in the investments.

The illustrative calculations compare the savings in this baseline case to the savings under three alternative scenarios. First, the worker is unemployed during a recession ("unemployment"). Second, the worker is unemployed three months before the recession starts, during the recession, and three months after the recession ends ("last hired, first fired"). And third, the worker is unemployed three months before the recession, during the recession, and three months after the recession, and the worker only gradually over the course of a year recovers to her original savings rate of 10 percent, once she is reemployed ("everything goes wrong").[28]

These three alternative scenarios probably still paint an optimistic picture of the effect of recessions on total savings accumulations. All three scenarios ignore the possibility that workers will take out loans from their own retirement savings accounts or withdraw money to pay their bills when they are unemployed. A growing number of people took loans from their 401(k) plans, for instance, during and after the Great Recession.[29] And withdrawals from retirement savings accounts tend to go up with unemployment spells.[30]

The illustrative calculations provide two separate figures to show the effect of unemployment timing on savings. One figure is simply the account balance in June 2014 that the hypothetical workers have accumulated over their 35-year careers. Comparing the balances between different scenarios provides a sense of the absolute impact of unemployment spells on savings balances.

The second number is the amount accumulated per each (inflation-adjusted, time-adjusted) dollar the worker has saved in her account. This number is the division of the total account balance in June 2014 by the sum of all dollars the worker has invested. Each past contribution is adjusted for price changes and the time that has passed since the money was invested.[31] The differences in savings per dollar invested from the baseline scenario capture the impact of the timing of unemployment relative to financial market movements. That is, it is an indicator of the effect of "buying high and selling low."

Table 7.1 shows the baseline scenario and its two relevant numbers—total account balance and savings accumulated per dollar invested. The baseline scenario shows an account balance of $421,659.50 after 35 years of saving and investing, which comes out to $3.46 for each dollar invested (Table 7.1).

Table 7.1 Savings effect of the interaction between labor and financial market risk exposure

Scenario	Baseline	Unemployment	Last hired, first fired	Everything goes wrong
	No unemployment	Unemployment during recessions	Unemployment during recessions, 3 months before and 3 months after recessions	Unemployment during recessions, 3 months before and 3 months after recessions
	No savings reduction	No savings reduction	No savings reduction	Savings reduction at start of reemployment, taking 1 year to recover
Balance in June 2014	$421,659.50	$297,975.59	$269,077.07	$247,096.30
Savings per dollar invested	$3.46	$2.96	$2.87	$2.83
Share of baseline (balance)		71%	64%	59%
Share of baseline (savings per dollar invested)		85%	83%	82%

Note: See text for discussion of simulations.

Table 7.1 then calculates the same numbers for the three alternative scenarios—unemployment, last hired and first fired, and everything goes wrong—and measures of the relative difference between each alternative scenario and the baseline case. Being unemployed during each recession drops the balance to $297,975.59—an almost 30 percent difference from the baseline (Table 7.1). The savings per dollar invested, though, drops only 15 percent from the baseline scenario to $2.96. The difference in these two numbers arises from the fact that savings per dollar invested also corrects for the time that has passed since the investment has been made. That is, the timing of unemployment relative to stock market fluctuations reduces the financial market gains a worker can expect in return for each dollar they invested by 15 percent, leading to a cumulative loss of close to 30 percent in total savings after compounded interest is factored in.

Being unemployed longer and taking time to recover to the full savings rate than is the case in the other alternative scenarios further shrink the account balance and the savings per dollar invested. The "everything goes wrong" scenario—which includes a long spell of unemployment and reduced savings rates—shows an account balance of $247,096.30—or 41 percent less than the baseline balance. And the savings per dollar invested drop to $2.83—or 18 percent less than in the baseline scenario. The losses of savings associated with the timing of financial and labor markets—when unemployment happens compared to financial market fluctuations—amount to substantial savings losses because workers end up buying high and selling low. The resulting loss of more than 40 percent in total savings reflects the combination of not being employed and thus not being able to participate in a retirement plan, of employers and employees reducing their contributions immediately following a recession, and of the inopportune timing of unemployment relative to financial market trends.

Conclusion

The increasing use of individualized savings—retirement accounts and housing—has tightened the link between labor and financial market risks. Households face obstacles to rebuilding their wealth in a recession and immediately afterwards, because they save in individualized savings vehicles. Unemployed workers can no longer participate in employer-sponsored retirement accounts and often do not have the resources to contribute to other individualized savings when times are tough. Employees and, to a lesser degree, employers cut back on their savings to make ends meet during tough economic times. Households then exacerbate the threats to their wealth with individualized forms of savings as they end up buying high and selling low since they do not have money available when stock and house prices, for instance, are relatively low.

The bottom line is that the increased use of individualized savings, mainly retirement accounts and owner-occupied housing, has made it harder for workers who experience labor market risks and those who are exposed to high labor market risks to save.

There are four main mechanisms by which labor market risks translate into lower savings. First, households increasingly rely on individualized savings rather than pooled investments such as DB pensions. Household savings are hence directly tied to the ups and downs of financial markets, which reflect the ups and downs of the labor market. Individual savings hence magnify labor market swings. Second, access to savings depends to an important degree on having a job, especially a job with a larger employer. The prioritization of employer-sponsored retirement savings creates a direct link between labor market risks and household savings. And third, participation in any form of tax-advantaged savings is entirely voluntary. Employers and employees will be more likely to cut their savings when economic times are bad than when they are good. And fourth, the tax code offers larger savings incentives to higher income earners. Adverse labor market risk will lower earnings for many people, reducing their tax incentives to save. Differences in labor market risk exposure then contribute to growing wealth inequality, since households with labor market risk exposure will save less, all else equal, than households with less labor market risk exposure.

It is important to note that most of these mechanisms that tie labor market risk exposure to financial market and savings outcomes are out of people's control. Weakening the link between labor market risk exposure, financial markets, and savings will ultimately require a different policy approach, for instance, by redesigning savings incentives to no longer disproportionately benefit higher income earners or by systematically accounting for risk exposure in savings.

CHAPTER EIGHT

The Pitfalls of Employer-Sponsored Retirement

How would you personally define what a secure retirement means to you?[1]

"Oh god, I was never even offered a 401(k). I'm not gonna have any retirement; only Social Security, that's it." (White man, 58 years old).

The United States directly provides fewer public benefits such as Social Security than other countries.[2] However, it foregoes a much larger share of tax revenue to incentivize private savings in addition to public benefits than is the case in other countries. The US welfare state as a result tends to be as large or larger than that in Western Europe,[3] with savings incentives—tax breaks for individual savings and insurance—taking on a much larger role.

These US savings incentives tend to be compartmentalized and hence fairly complex. Households can receive separate tax breaks for saving with their house by building up home equity, saving for retirement, saving for their children's education, and saving for health care, to name some of the most important saving purposes. The main thrust is that public policy encourages savings in a wide array of individualized savings. And people's individualized savings can be exposed to labor and financial market risks.

Public policy further exacerbates this risk exposure in the case of retirement savings by effectively inserting the employer as an unreliable middle man into people's savings decisions. US policy has long emphasized an approach of voluntary retirement savings. It is up to employers and employees to decide on whether and how much they want to save to supplement their Social Security income.[4] But voluntary participation encounters long-recognized behavioral and institutional obstacles such as complex savings incentives and savings instruments that can keep many households from saving enough for their future. Policymakers hence have devised tax incentives for employers to offer retirement plans as of the primary venues to get people to save more than they otherwise would. These savings incentives are meant to encourage employees to save for retirement to overcome the obstacles endemic to a voluntary system.

But relying on employers as the primary conduit for retirement savings can directly expose people's savings to labor market risks. First, access to retirement plans at work differs with employment arrangements. Those with lower labor market risk exposure typically have more access to employer-sponsored retirement plans than workers with more labor market risk exposure, who arguably need these savings the most. Second, primarily relying on employers to deliver retirement savings only works for wage and salary employees if their employer decides to sponsor a retirement plan—either in the form of a DB pension or DC savings accounts such as 401(k) plans. Employers in effect act as gatekeepers for retirement plans that enjoy preferential treatment in the tax code and thus offer some of the largest savings incentives. Many people who would like to save more may have limited access to tax-advantaged retirement savings. Third, employers may decide to sponsor a retirement plan, but they may lower the amount they contribute to their employees' retirement plans over time, especially during a recession when labor market risks become particularly acute. Relying on employers as the primary conduit for private retirement savings creates a link between labor and financial market risk exposure. Fourth, employees also need to increasingly decide that they want to participate in their employer's retirement plan and at what level. Enrollment in DB pensions is automatic, but enrollment in DC plans is usually not. People may not take advantage of all that the tax codes and employers have to offer, for instance, because they are not fully aware of their options or because they are more focused on paying their current bills than to save for retirement. Fifth, employees participating in a retirement plan at work may systematically incur too much financial market risk not only in their retirement savings but across all of their savings, largely because they may underestimate or misunderstand the risks associated with employer-sponsored retirement plans.

I briefly review the evidence in this chapter to show that each of these five problems associated with the employer-based savings system has increased over time. I offer some explanations for these growing problems. And I conclude this chapter with a short discussion of the relevant policy implications.

Policy Emphasizes Employers as Conduit for Private Retirement Policy

The logic of emphasizing employers as the primary venue for retirement savings results from the realization that standard neoclassical theory, on which the argument for pure voluntary participation typically rests, is flawed. These models often have not fully captured real-life obstacles to households saving for their future. For one, most models that rely on rational forward-looking individuals assume that all households can save for their future, regardless of their income levels. The empirical evidence indeed suggests that even the poor can save some money, but saving tends to be more difficult for lower income than for higher income earners.[5] And human psychology often prevents people from making optimal complex financial decisions, especially those that require people to forego certain and satisfying consumption today in exchange for more, but also more uncertain consumption in retirement.[6]

Policymakers have hence recognized that these obstacles will systematically keep a large number of people from saving enough for retirement on their own. Households will then need a reliable partner to nudge them to save more. Employers are seen as such potential partners as they may want to pursue their own goals—additional compensation for highly compensated employees, recruitment, and retention—for offering retirement benefits to some of their employees. Policy can thus take advantage of these overlapping interests between employees and employers, the argument goes, and make it easier for employers to help all employees save for retirement.

The tax code especially emphasizes employer-sponsored retirement benefits as the primary conduit for financial savings. It provides a number of tax breaks to employers to get them to offer retirement plans to their employees and some assistance to their employees for saving in such plans, for instance, through matching contributions to a 401(k) plan.

How exactly does the tax code try to get employers to offer retirement plans? Those saving for retirement at work typically receive a few tax breaks.[7] Employers and employees can contribute to a retirement plan and those contributions are not subject to federal income taxes nor are employer contributions subject to payroll taxes for Social Security and Medicare.[8] There is a maximum amount that employees and employers can contribute to retirement plans on a tax-advantaged basis.[9] Employees, for instance, could contribute a maximum of $18,000 to their employer's 401(k) plan in 2015 and deduct that amount from their income subject to federal income taxes. The total amount that employers and employees could contribute on a tax-advantaged basis to all of an employee's employment-based DC savings accounts was $53,000 in 2015.[10] The money contributed to retirement plans then grows because it earns capital income—capital gains and interest and dividend income. This capital income in DB pension plans and DC accounts is also not subject to taxation while the money stays in such retirement plans. Income paid out from DB pensions or withdrawn from DC accounts is then subject to personal income tax rates.

Policymakers have devised these tax breaks in such a way that they presumably encourage employers to offer retirement plans at work. The main tool in the tax code to encourage employers to offer a retirement plan is the maximum contribution limit for employer-sponsored retirement plans. The underlying assumption is that business owners and highly compensated managers both want to save the maximum amount of taxes and are the decision makers when it comes to offering benefits to their employees. Contribution limits for employees to employer-sponsored retirement plans, such as DB pensions and 401(k) account plans, are consequently higher than for individual savings plans such as IRAs.[11] Business decision makers—owners and managers—will enjoy greater tax breaks with a 401(k) plan offered to all employees, including managers and owners, than with an IRA outside of work. The maximum employee contribution limit is then an incentive to corporate decision makers to offer a retirement plan at work. Few employees will contribute the maximum, but business owners and managers with comparatively high incomes may find these maximum contributions especially attractive.[12] They then will presumably encourage their employers to offer a retirement plan at work so that they can take advantage of these maximum contributions (tax breaks).

And employers can make additional and often even larger tax deductible contributions to their employees' retirement plans than employees can. Business decision makers wanting to give highly valued and highly compensated employees, including themselves, extra compensation at a favorable tax treatment presumably will find the employer maximum contributions especially attractive and offer retirement plans to take advantage of these tax breaks.[13]

Policymakers then have put a few provisions into place to make sure all employees, not just the corporate decisions makers, who are well compensated, have access to tax-advantaged retirement plans from their employers. The rules in the tax code relating to maximum contribution limits for employer-sponsored plans exist to get employers to offer retirement plans in the first place. Other rules exist to make sure other employees, not just high-income earners, benefit from these retirement plans as well.

First, retirement plans have to be nondiscriminatory. The tax code caps the share of benefits that can go to highly compensated employees, defined as employees earning more than $120,000 in 2015.[14] That is, policymakers have designed tax code provisions to make sure employers share the benefits of a retirement plan between high-income earners and other employees.

Second, employers can receive some relief from proving that their retirement plans are nondiscriminatory if the plans contain particular features that support their employees' ability to save for retirement.[15] Such plans are then considered safe-harbor plans. The Pension Protection Act of 2006, for instance, created a new set of safe-harbor rules for 401(k) plans that meet a number of specific automatic features such as automatic enrollment and automatic escalation of employee contributions—contributions increase each year as share of earnings.[16] The tax code in essence offers employers a quid pro quo, so that employer-sponsored retirement plans that make it easier for all employees to save for retirement get some regulatory relief. Nondiscrimination and safe-harbor rules exist to nudge employers toward helping all of their employees to save for retirement, not just the well-heeled ones.

Evidence Highlights Current Approach's Failure

The aggregate data, though, suggest that incentives for employers to help employees save appear to work for an ever smaller share of the private sector workforce. Access to retirement plans at work has gradually declined since 2000 and employer contributions to their employees' retirement plans have also gone down over time.

Figure 8.1 shows the share of private sector workers working for an employer that offered (sponsored) a retirement plan at work, either as a DB pension or 401(k) plan.[17] This share peaked at 59.0 percent in 2000 and has trended downward since then, reaching 51.3 percent in 2013 (Figure 8.1). Just a little over half of the private sector work-force has had access to a retirement savings plan at work in recent years.

Even when focusing only on those workers who worked full time during the entire year, declining retirement plan access at work becomes apparent (Figure 8.1). The share of full-time, year-round employees working for an employer who sponsored a retirement plan peaked at 69.4 percent in 1998 and then trended downward, reach-ing 62.3 percent—less than two-thirds—in 2013. An even smaller

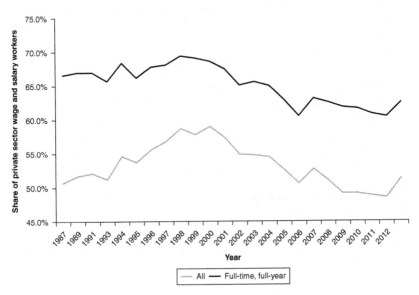

Figure 8.1 Private sector wage and salary workers with employer-sponsored retirement plan at work, select years from 1987 to 2012.

Notes: Numbers are share of private sector wage and salary workers in percentage. Includes all workers working for an employer who offers a retirement plan at work. Retirement plans include DB pensions and DC savings accounts.

Source: Craig Copeland, "Employment-Based Retirement Plan Participation: Geographic Differences and Trends, 2013," EBRI Issue Brief No. 405 (Washington, DC: Employee Benefits Research Institute, 2014), and Craig Copeland, "Employment-Based Retirement Plan Participation: Geographic Differences and Trends, 2012," EBRI Issue Brief No. 392 (Washington, DC: Employee Benefits Research Institute, 2013).

percentage of those workers actually participated in such plans, as I discuss below.

Not only has access declined, but private sector employers have put less money into their employees' retirement accounts. Figure 8.2 shows private sector employer contributions to DB pensions and 401(k) accounts as a share of private sector wage and salary payments.[18] Employers can make contributions on behalf of current and former employees. The share of total contributions to wages and salaries captures any potential crowding-out effects from contributions for former employees on contributions to current employees. This share reached a peak with 4.3 percent in 1993 and then trended downward reaching 3.6 percent in 2013, the lowest such share since 1985. This decline after 1993 marked a reversal of a trend toward increasing employer contributions in the preceding two decades, erasing about half of the gains made in the prior two decades. Employers would have contributed an additional $39 billion to their employees' retirement plans in

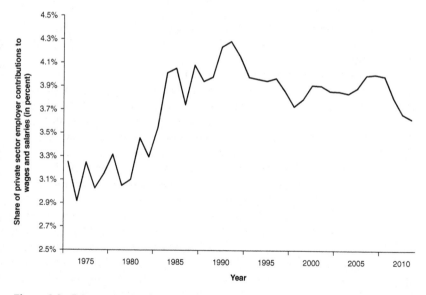

Figure 8.2   Private sector employer contributions to retirement plans as a share of wages and salaries, 1975–2013.

Notes: Retirement plans include DB pensions and employer-sponsored DC savings accounts. Contributions include all employer contributions on behalf of current and former employees. All figures in percentage of private sector wages and salaries.

Source: Bureau of Economic Analysis (BEA), "National Income and Product Accounts" (Washington, DC: BEA, 2014).

2013 if the share of employer contributions to wages and salaries in the private sector had stayed constant at the 1993 level.[19]

Uneven Access to Retirement Plans

The policy emphasis on employers helping their employees save for retirement can be both a help and a hindrance to increasing savings. On the one hand, employees clearly need some assistance to put money aside for the future in a world where such savings are purely voluntary and where risks are mounting and employers may be able to systematically offer such assistance.

But, on the other hand, employers become gatekeepers, who can limit access to retirement savings and associated tax benefits. Somebody has to be employed by an employer who has the means and the interest to offer a retirement plan to even have the possibility of getting access to an employer-sponsored retirement plan. And even then, employees often have to pay for the choices made by their employers on what types of plans are offered, for instance, by paying the fees and accepting some uncontrollable risk exposure associated with investment choices by the employer.[20]

The result is that employees with more labor market risk exposure often have less access to retirement plans at work than employees with less labor market risk exposure. That is, the self-employed, workers in small businesses, low-wage employees, employees in contingent employment arrangements—part-time, subcontracting, and temporary employment—as well as workers typically found in less stable employment arrangements (young, nonwhite, lower educational attainment, and lower income) tend to be much less likely than their counterparts to have a retirement plan through an employer.

Table 8.1 shows the sponsorship rates—the share of workers who work for an employer who sponsors a retirement plan at work—by a number of select characteristics, showing substantial variation in sponsorship rates. The variation tends to be especially large by employer size and by work status. Somebody working for an employer that has less than 10 employees, for instance, only had a 16.5 percent chance of having access to a retirement plan at work, compared to a 71.0 percent chance for somebody who worked for an employer that had 1,000 or more employees (Table 8.1). And part-time, part-year workers only had a 25.6 percent chance of having access to a retirement plan at work compared to 57.8 percent for full-time, full-year workers. Also younger

Table 8.1   Retirement plan sponsorship rates of private sector workers in 2013, by select characteristics

Characteristics	Sponsorship rate (%)	Participation rate (%)	Participation to sponsorship rate (%)
21–24 years	46.9	34.5	73.6
35–44 years	52.6	43.6	82.9
55–64 years	56.5	48.5	85.8
White	56.2	45.8	81.5
Black	50.2	36.6	72.9
Hispanic	34.7	25.5	73.5
No high school diploma	27.0	18.4	68.1
High school	45.7	34.5	75.5
Some college	51.3	38.7	75.4
College	61.0	51.7	84.8
Full time, full year	57.8	49.2	85.1
Part time, part year	25.6	9.1	35.5
$10,000 to $19,999 in annual earnings	31.7	15.2	47.9
$20,000 to $29,999 in annual earnings	43.4	30.4	70.0
$40,000 to $49,999 in annual earnings	61.8	52.9	85.6
$75,000 and above in annual earnings	71.4	66.9	93.7
Employer has fewer than 10 employees	16.6	13.2	79.5
Employer has 10–49 employees	33.4	25.8	77.2
Employer has 50–99 employees	49.2	38.3	77.8
Employers has 100–499 employees	59.9	47.2	78.8
Employer has 500–999 employees	62.4	49.8	79.8
Employer has 1,000 or more employees	71.0	57.0	80.3

Notes: All figures are in percentage. Sponsorship refers to the share of private sector wage and salary workers who work for an employer that sponsors a retirement plan at work for the respective subpopulation. Participation rate is the share of wage or salary employees who participate in a retirement plan at work. Employees need to work for an employer that sponsors a retirement plan before they can participate. All population groups only include people between the ages of 21 and 64 years, unless otherwise specified.

Source: Craig Copeland, "Employment-Based Retirement Plan Participation: Geographic Differences and Trends, 2012," EBRI Issue Brief No. 392 (Washington, DC: Employee Benefits Research Institute, 2013).

workers, workers with less education, lower income workers, and non-white and Hispanic workers had lower likelihoods of having access to a retirement plan at work than their counterparts.

Some employers, especially smaller businesses, tend to find themselves in economically more vulnerable situations than larger businesses and that instability is passed on to their employees in the form of less job security and fewer benefits. And even employers in stable industries have few incentives for offering a retirement plan to employees whom they do not expect to be working for them for long periods of time. Some workers consequently get less access to build-ing financial life rafts than others because of the way policy priori-tizes employer-sponsored retirement benefits over other retirement savings. But the affected workers also tend to be the workers who arguably need the most help to save for the future, precisely because they already face more labor market risks—working under financially more precarious circumstances—during their working years than is the case for other workers.

Employers Have Increasingly Cut on Retirement Benefits

The decline in total employer contributions to retirement plans shown in Figure 8.2 is thus not just an artifact of fewer plans being offered but also by employers becoming stingier with their contributions.

Consider what happens to employer contributions per active participant—those still employed with said employer—for 401(k) plans. Here I assume that all employer contributions are for active participants, largely because employers rarely make contributions in those retirement savings plans for those who no longer work for them.

Figure 8.3 shows two measures of the employer contribution per active participant from 1988, the first year for which complete data exist, to 2012, the last year for which complete data exist at the time of this writing. One measure adjusts past employer contributions for price changes that have occurred and the other measure adjusts for wage changes over time with the implicit assumption that employer contri-butions should have risen over time alongside their employees' wages and not just as prices in the economy went up. The data show that, regardless of the correction, these contributions per participant have gradually moved down. The decrease is more pronounced for wage-adjusted contributions than for price-adjusted contributions. Wages have grown a little faster than prices for much of the period from 1988 to 2012, but employer contributions even failed to keep pace with the slower growing prices never mind with wage growth (Figure 8.3). That is, employers have pulled back in how much they pay their employees in retirement benefits both by cutting access to retirement plans and offering fewer benefits in those plans.

Employers have cut back on offering retirement plans and on their contributions to their employees' retirement plans at a time when

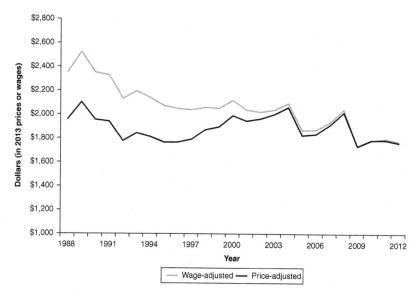

Figure 8.3   Employer contributions to DC plans per active participant, adjusted for wages or prices, 1988–2012.

Notes: Price adjustments are based on the Personal Consumption Expenditure Index from the BEA's NIPA, while wage adjustments are based on the BLS's ECI for wages and salaries for civilians in the private sector. Calculations only include private sector employers and private sector employment-based DC plans such as 401(k) plans.

Source: Based on Bureau of Economic Analysis (BEA), "National Income and Product Accounts (NIPA)" (Washington, DC: BEA, 2014); Employee Benefit Security Administration (EBSA), Department of Labor, "Private Pension Bulletin, Abstract of Form 5500—Historical Tables" (Washington, DC: EBSA, 2014); and Bureau of Labor Statistics (BLS), Department of Labor, "Employee Cost Index (ECI)" (Washington, DC: BLS, 2014).

profits rose. Companies hence had the means but not the desire to pay more employee benefits since the late 1980s and early 1990s.

This discussion highlights another albeit obvious pitfall of primarily relying on employers in encouraging employees to save for retirement in a system of voluntary retirement savings. This approach only works as long as employers want to offer benefits. Once employers became more reluctant to offer retirement benefits to their employees—as has been the case in the past few decades—strains start to show. Employees have less access to retirement plans at work, and total contribution rates to savings plans (including their own contributions and that from their employers) decline and employees' economic risk exposure increases.

Many Employees with High Labor Market Risk Exposure Do Not Participate in Retirement Plans at Work

Working for an employer that offers a retirement plan at work is only a first step. Employees also need to be eligible to participate, for instance, by having worked enough hours during a given period and employees increasingly have to decide to participate in an employer-sponsored plan. Eligible employees are automatically enrolled in DB pensions, but they still typically need to sign up for a 401(k) plan. Only a little less than 80 percent of private sector wage and salary workers who have access to a retirement plan at work actually participated in such a plan in any given year.[21] The ratio between participation and sponsorship varies very little by firm size, underlying the importance that having a retirement plan at work plays for actually saving for retirement (Table 8.1) and the danger of insufficiently saving for one's future that lurks in working for an employer who does not offer a retirement plan.

The gap, in contrast, between having access and participating varies more by variables other than employer size. The gap is generally larger among workers with more labor market risk exposure than among workers with less labor market risk exposure. Merely 47.9 percent of wage and salary workers with earnings between $10,000 and $19,999 with retirement plan access participated, compared to a full 93.7 percent for those earning $75,000 or more in 2013 (Table 8.1). And only 73.5 percent of workers between the ages of 21 and 24 years who had access to a retirement plan participated in one in 2013, compared to 85.5 percent for workers between the ages of 45 and 54 years. Further, a mere 72.9 percent of African American employees with retirement plan access participated in 2013, compared to 81.5 percent for whites.

The substantial gap between having a retirement plan at work and participating in one illustrates that voluntary participation comes with a heavy price tag. Many workers who already face substantial labor market risks will also face increasing economic insecurity in the future because they work for employers who do not offer retirement plans or because they do not participate in their employer's retirement plans. And the share of workers facing substantial labor market risks is going up, while the share of workers with access to retirement plans and those participating in a retirement plan have gone down, in part because policy has prioritized employer-sponsored retirement savings over other savings.

Household Financial Risk Exposure Has Increased Alongside the Growth of Retirement Savings Accounts at Work

It is not just that households may end up with fewer savings in the employer-sponsored system, when they encounter high labor market risk exposure. Financial market risk exposure can also be higher than it otherwise would be in part because of the reliance on employer-sponsored retirement benefits. The financial market risk exposure for people with DC plans and without DB pension plans has risen faster than the financial market risk exposure of people with DB pensions. The discussion below goes into more detail on how employer-sponsored retirement savings, especially in the form of DC plans, can contribute to people's financial risk exposure.

Employers with DB pensions make the investment decisions. Households are often unaware of the investments their employers are making in DB pensions and the risks associated with those investments. But the potential risk exposure for households is limited because employers will accept at least part of the financial risk if a pension plan becomes underfunded. And the Pension Benefit Guaranty Corporation insures many private sector DB pensions in case of employer bankruptcy.[22]

Employers with DC plans, in comparison, decide on the investment options for their employees and employees then typically decide how to manage financial risk exposure with these investment options. Americans can incur too much financial risk exposure in their 401(k) plans because the necessary financial decisions tend to be complex and the full consequences of potential mistakes are far off into the future. People often use rules of thumb rather than some complicated mathematical optimization strategy to make financial decisions when faced with complexity and long time horizons. Using rules of thumbs, such as allocating all investments equally across all investment options—for instance, by putting one-fifth of all assets into each of five mutual investment options, can expose people's savings to too much financial market risk.[23] And the potential consequences of too much financial risk exposure compound since households invest for long periods of time.

The potential for high financial risk exposure with employer-sponsored retirement plans does not stop there. People need to theoretically account for the financial risk exposure in their retirement savings plans, such as 401(k) plans, in their other savings such as housing. People who are relatively risk-averse, for instance, but have accepted a lot of risk in their 401(k) plan by investing heavily in stocks should in theory lower their risk exposure elsewhere. They could do so by putting savings into lower risk assets such as bonds and savings accounts rather than into another risky asset such as housing.

This proposition that households protect themselves from risk exposure in their employer-sponsored retirement plans by considering all of the financial risks they incur in other investments as well as with their debt is asking a lot from households. Households may not have all of the relevant information, and even if they did and knew how to use it, they may not be able to be fully protected against risks, in part because their savings and risk exposure depends on their employers' choices for a retirement savings plan.

The compartmentalization of savings that exists by design—getting employers to help employees to save for retirement, for instance, while people need to buy a house on their own—complicates financial decisions for households and can build obstacles to savings and risk protection. Household financial risk exposure has indeed grown over time, especially for older households near retirement.[24]

One particular indication that this increase in financial risk exposure has been happening outside of households' control is that financial risk exposure among near-retirees, who have a lot more wealth than younger households, has been increasing, even though their risk tolerance has declined.

This gap between rising risk exposure and falling risk tolerance among households with employer-sponsored DC plans suggests that Americans have found it increasingly difficult to protect their savings. Figure 8.4 provides a snapshot of household risk exposure and risk tolerance for older households with employer-sponsored DC retirement savings plans. It shows the share of households 50 years and older with high risk exposure and the share of households with above-average or substantial willingness to take financial risks. I define very high risk exposure as having a concentration of stocks and housing out of total assets of 75 percent or more and having a debt to assets ratio of 25 percent or more.[25] The figure shows that household financial risk exposure for those nearing retirement has increased, while older households' risk tolerance has gone down.

The primary explanation for this gap between risk exposure and tolerance is that households have encountered substantial obstacles in protecting their savings, as they participate in DC plans at work, while labor and financial market risks have gone up. The overreliance on employer sponsorship of retirement savings, which constitute one of

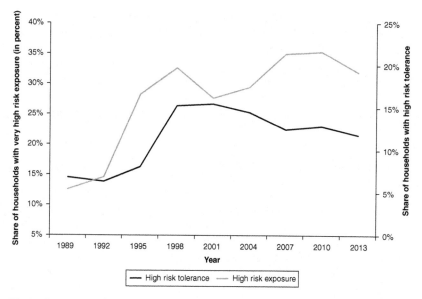

Figure 8.4   Financial risk tolerance and risk exposure of nonretired households 50 years and older, 1989–2013.

Notes: A household has a high risk tolerance if it indicates above-average or substantial financial risk tolerance. A household has high financial risk exposure if it has a ratio of risky assets—stocks and housing—out of total assets that is greater than 75 percent and a debt to assets ratio that is greater than 25 percent. The household sample only includes households 50 years and older, who are not retired, to capture the risk exposure of near retirees, and only households with employer-sponsored DC plans, but no DB pensions.

Source: Based on Board of Governors (BOG), Federal Reserve System, *Survey of Consumer Finances* (Washington, DC: BOG, various years).

the largest forms of private savings for households, constitutes such an obstacle to protecting retirement savings.

Policy Implications

This discussion highlights the shortcomings of policies that prioritize employer-based voluntary retirement savings over savings outside of the employer–employee relationship. This is not an argument to end employer-based retirement savings all together, but rather for improving the employer-based system and for putting nonemployment-based savings on an equal footing.

The data in Table 8.1, for instance, show that employers appear to be able to get their employees to enroll in retirement savings plans.

The ratio of participation to sponsorship is relatively stable across all firm sizes. It is just that smaller employers are much less likely to offer retirement plans than is the case for larger employers. Additionally, all employers have been cutting back on offering retirement plans and on contributing to those plans that are offered. Employees also can face substantial risk exposure across all of their savings because of a heavily compartmentalized system, which particularly sets apart employer-sponsored plans.

There are three separate policy implications from this discussion. First, employers can be unreliable partners in getting workers to save, especially when employers focus more heavily on their short-term profitability than on offering benefits to their employees. But people are likely to save more when they have a partner. That is, IRAs are not suitable supplements for employer-based benefits. Policymakers consequently want to find additional partners to get households to save more. Such partners could include nonprofits, governments, and financial institutions. Low-income savers, for instance, can receive some public savings matches for their savings in IDAs that are administered by nonprofits.[26] The federal government has created so-called MyRAs that are intended to make it easier for people to save for the future.[27] And a number of state governments including California have started to look into offering retirement savings plans to private sector employees who currently do not have retirement plans at work.[28] And the US Congress passed legislation in late 2014 to make it easier for banks to offer lottery-based savings accounts, whereby savers forego some interest on their savings in exchange for the possibility of winning large cash prizes.[29] Several potential partners other than employers exist to help households save more for the future as recent experiments illustrate.

Second, employees still need some encouragement to participate in savings accounts. Basically, policymakers and policy experts have started to discuss an end to complete voluntary participation. One direction is what could be called a "soft" end, while the other is a "hard" end.

The "soft" end to voluntary participation would require employers to offer some help for employees to save, but would leave employees the option not to participate. The proposal for an automatic IRA (auto-IRA) is one such "soft" end to voluntary participation. All employers who do not yet offer a retirement plan need to enroll their employees in payroll deduction to an employee's IRA. And employees can opt out of this payroll deduction if they do not want to participate.[30]

A "hard" end to voluntary participation would put in place a universal, required private savings add-on to Social Security. Proposals in this vein would require that all employees and, in some instances, employers contribute a small share of employees' earnings to a low-cost and generally low-risk savings accounts. The required contributions vary under these proposals, but tend to start around two to three percent of earnings. The mechanisms by which such proposals envision mitigating the risk to participants also vary. They can be either low-risk investment options such as treasury bonds or riskier investments with an explicit government guarantee against excessive losses.[31]

Third, the US savings system is highly compartmentalized. There is a myriad of tax incentives for different savings purposes, the largest of which are housing and retirement. This compartmentalization of savings for different purposes can lead households to unwittingly incur too much or too little risk in their savings. They either have too much of their future economic security at stake, or they are leaving money on the table by not foregoing potential earnings. A key solution then to overcome compartmentalization is to simplify tax-advantaged forms of savings, typically by creating a very small number—between one and three—of tax-advantaged savings accounts.[32] Reducing compartmentalization in savings should ultimately help households build more wealth over time by better protecting against financial risks.

Conclusion

The US system of savings requires households to save more outside of public benefits than is the case in other advanced economies, emphasizes voluntary participation in all savings including retirement savings, and hence prioritizes the delivery of retirement benefits through employers to help households reach one of their most important long-term savings goals. The employer-based voluntary system of private retirement savings works well for higher income workers who work for large employers that offer a retirement savings plan at work. But the system works especially poorly for employees with substantial labor market risk exposure—lower income workers, communities of color, and those working for smaller employers. Those workers who face disproportionately high labor market risks may end up with fewer savings than is the case for workers with less labor market risk exposure. And all workers with employer-sponsored retirement savings can incur high financial market risk exposure due to the compartmentalization of savings and the complex decisions necessary in such a system to adequately protect household savings. Policymakers can address these shortcomings by deemphasizing the role of employers, finding stronger ways to encourage households to save, and by overcoming the artificial compartmentalization between savings for separate purposes. All households, especially those facing the real-life waves of labor market risks, will eventually find it easier to build strong financial life rafts that can bring them to sunny shores, if policymakers enact these and a few other broad changes.

CHAPTER NINE

Upside-Down Tax Incentives

How would you personally define what a secure retirement means to you?[1]

"To have a number of investments and inheritance." (White woman, 84 years old)

Retirement is ultimately a costly proposition since people can spend decades without earning money from work and taking care of their loved ones and themselves. They hence need to save a lot of money outside of Social Security for their own future. Policy offers some help to people wanting to save for their retirement, but it provides the least help to those who face the largest risk exposure and thus greatest obstacles to saving more. The federal government already uses the tax code to incentivize people to save, typically through tax advantages for particular savings such as retirement savings in 401(k) plans. But these savings incentives are complex and favor higher income earners over those with lower earnings. The help that the tax code offers consequently does little to combat the growing retirement crisis since it fails to adequately target those who actually need help.

Savings incentives in the tax code exist for people to save for retirement, housing, health care, and children's education, although incentives to save for retirement and housing are much larger than other savings incentives in the federal budget. Employees can often defer tax payments for their and their employers' contributions to retirement savings vehicles such as 401(k) plans. Households can also deduct the interest paid on their mortgages for their primary or secondary residences from their taxable income. Capital gains are

generally not subject to federal income taxation until people withdraw the money from their savings accounts, and homeowners do
not have to pay any income tax on up to $250,000 in capital gains
from the sale of their primary residence, or $500,000 if they are
married. These tax advantages supposedly encourage more people to
save more money for their future than they would have saved absent
these tax incentives

The existing savings incentives in the tax code fall short in getting a lot of people to save, who otherwise would not have saved,
for three reasons. First, savings incentives are complicated, making it
unnecessarily difficult for people to understand them and thus actually hindering savings. For retirement savings alone, there are DB
pensions and a variety of DC savings plans. Additional savings plans
exist for health care and education. And households can deduct the
interest on their mortgages for their primary or secondary residences
if they itemize their deductions. Moreover, all tax-advantaged savings vehicles come with their own rules of who can save with them,
how much money people can save, which savings are protected from
bankruptcy, and when the tax advantages occur—during the contribution phase, during the investment phase, and during the withdrawal phase. This complexity often stands in the way of people
taking full advantage of all of the tax incentives to save available
to them, since complexity breeds confusion and confusion leads to
inaction, that is, no savings.

Second, each savings incentive for retirement, housing, health care,
education, and so on, primarily emphasizes a narrowly defined set of
savings goals. Existing rules make it difficult to use tax-advantaged
savings for purposes other than the intended ones. Households may
have retirement savings, for instance, they cannot fully access in an
emergency. And there are no meaningful incentives to build liquid
emergency savings. These limits can prevent people from saving for the
long term because they are worried they cannot have access to money
when they need it before then.

Third, savings incentives in the tax code are skewed toward higher
income earners. Many savings incentives occur in the form of deductions from taxable income. Such tax deductions lower the amount of
income that is subject to federal income taxation. But the US tax code
is progressive such that the amount of taxes owed increases with household income. The amount of taxes owed on the last earned dollar—a
household's marginal tax rate—goes up with income. The value of savings incentives then depends on the marginal tax rate and the marginal

tax rate is greater for higher than for lower incomes. The tax code, in fact, offers little or no incentives to lower income households who may not owe anything in federal income taxes but who may need the most help in saving more.

The complexity of existing savings incentives that favor select savings goals and help higher more than lower income earners leaves a substantial share of households, especially lower income ones, with no tax-advantaged savings and potentially contributes to growing wealth inequality. The existing savings incentives do not work for households that need the most additional help saving more: lower income households that have experienced the largest increases in economic risk exposure.

In this chapter, I discuss these three design flaws—complexity, select and limited savings goals, and favoring high-income earners—of savings incentives and present some basic calculations on the value of tax benefits to select types of households to illustrate the upside-down nature of existing savings incentives.

Design Flaws of Current Savings Incentives

Existing savings incentives are often deductions from taxable income. Employee and employer contributions into a tax-advantaged savings plan—primarily into retirement savings vehicles such as 401(k) plans and IRAs—typically reduce the taxable amount of income for employees. The same is true for interest payments on mortgages owed on primary residences. The money in a tax-advantaged savings vehicle then accumulates without households having to pay personal income taxes on the capital gains in the savings vehicle. Taxes are due, however, when money is withdrawn for retirement or other purposes, after households often have reaped large tax advantages for long periods of time.[2]

The federal government uses these tax incentives primarily to get people to save for retirement and to buy a house to live in, preferably without a mortgage, once they are retired, but similar tax incentives exist for health-care savings—into Health Savings Accounts (HSAs), for example, which allow people to pay for health-care costs that are not covered by insurance—and for children's college education, to subsidize tuition payments.

Three flaws in this system make it difficult for people who have the greatest need to save more to actually do so.

Complexity of Existing Savings Incentives Slows Savings

The federal tax code's incentives for retirement, housing, education, and health-care savings are so confusing that even people who would like to take advantage of them may be deterred from doing so.

The retirement savings system alone is a complex web of different options and varying incentives that make it difficult for households to navigate.[3] To know and maximize all available retirement savings incentives, for instance, households need to figure out which retirement savings options their employers offer, know the rules governing each such savings option and all alternative savings options, understand how saving in one savings plan could impact savings in another, estimate their marginal tax rates in the current tax year, project the marginal tax rates for the rest of their careers, and come up with a reasonable estimate for their retirement ages and their marginal tax rates in retirement. The average household must navigate similarly complex systems to decide on and set up a Coverdell Education Savings Account (ESA) or an HSA.

Giving households some choice is not, in and of itself, a flaw with savings incentives, but behavioral economics has shown that overwhelming consumers with excessive choices is effectively the same as providing no choice at all. Multiple studies show that too many choices in key decisions can overwhelm and frustrate consumers, resulting in consumers relying on heuristics—educated guesses—when making complex choices[4] or making no choice at all.[5] Individuals are even more likely to abstain from choosing anything altogether out of a fear of making a choice that could end up damaging the financial well-being of the household, for instance, by limiting access to savings in an emergency.[6] The existing policy approach basically says that Americans can build sturdy life rafts for their future by building them on their own out of multiple parts, once they have mastered different instructions for each part. Who would not want to do that?

Dedicated Savings Goals Limit the Protections Savings Can Offer

The complex system of US savings incentives encourages households to save for particular predetermined purposes. These include retirement, home ownership, college education, and health care, to name the most relevant ones.

Households can get access to some of their dedicated savings for other purposes, within limits. Current rules for 401(k) plans, for instance, allow for so-called hardship withdrawals, which include medical emergencies, prevention of eviction or foreclosure, tuition payments, purchase of a primary residence, funeral expenses, and some expenses for repairs on a primary residence. However, hardship withdrawals can only be taken while still working for an employer. Income loss due to unemployment, for instance, is thus not considered a hardship withdrawal. And the employee has to pay income taxes and typically a ten percent excise tax on any hardship withdrawal.[7] Households can also prematurely withdraw money from an IRA, as long as they pay the associated income taxes.[8] Excise taxes may apply if the reasons for withdrawal from an IRA do not meet specific criteria.[9] That is, the tax code includes financial hurdles to withdrawing money from dedicated retirement accounts prematurely and thus may make it harder for households facing increasing labor and financial market risks to protect themselves against these risks.

Households may alternatively access their dedicated tax-advantaged savings by taking out a loan. They could, for instance, borrow from their own 401(k) plans or they could ask for a home equity line on their owner-occupied home. There are, again, limits similar to hardship withdrawals, although there are no immediate tax penalties for taking such loans. Loans from 401(k) plans are consequently more prevalent than withdrawals.[10]

But there are additional hurdles to accessing dedicated tax-advantaged savings with a loan that limits this option. Most importantly, the chance to take a loan decreases when labor and financial market risks materialize and households are most in need of getting access to their savings through a loan. A household still has to work for an employer to take out a loan from its own 401(k) plan and typically has to repay a loan within 90 days after losing their job. Otherwise, tax penalties—income taxes plus a ten percent excise tax—apply.[11] This substantially reduces the value of so-called pension loans as a risk protection amid rising labor market risks. Job losses after all close off access to 401(k) loans. Similarly, banks become more reluctant to give households home equity lines when unemployment is increasing and when home prices are falling, although this is exactly the time when households need access to their illiquid savings tied up in their houses.[12]

Not only do people have limited access to their tax-advantaged assets for short-term needs, but there are only a limited number of options to build emergency savings on a tax-advantaged basis. Such programs to help households save more for their short-term needs often exist at the state and local government level, but are less prevalent at the federal level and hence do not enjoy the same level of tax benefits as savings programs for housing and retirement.[13]

The bottom line is that households need to build both long-term and short-term financial buffers that they can access when growing labor and financial market risks materialize but policy favors a limited number of long-term savings goals and offers little help with emergency savings. A large share of households, especially among vulnerable populations such as lower income households, communities of color, and single women, have consequently very few emergency savings.[14] Following a loss of income, 43.5 percent of US households would not have enough liquid assets to live at the poverty level for three months,[15] never mind maintain their standard of living.

Savings Incentives Skewed toward Higher Income Earners

The value of federal savings incentives in the tax code for retirement, housing, education, and health care generally increases with income, but the connection is complex. I hence first discuss the relevant real-life complexities in theory and then provide some illustrative calculations in the next section to demonstrate that the existing savings incentives are skewed toward higher income earners, even—or especially—when we account for the relevant real-life complexities.

Let us start with the simpler part of the discussion before delving into the complications. First, households deduct their retirement savings and mortgage interest from their current taxable income and thus reduce the amount of income subject to taxation. The tax code is progressive, such that higher income earners pay higher marginal taxes—the amount of taxes due on the last dollar earned—than is the case for lower income earners. Since higher income earners face higher marginal income taxes than lower income earners, they have a stronger incentive to reduce their taxable income than is the case for lower income earners with a deduction.[16] The highest tax bracket—for those annually making more than $406,750 individually or $457,600 jointly in 2014—is 39.6 percent.[17] Earners in this tax bracket would lower their current year tax liability by 39.6 cents for each dollar contributed to an eligible 401(k) or IRA and for each dollar paid in interest on a mortgage for a primary or secondary residence. A lower income earner, in comparison, faces a marginal tax rate of ten percent and thus saves only ten cents in current year income taxes for each dollar they contribute to a tax-advantaged asset. The same is true for contributions to eligible

Coverdell ESAs for anticipated college tuition expenses and eligible HSAs for savings toward medical care.

Second, capital income in tax-advantaged assets is not subject to either capital gains or income taxation—depending on the form of capital—as long as the money stays in a tax-advantaged asset. Again, higher income earners benefit more from this tax advantage than lower income earners because they save more in taxes, as long as the money is locked away in tax-advantaged savings.

Current savings incentives contribute to a pronounced imbalance in who benefits from them and who does not. In 2013 the federal government forewent about $137 billion in revenue annually from tax expenditures for retirement savings alone. However, only 18 percent of this foregone revenue went to the bottom 40 percent of earners, while 51 percent accrued to the top 20 percent of earners, with over 75 percent of this tax incentive going to the top ten percent of earners.[18] Importantly, this unequal distribution of tax incentives is a snapshot of only one year's benefits offered to households by allowing them to deduct their contributions to tax-advantaged assets and by not taxing capital income in tax-advantaged assets that year. But the picture gets more complex when looking at a longer time horizon.

There is an offsetting tax cost—expected tax payment—to households and this is where things start to get complicated. People eventually may have to pay income taxes on the money they withdraw from their tax-advantaged savings. Some experts hence refer to these savings incentives as tax deferrals, rather than tax breaks or tax shelters, since households eventually are supposed to pay taxes.[19]

There is an argument that looking only at the tax benefits when households contribute and invest money in tax-advantaged savings assets overstates the benefits to high-income earners, because it ignores their future tax payments. The Investment Company Institute's (ICI) Peter Brady laid out the argument against the link between tax incentives and inequality in great detail in 2012.[20] This argument says that the initial benefit and the ultimate tax payments offset each other to a large degree, such that savings incentives favor rich households only somewhat.

This ultimately overly simplistic and thus misleading logic goes as follows. The tax payments upon withdrawal will vary again with income, in the same way that the initial tax benefits varied with income, since the tax code treats withdrawals as personal income. Higher income earners will pay higher income taxes than lower income earners when they withdraw their funds, because the tax code is progressive with higher marginal tax rates for higher than for lower incomes. Future tax payments upon withdrawal will offset the initial tax benefits. And the offsetting effect upon withdrawal is larger for higher income earners than for lower income earners due to the progressiveness of the US tax codes. So, yes, high-income earners receive larger tax benefits upfront, but they will also pay much higher taxes in the future, according to this argument.

This is not to say that there are no tax benefits from tax deferral when all is said and done and both initial tax benefits and future tax payments are counted, even in this view. And the net tax benefits are typically much larger for higher income than for lower-income earners, as I discuss below. The main benefit is that households can generate investment earnings on a larger investment than would be the case without initial tax incentives. That is, households benefit from the power of compounded interest on a larger initial investment by deferring taxes. Higher income earners still get more value from this tax-free compounded interest effect, because they get to keep and invest more money upfront that otherwise would have gone to the government than is the case for lower income earners.

The size of the net tax benefit—tax benefits minus expected future tax payments—from deferring tax payments into the future depends on some real-life complications that tend to favor higher income earners' savings. High-income earners consequently tend to benefit multiple times more from tax deferrals than lower income households.

So, what are these real-life complications?[21] First, households will have varying opportunities to put money into tax-advantaged assets, not just because some households have more money to save than others. High-income earners, for instance, are also those who are most likely to have access to an employer-sponsored retirement savings plan in the first place. Similarly, higher income earners are more likely to get access to HSAs—through so-called cafeteria benefit plans—and other benefits such as tax-advantaged parking, transportation, and child-care expenses from their employers.[22] Since employer-sponsored retirement plans typically offer employees the chance to make larger tax-advantaged contributions than is the case in other retirement plans, higher income earners often can deduct more total dollars on a tax-advantaged basis than is the case for lower income and middle income households.

Second, households' marginal tax rates can decline when people reach retirement, because their income decreases and because older households can enjoy additional tax breaks not available to younger households.[23]

Lower future marginal tax rates mean lower future tax payments and thus fewer offsetting tax payments in the future against the initial tax benefits, boosting the unequal nature of existing savings incentives. And, high-income earners have high marginal tax rates to begin with and those marginal tax rates have more room to fall than is the case for lower initial marginal tax rates for lower income earners.

In some instances, withdrawals from tax-advantaged savings are not subject to personal income tax at all. Households do not pay taxes on money from ESA used for tuition or from HSAs used to pay medical bills, for example. The net benefit from tax deferrals depends in part on the gap between the marginal tax rate when households contribute money to tax-advantaged assets and the marginal tax rate when they withdraw their savings. That means that high-income earners see the biggest net benefits in cases when the marginal personal income tax rate on withdrawals is zero because they experience the largest marginal tax rate difference.

Third, the benefit from tax deferrals depends in part on tax-free compounding of interest. And the longer the interest compounds, the larger the net benefit to the household. Higher income earners may start to save earlier and withdraw savings later in life than would be the case for lower income households,[24] simply because they have more income. Such longer investment periods imply longer interest compounding periods and greater tax benefits from deferring tax payments. Higher income earners thus are better able to take advantage of tax-free interest compounding than is the case for lower income households.

Fourth, the net tax benefits increase when not all money is withdrawn. Households often die before they spend all of their money, leaving large tax benefits to their heirs.[25] And higher income households are more likely to leave money in tax-advantaged assets to their heirs than is the case for lower income households.[26] Existing tax incentives may then transmit wealth inequality from one generation to the next.

Existing savings incentives disproportionately favor higher income earners. As a first stab at showing the inequality of tax incentives, I use the estimated amount of net pension contributions and earnings on retirement accounts plus the value of the mortgage interest deduction—as a share of after-tax income, by income percentile, in 2013 in Figure 9.1. The data show that the contemporaneous benefit of tax deductions—as a share of income—increases sharply with income levels. High-income earners benefit multiple times more from these savings incentives than lower income earners, relative to their incomes. That is, actual tax benefits rise faster than incomes. Households in the top fifth of the income distribution, for instance, on average receive savings incentives equal to an estimated 3.1 percent of their income, almost twice as much as the 1.8 percent for households in the fourth-fifth of the income distribution (Figure 9.1).[27] And households in the bottom fifth of the income distribution receive only a fraction of those benefits with an average of 0.4 percent of average tax income.

This figure highlights the unequal distribution of current tax deductions, but it does not include the offsetting effect of future tax payments, nor does it show the various factors contributing to the disproportionate tax benefits among high-income earners. I consequently use a few illustrative calculations in the next section to demonstrate how a wide range of factors can contribute to higher income earners reaping larger benefits from the existing savings incentives than lower income households can.

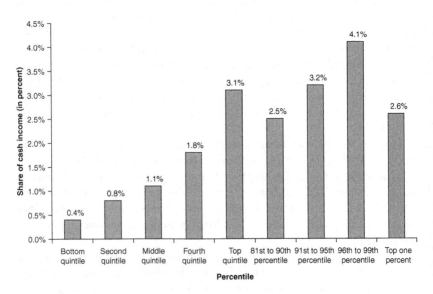

Figure 9.1 Net pension contributions and earnings and mortgage interest deduction as a share of after-tax income, by income percentile, 2013.

Note: All figures in percentage.

Source: Congressional Budget Office (CBO), "The Distribution of Major Tax Expenditures in the Individual Tax System, Table 2" (Washington, DC: CBO, 2013), accessed March 5, 2015, http://www.cbo.gov/sites/default/files/43768_DistributionTaxExpenditures.pdf

Before I do show these simulations, though, it is important to point out that there does not appear an offsetting macroeconomic effect—more total savings—from these unequal tax incentives, favoring high-income earners over low-income ones. Research shows that higher income earners, on average, largely replace nontax-advantaged savings with tax-advantaged savings. That is, higher income earners would save similar amounts without savings incentives.[28] The federal government probably spent as much as $92 billion in fiscal year 2013 on retirement savings incentives for the top quintile of earners alone without actually increasing personal savings beyond where savings would have already been.[29] The existing tax-advantaged savings serve as tax shelters for higher income earners, but do not raise savings in a meaningful way and offer little help to lower and middle income households most in need of additional savings at a time of rising risk exposure. Existing savings incentives basically give sturdy new life rafts to those Americans who already have life vests, but do little to help those who need it the most.

Illustrating the Workings of Existing Savings Incentives

Some of the complexities of existing savings incentives and their impact on wealth distribution are best illustrated with a few simplified calculations of the net tax benefits—tax benefits minus tax payments—for a range of hypothetical households.

Let us review the discussion of how the tax deferrals work and the related complexities:

- The net benefit of tax incentives arises from deferring tax payments into the future and letting tax-free contributions earn tax-free compounded interest.
- Higher income earners get a higher net benefit because they get a larger tax break on their initial contribution, on which interest compounds.
- The net benefit is larger when households can contribute more to a tax-advantaged asset, for instance, because they work for an employer who sponsors a retirement plan.
- The net benefit increases when a household's marginal tax rate is lower when they withdraw savings than when they contributed money to a tax-advantaged asset.

- The net benefit is larger when households can wait longer and let interest compound for longer periods.
- The net tax benefit is larger when money is not withdrawn, but passed on to the household's heirs.

I account for all of these aspects in my simulations, other than the last one—passing on one's savings to an heir—since it would require making assumptions for more than one generation.

My calculation here focuses on two types of retirement savings plans—an IRA and a 401(k) plan—to keep the discussion simple. Higher-income earners often can have access to multiple retirement plans at work, for instance, because both spouses of a couple with two earners have a 401(k) plan or because employers offer a 403(b) plan—a retirement plan akin to 401(k) plan in nonprofits—and a tax deferral plan known as 457 plan.[30]

My illustrative calculations require a few assumptions to get started. First, I make some assumptions about the amount that is being contributed and the length of time for which the contribution is invested. I assume a household contributes $5,500 annually to an IRA as the baseline scenario, to which I compare my other scenarios to illustrate the effect of key differences. This amount is likely too high for low-income earners and too low for high-income earners. That is, the initial comparison already overstates the gap in net tax benefits between low- and high-income earners. I then assume that the household invests the contributions for 25 years, before withdrawing all of the contributions and the returns earned on them and paying personal income taxes on these withdrawals.[31]

Second, the value of the tax incentives depends on the households' marginal tax rates at three different points in time. These include the households' marginal tax rate when it makes the contribution. This constitutes a tax benefit, because the contribution is not subject to federal income taxes. It also includes the marginal tax rate during the investment period as another tax benefit, since the income earned on the investments is not taxed during that time. Finally, it includes the marginal tax rate when the money is withdrawn as an offsetting tax burden, since withdrawals are subject to income tax. For the baseline example, I assume that all marginal tax rates are equal to 25 percent.

Third, the value of the tax incentives depends, to some degree, on the rate of return the household can earn on its contributions. I assume that the household can earn a nominal rate of return of six percent on average for the 25 years during which the money is invested.

I then calculate something called the net present value of the deferral benefit. The appendix contains the exact formula, taken from the work by Peter Brady at the Investment Company Institute.

The intuition of this calculation goes as follows. It adds the tax benefit of deducting the tax contribution from income taxes, plus the tax benefits from not paying federal income taxes on the earnings on the contributions during the investment period, minus the income taxes paid on the withdrawal when the entire contributions, plus accumulated rates of return, are withdrawn. It adjusts each tax benefit and tax burden by a process called discounting, so that all amounts are comparable to each other, regardless of how short or how long taxes have been deferred. These adjusted amounts of tax benefits and tax burdens are the amounts the household would have to set aside (or, in the case of tax burdens, receive) today that would amount together with the expected interest rate—the discount rate—to the future dollar amounts calculated as nominal tax benefits and tax payments. I assume that the discount rate is equal to six percent.[32] The sum of the adjusted two tax benefits, minus the future tax burden, shows the total value of deferring taxes into the future.

I focus my discussions on the total value of the net tax benefit of deferring tax payments into the future as the key metric, rather than alternative measures such as the deferral benefit per dollar deferred. Higher income earners will enjoy larger total net benefits not only because of higher incomes but because of other factors in the US savings landscape, such as increased access to employer-sponsored retirement plans. Calculating the deferral benefit per dollar ignores these other factors and naturally downplays the differences of net benefits by income. I report the deferral benefit per dollar only for completeness sake, but consider the total value of the net tax benefit to be a better measure of tax deferral benefits.

Table 9.1 shows some of these key assumptions and then presents the total deferral benefit for the baseline scenario and a few alternative scenarios that I discuss below. The first line in Table 9.1 shows the baseline scenario with a total tax deferral benefit of $1,236.42 for a contribution of $5,500 in 2015.

Now, I create alternative scenarios to show the effect of different inputs on the value of the tax deferral by income. First, I create a scenario for a low-income household with a constant marginal tax rate of 10 percent. All other inputs into the calculation remain the same. Only the marginal tax rates change. The deferral benefit now drops to

Table 9.1 Simulated net tax benefits of tax deferral under varying assumptions (in 2015 dollars)

	Tax rate at deferral	Tax rate at withdrawal	Deferral benefit per dollar invested	Total deferral benefit	Ratio of total benefit to baseline benefit
Baseline scenario, $5,500 deferred	25.0%	25.0%	22.5%	$1,236.42	–
Low-income earner, $5,500 deferred	10.0%	10.0%	11.9%	$654.89	53.0%
High-income earner, $5,500 deferred	39.6%	39.6%	26.1%	$1,437.22	116.2%
High-income earner, $18,000 deferred	39.6%	39.6%	26.1%	$4,703.61	380.4%
High-income earner, $23,500 deferred	39.6%	39.6%	26.1%	$6,140.83	496.7%
High-income earner, $23,500 deferred, marginal tax rate declines at retirement	39.6%	25.0%	40.7%	$9,571.83	774.2%
High-income earner, $23,500 deferred, all invested in stocks, marginal tax rate declines at retirement	39.6%	25.0%	29.6%	$6,946.99	561.9%
High-income earner, $23,500 deferred, all invested in stocks, marginal tax rate declines at retirement, deferral period is 35 years	39.6%	25.0%	34.5%	$8,096.06	654.8%

Notes: Benefits of tax deferral calculated as net present value. Discount rate is equal to government interest rate, which is set equal to six percent nominally. All tax rates are marginal tax rates. Deferral period is 25 years, unless otherwise stated.

Source: Based on Peter Brady, "The Tax Benefits and Revenue Costs of Tax Deferral" (Washington, DC: Investment Company Institute, September, 2012).

$654.89, or about half of the tax deferral benefit for a middle income earner (Table 9.1).

Second, I create a scenario for a high-income household with a constant marginal tax rate of 39.6 percent. This is again the only assumption I change in this example. The deferral benefit now totals $1,437.22 or 16 percent more than the benefit for middle income earners (Table 9.1).

But, high-income earners can benefit under the current system of tax incentives in a number of other ways, which are often not available to lower income earners. I hence show a few additional calculations to illustrate these benefits to high-income earners.

I first assume that a high-income earner has access to a 401(k) plan through an employer and contributes the maximum amount of $18,000 in 2015 instead of the maximum of $5,500 to an IRA. High-income earners are much more likely to have access to an employment-based retirement plan than lower income ones. That is, an IRA is a good approximation of the retirement savings reality for lower and middle income earners and a 401(k) plan reflects the typical situation for high-income earners. The total tax deferral benefit now is $4,703.61 or almost four times the benefit in the baseline scenario. That is to say that the value of sheltering retirement savings from taxes is greater for higher income earners than for lower income ones, to a large degree, because higher income earners are more likely to have access to employer-sponsored retirement plans with greater contribution limits than is the case for IRAs.

The total tax benefit increases even further if a high-income earner has access to more than one retirement plan. I now consider some-body who has access to both a 401(k) plan through an employer and a Simplified Employee Pension IRA through a consulting business. The combined contributions to both plans increase to $23,500 for the pur-poses of this example.[33] This total contribution is higher than the total annual earnings of many low-income earners. The tax deferral benefit increases to $6,140.83 in this example, which is five times the total tax deferral benefit in the baseline scenario (Table 9.1).

High-income earners benefit from tax deferral because they are more likely to have access to employer-based retirement savings plans, because they are more likely to have more than one retirement savings plan and because they are more likely to have enough extra income to make substantial contributions to tax-advantaged retirement plans.

Higher income earners may also benefit from deferring taxes on their income if their marginal tax rate declines over time. In the next sce-nario, I assume that the high-income earner's marginal tax rate indeed declines over time. The high-income earner in this example already pays the highest marginal tax rate when she makes the contribution, so her marginal tax rate can only decline. I assume that her marginal tax rate drops to 25 percent at the time when the money is withdrawn. The tax deferral benefit increases to $9,571.83 in this case, which is almost eight times the benefit in the baseline scenario (Table 9.1). Tax payers can benefit from tax deferrals if their marginal tax rates in retirement are lower than their marginal tax rates during their working years.

This decline in marginal tax rates is more likely to occur for higher than lower income tax payers simply because higher income tax payers already pay high marginal tax rates when they contribute to their retirement accounts. Using tax-advantaged retirement savings is more attractive to higher than lower income earners simply because their marginal tax rates are more likely to fall over time as they start from higher marginal tax rates to begin with.

There is one complicated but limiting effect in the tax code, though, that especially applies to higher income earners. The tax benefit during the deferral period depends on how savers invest their money. If the money is invested in stocks, the tax rate that high income tax payers save is not their foregone marginal personal income tax rate, but the tax rate on long-term capital gains and dividend payments, which is equal to 20 percent. But a lower tax rate during the savings period that high-income earners would have paid, if their savings had not been in tax-advantaged accounts, also means that the value of the tax deferral declines. I again assume that the marginal tax rate at withdrawal is lower with 25 percent than the marginal tax rate at the time of contribution with 39.6 percent. The tax benefit now still totals $6,946.99 or almost six times as much as in the baseline scenario (Table 9.1).

I add one final aspect to this same calculation. Higher income households may be more likely to invest their money for longer periods of time than is the case for lower income households. This would allow them to benefit from tax-free interest compounding longer. I now assume that high-income earners can defer tax payments for 35 years instead of 25 years. Because all numbers in Table 9.1 are adjusted for time passed, they are directly comparable with each other even though the deferral period is a decade longer than in the other calculations. The marginal tax rate in this example declines from 39.6 to 25 percent and all money is invested in stocks with a capital gain and dividend tax rate of 20 percent. The household now sees a total net benefit, from contributing $23,500 in 2015, of $8,096.06, or six-and-a-half times the net benefit in the baseline scenario (Table 9.1).

The lessons from these simulations are clear. First, households need to navigate a complicated system of rules to maximize their tax benefits. They need to understand which savings plans they have available, how much they can contribute, how to invest their money, how long to keep their money in a tax-advantaged asset, and how their decisions interact with current and future tax rates for personal income and capital income. Second, higher income earners benefit a lot more from savings incentives since they are more likely to have access to them, they pay higher tax rates, they can wait longer before withdrawing their money, and they, presumably, understand these incentives better, allowing them to better utilize the interactions between savings rules and current and future tax rates than is the case for lower income households.[34]

Conclusion

Households have experienced an increase in labor and financial market risk exposure. This is especially true for lower and middle income households. Households could, and theoretically should, respond to this increase in risk exposure by building up more savings cushions. Policy has in fact designed a number of savings incentives in the tax code to presumably make it easier for households to save for retirement, housing, education, and health care, to name the most important purposes. But, the resulting system of savings incentives has three flaws. It is complex, it does not fully address the short-term savings needs of households increasingly exposed to economic risks, and it offers substantially more valuable benefits to higher than to lower income earners. Households that most need to save in order to protect themselves from the growing risks and to counter their increasing economic risk exposure receive the least help from the existing savings incentives.

Appendix

The calculation of the net present value of the net tax benefit of tax deferral is taken from ICI's Peter Brady's work and follows the development by other researchers[35]:

$$R_D^{PV} = t_0^0 + \sum_{n=1}^{T} \frac{t_0^d r_c [(1-t_0^0)(1+r_c(1-t_0^d)^{n-1}]}{(1+r_g)^n} - \frac{t_0^T (1+r_c)^T}{(1+r_g)^T}$$

The equation calculates the net present value of one dollar that has been deferred from paying taxes, R_D^{PV}. The other relevant variables in this equation are defined as follows:

t_0^0 = marginal income tax rate when the initial contribution is made

t_0^d = marginal income tax rate during the deferral period, when the money is invested

t_0^T = marginal income tax rate when money is withdrawn

r_c = rate of return earned on the investments during the deferral period

r_g = government interest rate, which is equal to the discount rate

T = length of deferral

The equation has three separate parts on the right hand side. The first, t_0^0, is the tax benefit from deducting the initial contribution from taxable income in the first year. The second part, after the summation sign, shows the tax benefits from earning tax-free compounded interest on the investment over the deferral period, T. And the third part after the minus sign shows the tax burden the household has to pay when withdrawing money from the tax-advantaged asset.

CHAPTER TEN

Sidelined: The Millions Who Are Left Out

How would you personally define what a secure retirement means to you?[1]

"To just have plenty of money saved up. To have a good 401(k), good life insurance, a nice bank account." (White man, 36 years old)

Economic risks have gone up for households over the past 30 years. Wages and salaries have become more volatile, unemployment spells have become longer, stock prices have undergone wider boom and bust cycles, and house price swings have become more dangerous as households have become mired in debt. And households increasingly have had to manage their savings on their own to avoid too much exposure to these risks as DB pensions have disappeared, Social Security's benefit growth has slowed, and individualized savings such as 401(k) plans, IRAs, and housing have become ever more widespread.

Households have to save more money than in the past to counter the combination of growing risks and rising risk exposure. But this very combination of rising risks and increasing risk exposure has made it more difficult for households to save more. Key challenges for households include economic obstacles such as low and increasingly unstable income, as well as behavioral hurdles such as problems making increasingly complex financial decisions on their own.

These obstacles are a key rationale for public policy to help people save with individualized savings by offering employers tax breaks to encourage employees to save more, especially for retirement and by giving employees tax breaks for saving on their own.

But these policies work well for a few, do not work at all for many, and are inadequate for most households. That is, most households tread water with their savings, while only a few have stable and secure financial life rafts. The prioritization of employer-based retirement savings in savings incentives, for instance, results in the de facto exclusion of many of the very households that have the greatest risk exposure and need the most help in saving. And savings incentives offer few or no benefits to low-income households that often experience the most economic risk exposure and thus have the greatest need for more savings.

Policy thus has created uneven risk protections in stormier times. The existing policies are most effective for households that have comparatively high incomes. Employer-based retirement benefits and existing tax breaks work least effectively for lower income households.[2] Yet, those are the same households that have experienced disproportionate increases in labor market risk exposure and some financial market risk exposure and hence need the added risk protections from additional savings.

I present data in this chapter that shows in some detail who benefits and who does not from existing savings incentives for different forms of savings.[3] The summary data show that current policies consistently fall short in offering most households the risk protections they need. First, only a small share of households fully benefit from the myriad of savings incentives, while a substantial share of households receives no savings incentives at all. Wealth inequality has consequently also grown. Second, the share of households saving with tax-advantaged savings has not increased, despite large-scale policy changes meant to broaden the share of households who save. Third, households that do not benefit from savings incentives are also more economically vulnerable than households that do benefit. And fourth, the household groups least likely to benefit from savings incentives are nonwhites, Hispanics, households with no college degree, and households with incomes at the bottom of the income scale.

The trifecta of financial insecurity—lack of savings coverage, rising wealth inequality and thus insufficient savings for many, and increasing risk exposure—follows from policy design shortcomings. The lack of progress on savings coverage, through tax-advantaged saving, follows from the prioritization of employer-sponsored benefits, which can exclude many savers. Further, tax incentives are skewed toward high-income earners. And increasing financial and labor market risk exposure follows from a growing emphasis on individualized savings, for which households receive little help in protecting their savings. Households consequently have not made meaningful strides toward more savings and better risk protections at a time of growing risks over the past 30 years.

The Concentration of Tax-Advantaged Savings

Public policy encourages households to save by offering tax breaks for a number of different savings vehicles, although retirement savings and housing receive the largest tax breaks. Other tax incentives exist for education, health care, and life insurance. Households enjoy tax advantages for savings in DB pensions, 401(k) plans, IRAs, housing, Coverdell ESAs, HSAs, and some types of life insurance. Most savings eventually will go to pay for households' retirement as they age, no matter what the stated savings goal is called. But households have uneven access to these tax-advantaged savings. For one, households can gain easier access to some retirement plans if their employers offer such plans. Second, tax incentives structured as deductions of savings from taxable income offer larger incentives for higher income earners and fewer or no incentives to lowerincome households.

Consistent data on tax-advantaged savings exist in the *SCF* for DB pensions, 401(k) plans, IRAs, housing, and the cash value of life insurance policies from 1989 to 2013. Data on whether a household has a Coverdell ESA or a HSA is combined with data on whether a household has a 529 education savings plan only for the years from 2004 to 2013. I hence focus on the main five types of tax-advantaged savings vehicles—DB pensions, 401(k) plans, IRAs, home equity, and cash value of life insurance policies—in this discussion and report additional information on education and health savings in the appendix.

Figure 10.1 shows the shares of households with no tax-advantaged savings and with three or more tax-advantaged savings. The data show that close to one-fourth of households, 23.5 percent to be exact, had no tax-advantaged savings in 2013, while one-fourth, 27.1 percent, of households had three or more tax-advantaged savings (Figure 10.1).

These shares change with age, although large gaps persist. About one-sixth, 13.4 percent, of households 50 years and older had no tax-advantaged savings, 48.5 percent had one or two tax-advantaged savings, and 38.1 percent of households had three or four tax-advantaged savings in 2013.[4]

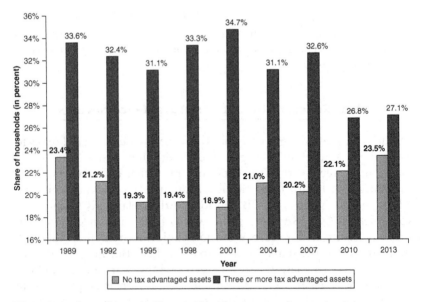

Figure 10.1   Share of nonretired households without any tax-advantaged savings.

Notes: All figures are in percentage. Sample includes only nonretired households. Tax-advantaged savings options include owner-occupied housing, DB pensions, IRAs, 401(k) plans, and life insurance policies, as long as they have a positive cash value. The difference between the two groups shown here is households with one or two tax-advantaged savings. They make up the largest group in any given year, but there is again no clear up or down trend over time. Adding this third group to the figure makes the presentation unnecessarily unwieldy without adding any information.

Public policy benefits are highly concentrated among a minority of households, while a sizeable share of households do not fully benefit from the tax incentives. The primary tool to help households build stable and secure savings—tax incentives—has hence left many households treading water.

Long-Term, Large-Scale Changes in the Way We Save Do Not Bring More Opportunities

Figure 10.1 also shows no improvement over time. Savings policy in the United States since the 1980s has tried to get more people to save for their future by offering a variety of tax incentives. Yet, the trend in households with no tax-advantaged savings—an approximation for measuring the first goal of getting more people to save—has actually been growing since 2001. By 2013, the share of households without any tax-advantaged savings was at the highest level on record, dating back to 1989 (Figure 10.1). At best, this trend suggests no improvement in the share of savers, and at worst it shows that the share of households with tax-advantaged savings has actually declined since the early 2000s.[5] Tax incentives have definitely not created a groundswell of new savers, even though increasing risks and rising risk exposure have created a need for many more households to save for their future.

At the same time, the share of households with three or more tax-advantaged savings has fallen to a little over one-in-four in the aftermath of the Great Recession of 2007 to 2009, which is the lowest level on record, dating back to 1989 (Figure 10.1). That is, access to tax-advantaged savings seems to have become more concentrated over time.

The lack of progress in getting more people to have tax-advantaged savings is surprising since the period was marked by a growing emphasis on individual savings that carry many tax advantages, which theoretically should have made households more aware of the various tax breaks that exist, especially for retirement savings. The share of households with DB pensions has declined, while the share with 401(k) plans has grown. These two trends just offset each other. In the end, the shares of households with no tax-advantaged savings did not consistently fall over time and, in fact, increased after 2001 (Figure 10.1).

The bottom line is that public policy efforts have been unsuccessful in broadening the circle of savers over the past decades, even though public policy put a greater emphasis on individualized savings that were meant to incentivize more people to save by getting people more directly involved in retirement savings and by offering them more savings choices.

Fewer Tax-Advantaged Savings Go along with More Economic Insecurity

The data further suggest that having tax-advantaged savings correlates with a number of beneficial indicators. Households with three or more tax-advantaged savings tend to have more wealth and less financial and labor market risk exposure. Many households with no or only a few tax-advantaged savings, in comparison, face a more insecure financial future.

Tax-Advantaged Savings and Wealth-to-Income Ratios

Table 10.1 summarizes a number of key economic security indicators for households, categorized by the number of tax-advantaged savings forms they have. The table first presents the ratio of wealth to income. This is a key economic security measure meant to highlight personal economic security since wealth is meant to replace income when somebody retires, which is the main reason for people to save. Next, the table shows the share of households with very high risk exposure. I define very high risk exposure as having a share of risky assets—stocks and housing—out of total assets that is greater than 75 percent and a debt to assets ratio that is greater than 25 percent. This measure summarizes the key indicators of financial risk exposure, and the conclusions in this book do not depend on the specific thresholds chosen for the definition of very high risk exposure. Third, as a particular and novel measure of financial vulnerability, I show the share of households that have 401(k) plans and that have loans from such plans. Households with DB pensions, for instance, could not borrow against their pensions and thus could not reduce their future savings with such loans. And such loans tend to lower retirement wealth in the future.[6] Fourth, I look at the unemployment rate and the length of unemployment (available only from 1998 onward) as indicators of labor market risk exposure.

The data in Table 10.1 show that households with more tax-advantaged savings also had a lot more wealth and, on average, substantially less financial and labor market risk exposure. The median wealth-to-income ratio for households with three or more tax-advantaged savings was 297.0 percent in 2013, compared to 90.1 percent for households with one or two tax-advantaged savings, and zero for households with no tax-advantaged savings. Having tax-advantaged savings should not directly equate to no wealth since households can save in a wide variety of nontax-advantaged savings forms, such as savings accounts. Practically, though, it appears that having tax-advantaged savings is equal to having wealth for the typical household (Table 10.1).

The wealth-to-income trends further suggest that full access to tax-advantaged savings may have contributed to rising wealth inequality. Households with three or more tax-advantaged savings had not only a greater wealth-to-income ratio than households with just one or two tax-advantaged savings for the entire period from 1989 to 2013 (Table 10.1). But the wealth gap between households with several

Table 10.1 Select indicators, by number of tax-advantaged savings

Year	1989	1992	1995	1998	2001	2004	2007	2010	2013
Median wealth to income (%)									
No tax-advantaged assets	0.0	0.0	0.0	0.0	0.0	0.0	0.0	0.0	0.0
One or two tax-advantaged assets	102.3	104.4	107.4	99.1	109.7	116.6	133.2	90.7	90.1
More than two tax-advantaged assets	235.7	218.5	229.6	272.8	292.6	341.1	359.9	307.4	297.0
Ratio of median wealth for households with more than two taxadvantaged assets to households with one or two tax-advantaged assets	230.5	209.3	213.8	275.3	266.7	292.5	270.2	338.8	329.8
Average share of households with very high risk exposure (%)									
No tax-advantaged assets	0.1	0.2	0.6	0.8	1.3	1.2	0.6	0.5	0.3
One or two tax-advantaged assets	27.3	28.7	32.7	32.5	31.9	41.5	37.4	40.7	37.5
More than two tax-advantaged assets	28.5	30.0	33.3	31.9	33.0	34.0	34.7	34.3	30.6
Average share of households with 401(k) plans and loans from their 401(k) plans									
One or two tax-advantaged assets	0.2	9.9	11.4	13.1	13.1	13.4	11.5	15.6	15.5
More than two tax-advantaged assets	5.4	7.1	9.8	12.9	9.0	9.6	9.7	9.1	10.5
Average share of head of households who are unemployed									
No tax-advantaged assets	9.0	11.0	9.8	9.5	7.1	6.9	9.3	11.9	12.3
One or two tax-advantaged assets	3.5	4.9	2.7	3.2	2.4	3.2	3.4	5.7	5.0
More than two tax-advantaged assets	0.5	1.1	0.6	1.3	1.2	1.3	1.1	1.7	2.1
Average length of unemployment of head of household (in weeks)									
No tax-advantaged assets	n.a.	n.a.	n.a.	7.40	6.40	7.74	7.20	12.73	10.26
One or two tax-advantaged assets	n.a.	n.a.	n.a.	3.95	2.87	4.67	3.42	7.07	5.09
More than two tax-advantaged assets	n.a.	n.a.	n.a.	1.66	1.94	2.25	1.44	3.63	2.36

Notes: The calculations rest on five potential tax-advantaged savings: DB pensions, 401(k) plans, IRAs, housing and life insurance policies if they have positive cash values. Households have very high risk exposure if their risky asset—stocks and housing—amount to more than 75 percent of all assets and if their debt is greater than 25 percent of assets. Very high risk exposure is calculated only for households with any assets. Sample includes only households that are not retired. The share of households with 401(k) loans is only calculated for households with 401(k) plans. n.a. indicates that data are not available.

tax-advantaged savings and those with one or two such assets has also grown from a ratio of about two to one in 1989 and 1992 to a ratio of well above three to one in 2010 and 2013.[7] That is, the concentration of tax-advantaged savings appears to have contributed to growing wealth inequality and rising retirement income adequacy among those who do not have full access to tax-advantaged savings.

Tax-Advantaged Savings and Financial Market Risk Exposure

Households with three or four tax-advantaged savings typically had a lower likelihood of having very high financial market risk exposure. They also had a lower chance of having taken out a loan on their 401(k) plans in most years, which not only indicates less risk exposure but also suggests more retirement savings in the future. And the gap in these exposure measures substantially widened after the Great Recession of 2007 to 2009, alongside a growing wealth gap. That is, financial market risk exposure and household wealth move in opposite directions. When financial market risk exposure is high, wealth is low and vice versa; when financial market risk exposure is low, wealth is high.

Tax-Advantaged Savings and Labor Market Risk Exposure

But that is not all. Households with several tax-advantaged savings also had less labor market risk exposure than other households (Table 10.1). Their unemployment rate was regularly a fraction of other households' unemployment rate, hovering between one and two percent for most of the years from 1989 to 2013. Households with one or two tax-advantaged savings generally had an unemployment rate that was three to four times as large as this. An even greater disparity shows up for households with no tax-advantaged savings that had an unemployment rate that was often at least ten times as large as the unemployment rate for households with three or four tax-advantaged savings. The differences in the length of unemployment are also systematic, such that households with three or more tax-advantaged savings tend to be unemployed for much shorter periods of time than other households (Table 10.1). And again, labor market risk exposure and household wealth move in opposite directions. Higher labor market risk exposure goes along with less wealth, and lower labor market risk exposure goes along with more wealth.

Tax-advantaged savings go along with growing wealth and thus rising retirement income adequacy among higher-income earners. This may reflect the very fact that these tax-advantaged savings offer greater tax benefits to higher income than for lower income earners. And the concentration of savings and retirement income security may reflect the prioritization of employer-sponsored retirement benefits, given that two out of four tax-advantaged savings—DB pensions and 401(k) plans—depend on employers offering such benefits to their employees. It is also possible that tax-advantaged savings are concentrated among households that face less labor market risk exposures, which may make it easier for households to plan for their future, take better advantage of the complex and myriad tax-advantaged savings instruments, and thus better reduce their financial risk exposure and save more for their future with the help of the tax code. The confluence of policy design flaws and risk exposure differences clearly creates a system of economic protection that works for the lucky few—about one-fourth in my data—but not the overwhelming rest of households that are left treading water and worrying about their future incomes in retirement.

Most Vulnerable Households Have Few
Tax-Advantaged Savings

Who are those lucky few households that do not have to worry about their retirement? Table 10.2 summarizes the demographics of households with no tax-advantaged savings, with one or two tax-advantaged savings, and with three or four tax-advantaged savings. The table summarizes the data for the entire period from 1989 to 2013 without additional breakdowns by years because the demographics in each group changed very little over time.[8]

The demographic differences between the groups of households with and without tax-advantaged savings are striking (Table 10.2). More than four in five households (85.6 percent) with three or more tax-advantaged savings, for instance, are white. Comparatively, only a little over half of households, 52.1 percent, without any tax-advantaged savings are white (Table 10.2). And 54.4 percent of households with three or more tax-advantaged savings have at least a college degree, while most households with no tax-advantaged savings have no college education (Table 10.2). Furthermore, the number of tax-advantaged savings increases with household income, so that 45.8 percent of

Table 10.2 Population composition of households, by number of tax-advantaged savings and time period

Household characteristics	No tax-advantaged savings (%)	One or two tax-advantaged savings (%)	Three or four tax-advantaged savings (%)
Race/ethnicity			
White	52.1	72.1	85.6
Black	22.4	13.8	7.9
Hispanic	19.9	9.8	3.0
Other	5.6	4.4	3.6
Educational attainment			
No high school/GED	25.3	14.2	4.4
High school/GED	35.8	33.7	24.1
Some college	20.8	19.5	17.1
College	18.2	32.5	54.4
Income level			
Bottom quintile	50.3	15.6	1.7
Second quintile	27.5	22.0	5.9
Middle quintile	14.6	25.1	16.1
Fourth quintile	5.8	22.4	30.5
Top quintile	1.8	15.0	45.8
Financial planning horizon			
Less than a year	77.6	64.5	45.1
One to five years	15.9	22.7	32.7
More than five years	6.5	12.8	22.2

Notes: All figures are in percentage. The calculations rest on five potential tax-advantaged savings: DB pensions, 401(k) plans, IRAs, housing and life insurance policies if they have a positive cash value. Households have very high risk exposure if their risky asset—stocks and housing—amount to more than 75 percent of all assets and if their debt is greater than 25 percent of assets. Sample includes only households that are not retired and that have one or two tax-advantaged savings. All demographic characteristics refer to the head of household.

households with three or more tax-advantaged savings had incomes in the top fifth of the income distribution. In comparison, more than half, 50.3 percent, of households without any tax-advantaged savings had incomes in the bottom fifth of the income distribution (Table 10.2). And households with three or more tax-advantaged savings also tend to take a longer view of the future, which can help them to take advantage of complex savings opportunities and better manage their risk exposure. More than one-fifth, 22.2 percent, of households with more than two tax-advantaged savings had a financial planning horizon of five years or more, compared to only 6.5 percent of households with no tax-advantaged savings (Table 10.2).

Conclusion

The bottom line is that the groups of households that tend to be especially vulnerable in the labor market are also the ones that have the least protections from tax-advantaged savings. Strikingly, this conclusion has not changed over time, even though as labor market risks have increased, especially for vulnerable populations; their need to save more has grown and policymakers have instituted large-scale changes, presumably to make it easier for households to save.

The inverse is also true. Groups of households that generally have less labor market risk exposure tend to be the ones who benefit more from tax-advantaged savings. They tend to be more likely to work for employers, for instance, that offer retirement benefits. They also tend to have higher incomes and thus value savings incentives in the tax code more than their counterparts. And they tend to have less overall risk exposure, which on average allows them to relax a little more about their future and hence take a longer term view, which in turn translates into more saving. Consequently, existing policies especially help those households that least need the assistance.

Policy hence contributes to growing wealth inequality and rising retirement income inadequacy. The lack of change, especially the absence of increasing share of households with any tax-advantaged savings, is one of the clearest signs that policy has not worked as intended. Existing policies clearly work for households that need the protections the least, but they fail for households that need the extra help from public policy. On the other hand, policy has extended a strong helping hand to households that already are in the best situation to build wealth, because they are well educated, earn higher income, and face fewer economic risks than their counterparts. The result is a growing inequality in wealth and economic risk exposure, which policy fails to address in a systematic and substantial way. Those who already have state-of-the-art survival suits to protect against the turbulent seas of rising risks also get secure and stable financial life rafts, while those without them need to sink or swim.

This broad policy failure can be traced to a number of particular design flaws in the way US policymakers have tried to get households to save more. First, the prioritization of employer-sponsored benefits in retirement savings has left a growing share of households ill-prepared for their retirement. Second, incentivizing household savings by making some forms of savings deductible from taxable income favors higher income households over others and offers little or no help to households that need the most help to save more for their future. Third, the complexity of and artificial divisions between savings incentives actually impede retirement savings for the average households and, instead, create outsized opportunities only for the savviest and most patient savers. Fourth, the emphasis on individualized savings in retirement plans and through housing as the primary tools to save for retirement outside of Social Security has exposed many households to more risks, just as those risks have grown and contributed to slow growing savings and increasing retirement income insecurity.

Appendix

The *SCF* has included information on additional tax-advantaged savings since 2004. The *SCF* specifically includes one variable on whether a household has an education account—529 or Coverdell ESA—or a HSA. The information is combined so that whether these are education or health savings accounts is unclear.

I provide some additional information in Table A10.1 to show that the inclusion of this additional information does not alter the conclusions in the text. Table A10.1 specifically shows the distribution of tax-advantaged savings when education and health-care savings accounts are excluded (taken from Figure 10.1) and when they are included. The shares of households with no accounts are slightly smaller from 2004 to 2013, when education and health-care accounts are included, but still 23.4 percent of all households had no tax-advantaged savings in 2013 (Table A10.1). In 2013, the share of households with one or two tax-advantaged savings falls from 50.1 percent, without health and education accounts included, to 48.7 percent, with health and education account included (Table A10.1). The shares of households with three or more tax-advantaged savings obviously increase when I include education and health-care accounts, but the bulk of this increase—generally 80 percent—comes from the decline in the share of households with

Table A10.1 Distribution of tax-advantaged assets, by number of assets and year

Year	Without education and health-care accounts			With education and health-care accounts		
	No account (%)	One or two accounts (%)	Three or more accounts (%)	No account (%)	One or two accounts (%)	Three or more accounts (%)
2004	21.4	48.7	29.9	21.0	47.0	32.0
2007	20.7	48.2	31.2	20.2	46.4	33.4
2010	22.4	52.0	25.6	22.0	50.3	27.7
2013	23.8	50.1	26.1	23.4	48.7	27.9

Notes: All figures are in percentage. Sample includes only nonretired households. Tax-advantaged savings options include owner-occupied housing, DB pensions, IRAs, 401(k) plans and life insurance policies (as long as they have a positive cash value). Education and health-care accounts include 529 savings plans, Coverdell ESAs, and HSAs.

one or two tax-advantaged savings, not from a substantial change in the share of households with no tax-advantaged savings. That is, health and education accounts tend to be especially prevalent among households that already own other tax-advantaged savings and do not create new tax-advantaged savings opportunities for those who have none.

Moreover, the trends do not change when I include health and education accounts. The share of households without any tax-advantaged savings grows over time, while the share of households with three or more accounts falls in the aftermath of the Great Recession in 2010 and 2013 (Table A10.1).

That is, the availability of a myriad array of tax-advantaged savings does not increase the circle of savers.

CHAPTER ELEVEN

Charting a New Course

How would you personally define what a secure retirement means to you?[1]

"Not having to worry about what you're going to eat or pay your bills." *(White man, 70 years old)*

People increasingly face insecure futures in retirement because policy has contributed to households' rising risk exposure just as labor and financial risks have grown. The result has been that savings have become less stable—households cannot be sure that their savings will be available when they need them—and that wealth inequality has grown—a few households have seen substantial gains in their savings, while most households struggle with saving for their future. This situation is akin to being on a boat in a brewing storm, where the rich get state-of-the-art survival suits and life rafts, while middle- and low-income households need to find ways to sink or swim as they tread water.

Policymakers—federal and state lawmakers and regulators—can help most households build more stable and more secure life rafts by addressing five specific policy shortcomings. These include first the erosion of Social Security's protections and the decline of DB pensions. Next, policy has prioritized employer-sponsored retirement savings over other savings, which has limited access to savings for many households. Further, tax incentives are heavily skewed toward the wealthy, offering little or no assistance to low-income households that arguably need the most help to save since they experience the largest risk exposure. Moreover, tax incentives and savings options are overly complex, which makes it difficult for most households to save more and to protect their savings. Finally, policy has put no or very little emphasis on helping households better manage their risk exposure, just as labor and financial market risks have become more pronounced.

These five problems lead to five important implications that can inform new solutions. I briefly present each implication and discuss some examples of new solutions that follow from each implication. This discussion is meant to offer some sense of what policymakers could do without overburdening the discussion with too many details.

Updating Social Security

Labor and financial market risk exposure is widespread and has often grown, while jobs and wages have become less stable and financial markets have gone through greater booms and busts than in the past. This widespread risk exposure in an era of growing economic risks requires that Social Security offers a strong, universal risk protection.

This means updating Social Security benefits, especially for vulnerable populations such as lower income households, households with little education, and communities of color.

Social Security specifically offers households some protections from labor market risk exposure. Its benefits are progressive such that lower lifetime earners receive relatively higher benefits for each dollar they paid into the system than people with higher lifetime earnings.[2] Households that experienced more unemployment spells and slower wage growth during their careers will receive somewhat higher benefits relative to the payroll taxes they paid. Social Security benefits hence counteract rising labor market risks.

And Social Security benefits do not fluctuate with booms and busts in financial markets.[3]

Updating Social Security would further increase households' protections from labor and financial market risks. There are several ways in which Congress could update Social Security. The following discussion highlights a few key examples that have gotten attention from members of Congress in recent years.[4]

First, Congress could establish a special minimum benefit that would create a meaningful income floor in retirement. With this special minimum benefit, somebody who has paid for 30 years into Social Security would receive a benefit that was equal to at least 125 percent of the federal poverty line. The value of the special minimum benefit would grow each year with average wage growth, so that its risk protection does not erode over time. Workers with more than ten years—the minimum number of years necessary to receive Social Security benefits—but fewer than 30 years of paying into Social Security would receive a prorated minimum benefit.[5] This new special minimum benefit would especially help low-income households and communities of color, who have few or no tax-advantaged savings, and who hence disproportionately have to rely on Social Security.

Second, Congress could increase benefits for all beneficiaries who reach age 85 years. This would be especially impactful for those who are most at risk of running out of savings in retirement, such as low-income households. Specifically, Social Security could raise benefits by an amount equal to five percent of the average benefit.[6] Each beneficiary would receive the same dollar amount as permanent benefit increase. This increase would then offer a greater monthly benefit improvement for lower income beneficiaries than for higher income ones and is thus well targeted to those beneficiaries with the greatest need.

Consider, for example, the effect of this update when the average monthly benefit is $1,500. Every beneficiary who is 85 years old and receives her or his own retirement benefit, would receive an additional $75 per month or $900 per year (5 percent of the average monthly benefit) in this case. Since the increase is the same for all those who qualify, a beneficiary who had initially a monthly benefit of $1,000 would consequently receive a benefit increase of 7.5 percent and a beneficiary with an original benefit of $2,000 would receive a benefit increase of 3.75 percent at age 85.

Third, Congress could improve survivorship benefits. Under this proposed update, the surviving spouse of a beneficiary couple could receive as much as 75 percent of the combined benefits for both spouses, as long as certain conditions are met; for instance, the new benefit could not exceed the benefit of an average-wage earner.[7]

This benefit would be especially helpful to the surviving spouse of a low-income couple. The benefit improvement relative to current benefits is again best explained with an example. Assume a couple with two lower income earners, who both receive $15,000 in annual benefits from Social Security, for a combined benefit of $30,000. When one spouse dies, the other one receives only her own benefit of $15,000 but no additional survivorship benefit. The updated benefit would give her an annual benefit of $22,500 (the equivalent of 75 percent of $30,000) and thus an additional $7,500 per year.[8] This benefit improvement would not apply to high income earners, but only help those with benefits at or below the average benefit.

Congress can update Social Security in targeted ways that are especially beneficial to households that experience particularly large labor and financial market exposure.[9]

Create New Savings Opportunities Outside of the Employer–Employee Relationship

Federal and state lawmakers could make saving easier as one way to protect against rising risks. One important step would be to create more low-cost, low-risk, and easily accessible savings options outside of the employer–employee relationship. This means that Congress and state legislatures will want to identify additional partners—other than employers—that can get households to save more for their future. Governments—state and federal—could play this role.[10]

The idea of having state (and federal) governments sponsor savings options for private sector workers grows out of three realizations. First, households need help in saving with low-cost and low-risk options, since they otherwise incur too many costs, face too much risk exposure and end up saving too little for retirement. But second, the current policy emphasis on getting employers to offer such help to their employees in saving for retirement has shown substantial gaps, leaving many households with too few savings. And third, states have the resources and expertise to offer retirement savings options to private sector workers since they already offer retirement savings to public sector employees and often sponsor education savings to all households. Having states sponsor a retirement savings option may be a suitable option to offer households more low-cost, low-risk savings

The specific design of a state-sponsored retirement plan can vary depending on a few key choices that Congress and state legislatures need to make. I will only focus here on the design choices that lawmakers face[11] and on how particular choices relate to households' economic risk exposure:

Coverage

Congress and state legislatures could leave participation in a state-sponsored retirement plan voluntary, but simply set up a new low-cost, low-risk standardized savings option that employers and employees could participate in, if they wanted to.[12]

Alternatively, Congress and state legislatures could set requirements for employers and employees to participate in a newly created state-sponsored retirement savings plan if they do not already offer retirement benefits to their employees. Congress and state legislatures could, for instance, require that all employers enroll their employees through payroll deduction in a state-sponsored retirement savings plan, unless they offer a DB pension or 401(k) plan to their employees.

More requirements for employers and employees to participate will lead to more people saving more money than they otherwise would have. And more people saving more money will increase their financial risk protections outside of Social Security.

Savings Amounts

Congress and state legislatures could further leave the amount of savings up to employers and employees or they could require that employees have to make a minimum contribution to the state-sponsored retirement plan. Most proposals, including my own, envision a contribution rate of two to three percent of payroll.[13] And, many proposals would automatically enroll all employees in a state-sponsored plan with a minimum contribution rate, but allow people to opt out of making their contributions and consequently not participate in the state-sponsored plan.

More required contributions, even with an opt-out option, will increase household savings relative to the current voluntary opt-in approach for retirement savings outside of the employer–employee relationship. A number of people will not opt out, who otherwise would not have saved at all.

Investment Options

The primary challenge in investing money that households have saved is to strike a balance between households' legitimate desire to earn a rate of return on their savings and the risk exposure that households face and the associated fees for their investments.

Households could invest in existing vehicles, such as mutual funds held in Individual Retirement Accounts (IRAs), but also in novel investment tools such as pooled funds run by private entities or by states, for instance, through their public employee pension systems.[14]

Congress and state legislatures can strike the balance between rates of return, risk exposure and fees by limiting investment options in IRAs to low-cost, low-risk ones.[15] Alternatively, states can exercise more direct control over households' risk exposure and fees if they select some private financial institutions to offer only a range of low-risk, low-cost investment options. And, they could combine a lot of small savings amounts into one big investment pool and invest this pool in a prudent manner themselves. Pooling investments in a state-sponsored privately run or in a publicly run investment pool will likely reduce costs and financial risk exposure more than would be the case with just helping individuals select appropriate low-cost, low-risk options in an IRA.[16]

Payout Options

Households will eventually have to spend the money they save and helping them to convert their accumulated savings into low-cost, low-risk streams of retirement income can reduce their financial market risk exposure in old age because they can count on the money being there. People could rely on investment products such as life insurance companies' annuities to turn their savings into regular streams of income that ideally do not run out while they are alive. Some proposals similarly try to mimic the lifetime payout stream from a DB pension.[17] If such secure streams of lifetime income are part of a state-sponsored retirement plan, households' risk exposure in retirement will be reduced.

The exact choices that Congress and state legislatures will make on each of these points will depend on factors such as the political feasibility of particular proposals and the parameters set by federal regulations, not just on a state's policymakers' desire to increase the risk protections through additional savings for their private sector workers.

Better Targeting Savings Incentives to
Lower Income Households

Tax incentives to save help high-income earners more than they do lower income ones. Savings incentives could be more efficient if they better target lower and middle income households than is currently the case. More efficient savings incentives could raise savings, particularly among lower and middle income households that face more economic risk exposure than higher income ones.

Households could receive a refundable tax credit as a match to their savings rather than deducting their contributions to savings accounts from their taxable income. Every household qualifies for the same credit, regardless of how much money they owe in federal income taxes, as long as they save the minimum amount necessary to receive the full credit.

I detailed this idea in a proposal I called (together with my former colleague Sam Ungar) the Universal Savings Credit.[18] This Universal Savings Credit would be a flat matching percent of all annual savings up to a predetermined limit. Each household could, for instance, receive one dollar as a credit for each five dollars that they saved.

An example will help show the potential effect of switching from the existing system to the Universal Savings Credit. Currently, a household receives a tax benefit by deducting the contributions to a retirement savings account, for instance, from their taxable income. With this deduction, a taxpayer with a top marginal tax rate of 15 percent, who contributes $2,000 to a 401(k) account lowers the amount of income taxes he or she owes by $300—15 percent of $2,000. The total savings of $2,000 in one year then includes $1,700 of income that the taxpayer would have had even after paying federal income taxes and an implicit government contribution to his or her savings account equal to $300, "paid" for with foregone tax revenue. The government subsidizes each dollar contributed to a savings account with 17.6 cents—$300 relative to $1,700—in tax incentives.

To save $2,000 with a tax credit, in comparison, a household would need to contribute less money upfront. This will be particularly beneficial to lower and moderate income taxpayers who have less income to save. With a tax credit, the household contributes to a savings account and the government provides a proportional contribution to that savings account in the form of the tax credit at the end of the year, when the household files its taxes. The household in the above example, wanting to save a total of $2,000, would initially contribute $1,700, then claim $300 in tax credit—assuming that the credit rate is 17.6 percent—and add that credit to her savings accounts. A household with a top marginal tax rate of 15 percent would need to receive a matching credit equal to 17.6 cents of each dollar saved to be as well off with the Universal Savings Credit as as with the current pretax deductions of contributions.[19]

The Universal Savings Credit could be structured such that most taxpayers will be as well off or better off with a uniform, universal and refundable credit than they are with current tax deductions.[20] Most proposals to convert tax deductions into tax credits envision tax credits of about 15 percent to 20 percent across the board to all taxpayers, up to a predetermined maximum annual savings amount.[21] This is generally enough to make the overwhelming majority of households at least as well off as with the current tax deductions.

Households, especially lower and middle income ones, will likely see substantial improvements in their risk protections from a refundable credit such as the Universal Savings Credit as compared to the current system of tax deductions. They will get more help from the tax code for saving than they do with the current system, which disproportionately benefits higher income household and offers little help to those who need it the most. This should lead to more people saving and help many households save more money than they currently do.

Simplifying Savings

Current savings incentives apply for a number of different goals in a number of different savings options. This makes savings incentives complex, which impedes household savings and contributes to high financial risk exposure. Simplifying savings incentives through tax reform by Congress will lead more households to save, increase the amount that households save, and facilitate households finding better risk protections.

A universal, uniform and refundable credit such as the Universal Savings Credit could help overcome the current compartmentalization.[22] Households could use the Universal Savings Credit to save for anything that they wanted, education, homeownership, health care, emergencies and retirement. They could put the Universal Savings Credit into existing savings.

And, the Universal Savings Credit could lead to a proliferation of new savings vehicles. With improved savings incentives, household may start to shop around for savings vehicles that better meet their needs than existing savings plans. Banks and insurance companies, for example, could respond to this growing demand by offering a range of savings plans that currently do not exist, but that could offer better risk protections than current options.[23] And, state policymakers could encourage the creation of new low-cost and low-risk savings options along the lines I discussed earlier in this chapter. The Universal Savings Credit would apply to all of them, as long as they offer low-cost, low risk savings to households.

All savings vehicles to which households could apply their Universal Savings Credit would operate with a uniform maximum contribution amount and a uniform credit for contributions.[24] Contribution rules, for instance, will be the same for IRAs and for 401(k)s. This would simplify savings, raise savings and lower risk exposure by making it easier for households to protect their savings between different savings vehicles since the rules would all be the same.

Congress could also establish consistent rules for when households can withdraw money from their tax-advantaged savings. Households, for instance, could withdraw money from any tax-advantaged savings for reasons other than retirement, when they need the money. Allowable reasons for withdrawals from tax-advantaged savings could match the reasons for existing allowable withdrawals from retirement savings accounts, including retirement, down payment for a primary residence, an unemployment spell, medical bills, and educational expenses. Households could only withdraw the actual amount necessary before age 62. Starting at age 62, households could withdraw all of their money for retirement income. This makes savings a lot more flexible and thus would likely encourage households to save more since they no longer have to worry whether or not their savings are available, when they need them.[25] Streamlining savings incentives will also make it easier for households to manage their financial risk exposure since households no longer need to save in a wide variety of savings accounts for different purposes, but rather could put all of their money into one single savings vehicle.

Making Risk Protections Integral Parts of Household Savings

The proposals to improve savings so far would improve households' risk protections largely by increasing savings. They would also in some instances directly lower risk exposure, too. For example, simplifying savings would allow households to better manage their total risky asset allocation. Households still would have to manage their own financial risk exposure, but it would be easier to do so than is currently the case.

Congress, state legislatures, as well as federal and state regulators can do even more to help households better manage their financial risk exposure with individualized savings. These policymakers specifically could make risk protections an integral part of savings policy.

Requiring Risk Disclosure

Federal and state regulators of savings options such as mutual funds and insurance policies, for instance, could require consistent, comprehensive and comparable risk disclosure for all financial investments. Many social scientists and business researchers already use standard statistics to calculate the riskiness of investments. And, many people already rely on statistics in their everyday lives from reading the sports pages to making medical decisions. Disclosing risk in financial products, such as the mutual funds that a worker could invest in in their 401(k) plan, is hence an easily implementable and understandable step.[26]

Regulators could even require a simple graphical disclosure of financial risk exposure. Such a simple graphical disclosure could, for instance, be an arrow pointing to the riskiness of a particular investment on a scale between low and high risk.[27] Such an approach will visualize the risk exposure associated with a particular investment and make it easier for households to protect their savings.

Making Low-Risk Investment Options the Default

Another approach would turn the behavioral obstacles to households managing their risk exposure into opportunities to improve risk protections. One of the most common behavioral obstacles is inertia, for example, in the face of systematic complexity. Households simply fail to make active savings and investment choices to manage their financial risk exposure because they are overwhelmed by the information that they need to process to make a decision.

Investment options that automatically manage households' risk exposure would take advantage of this inertia. Households would not have to make any decisions to maintain and even to lower their financial risk exposure over time. Such products already exist with so-called model portfolios and life cycle funds. Model portfolios, for instance, maintain a constant ratio of stocks out of total financial assets, such as 50 percent in a mutual fund, regularly rebalancing the portfolio as stock prices change. And, life cycle funds gradually reduce the allocation of stocks and thus financial market risk exposure in a mutual fund as an investor gets older.

Congress and state legislatures as well as regulators can encourage households to invest in safe and guaranteed investments by making these and other low-cost, low-risk investment options the default in tax-advantaged savings accounts. Default options apply, when households fail to make investment decisions. Their money will automatically be allocated to these default options.

The US Department of Labor has already issued guidance on the use of some default investments for 401(k) plans that offer positive rates of return and minimize risk.[28] This approach can be applied to other tax-advantaged financial savings vehicles and thus make it easier for households to manage their financial risk exposure.

Encouraging Risk-Minimizing Payout Options

In a similar vein, regulators could encourage the use of secure payout options in retirement accounts that minimize household risk exposure. Such payout options could include managed withdrawals as well as annuities—life insurance products that offer a lifetime stream of income. Greater use of such payout options will reduce retirees' risk exposure. Federal regulators, for instance, at the Department of Labor could develop regulations to encourage greater use of safe payout options in existing retirement accounts.[29]

Incentivizing Homeowners' Savings Outside of Housing

The discussion so far has left out the risk exposure in housing. Households are exposed to risks with their housing because they often have few savings outside of their house, such that, if anything goes wrong with their jobs, their mortgage or their house, they have nothing to fall back on and could end up losing their house. And, they borrow large mortgages to pay for their house, which can quickly lead to a detrimental spiral that could end up with them losing their house, if they lose a job, their wages fall or interest rates rise and they fall behind on making their mortgage payments.[30] Lower and middle income households, communities of color, and households with less education are more likely than their counterparts to have few savings outside of their house and to owe relatively large mortgages in comparison to the value of their house.[31] Saving more outside of one's house will create a buffer in the event something bad happens and protects the savings in a house for people's retirement. Households could continue paying their bills, including their mortgages, if they lost their job, for instance, so that they would not lose their house, too.

There are two possible approaches to get households to save more outside of their house. A first approach could start with converting the current mortgage interest deduction to a refundable credit akin to the conversion of tax deductions for savings accounts into the Universal Savings Credit. A household would receive a credit proportional to the amount of interest they paid on their mortgage, which could be put in a nonhousing designated savings account.[32] Similar to the proposed Universal Savings Credit and to the existing mortgage interest deduction, there would be an upper maximum of interest payments that could qualify for this credit. And as with the proposed Universal Savings Credit, the credit rate could be made progressive, so that it is higher for lower income earners. Importantly, policymakers could offer a higher credit rate to those borrowers with a mortgage, who put a specific share of the credit into a designated savings account.

An example may again help to show how such a new homeowner's credit would work. Let us assume that the conversion of the current mortgage interest deduction to a flat credit leads to a uniform credit rate of 20 percent of the amount of interest paid on a mortgage, if they do not save additional money.[33] A borrower who pays $1,000 in interest each month, would receive $200 per month or $2,400 for a year. Households could then qualify, for example, for a 25 percent credit rate if they put a minimum share, for instance 40 percent, of this credit into a designated savings account. A household who pays $1,000 per month in interest on a mortgage, could receive a credit worth $250 per month or $3,000 per year, if they put at least $100 per month or $1,200 for the year into a savings account. In this example, half of these savings ($600) outside of the house would come from the higher tax credit and the other $600 would come from the household. The household would save both in housing and outside of housing in this scenario.

A few steps could be taken to make saving outside of housing using this credit as easy as possible. First, borrowers could be responsible for saving part of their credit, but not have to figure out the minimum amount of savings needed to qualify for the higher credit rate. Mortgage companies could be required to disclose to borrowers how much they would need to save each year to qualify for the extra tax credit when they borrow a new mortgage or refinance an existing one. Also, if the savings amount were reported back to a household at tax time from their banks then they would not have to keep track of how much money they saved in a given year. Finally, households could use their savings that qualify for the additional tax credit at any time after a minimal waiting period of, for example, six to twelve months, for whatever purposes they want. This flexibility in using their savings will likely lead many households to save the extra money. And, given that households' financial decisions tend to be heavily influenced by inertia, it is reasonable to believe that many of the additional savings will actually remain in a savings account for some time, even without a waiting period.[34]

A redesigned tax incentive for homeowners could be used for savings outside of housing and improve households' risk exposure.

Congress could use an alternative approach to getting households to save outside of housing, if they implemented the Universal Savings Credit or some refundable credit like it. Policymakers could instruct the Internal Revenue Service to allow households to automatically deposit their tax refunds into tax-advantaged savings. Such an approach would increase savings outside of housing for all households because such savings would be both easy and tax-advantaged and because all households could qualify for the same maximum tax credit.

While there are several different ways to go about it, making risk protections integral to individual savings could reduce households financial risk exposure. Current savings policy fails to do this.

Conclusion

Households want to and need to save for their future, but they have been increasingly unable to do so. A number of poorly designed policies have stood in their way. Rather than having access to sturdy life rafts when their boat sinks in the increasingly turbulent seas of labor and financial market risks, many households have been left to sink or swim.

Policymakers—federal and state lawmakers and regulators—can heed the major lessons of the past three decades on what has not worked, why households ended up with high risk exposure, and how that risk exposure has translated into low savings and inadequate retirement income and build stable and secure financial life rafts for all—not just the lucky few.

This will require a large rethinking of public policy directed at households' savings. I have outlined a number of concrete policy steps in this chapter that would create real economic security for most households by helping them save more and by better protecting those savings. Without such a systematic rethinking in how the United States helps households save and build economic security for their future, households will feel the aftershocks of today's economic insecurity for decades to come and will feel like they are treading water well into their old age.

NOTES

1 The Elusive Goal of a Secure Retirement

1. All quotes taken from *Retirement Security 2015: Roadmap for Policy Makers: Americans' Views of the Retirement Crisis*, a biennial public opinion research conducted by the National Institute on Retirement Security and Greenwald & Associates, March 2015.
2. Katherine Porter, "The Damage of Debt," *Washington and Lee Law Review* 69, no. 2 (2012); Claire M. Renzetti, "Economic Stress and Domestic Violence" (Harrisburg, PA: VAWnet, a project of the National Resource Center on Domestic Violence, September, 2009).
3. Christian E. Weller, "Raising the Retirement Age for Social Security: Implications for Low Wage, Minority, and Female Workers" (Washington, DC: Center for American Progress, 2005); Monique Morrissey, "Beyond 'Normal' Raising the Retirement Age Is the Wrong Approach for Social Security," EPI Briefing Paper no. 287 (Washington, DC: Economic Policy Institute, 2011); Maria Heidkamp, William Mabe, and Barbara DeGraaf, "The Public Workforce System: Serving Older Job Seekers and the Disability Implications of an Aging Workforce" (New Brunswick, NJ: NTAR Leadership Center, John J. Heldrich Center for Workforce Development, 2012).
4. There is one corporate governance argument that links rising labor and financial market risks with increasing risk exposure. Addressing the causes of macroeconomic fluctuations in addition to discussing policies to improve household risk protections is beyond the scope of this book. See William Lazonick, "Labor in the Twenty-First Century: The Top 0.1% and the Disappearing Middle Class," in Christian E. Weller, ed., *Inequality, Uncertainty and Opportunity: The Varied and Growing Role of Finance in Labor Relations* (Ithaca, NY: Cornell University Press, 2015).
5. See Christian E. Weller and David Madland, "Keep Calm and Muddle Through" (Washington, DC: Center for American Progress, 2014) for a more detailed discussion of the consequences of inadequate retirement savings.
6. For a summary of John Maynard Keynes's discussion of savings motives, see Martin Browning and Annamaria Lusardi, "Household Saving: Micro Theories and Macro Facts," *Journal of Economic Literature* 34, no. 4 (1996): 1797–1855.
7. See Camilo Mondragon-Velez, "How Does Middle-Class Financial Health Affect Entrepreneurship in America?" (Washington, DC: Center for American Progress, May 2015), for some of the relevant literature and for data on the importance of household savings for the growth of entrepreneurship among older households.
8. This is merely an illustrative example. The specific savings needs will differ by household characteristics. For details and a discussion of some of the relevant factors determining required savings, see Fidelity Brokerage Services, "'How Much Do You Need to Retire?' Fidelity Viewpoints" (Smithfield, RI: Fidelity Brokerage Services, January 30, 2014),

accessed May 4, 2015, https://www.fidelity.com/viewpoints/retirement/8X-retirement-savings

9. Fidelity Brokerage Services, "How Much Do You Need to Retire?"

10. Combining these four savings forms—Social Security, DB pensions, financial assets, and nonfinancial assets—often feels strange because the way these savings are reported is not directly comparable. Benefits from Social Security and DB pensions are generally expressed as expected future payments, while savings in financial and nonfinancial assets is expressed as lump sums. A typical DB pension benefit will be something like 1.5 percent times the number of years of service times an employee's final pay. Someone who retires with a salary of $50,000 after 20 years working for a company with a DB pension in this example will receive $15,000 each year or $1,250 each month for the rest of her life. In comparison, the value of a 401(k), IRA, or house is reported as one single lump sum, not as a stream of future payments. Researchers often convert expected Social Security and DB pension benefits into a lump sum. To express future expected benefit payments as a lump sum, one first needs to estimate the monthly benefit one can expect to receive from Social Security or a DB pension. Assuming a retirement age of 67 years and maximum life expectancy, researchers can then calculate how much income a beneficiary will receive from this particular source over the course of a life time. Using a calculation called discounting, researchers can figure the amount a household would need to set aside today (or at any point in time) to generate, together with expected future incomes, this stream of future income payments. Researchers can then express all forms of savings in a similar way, making them comparable with each other. See Christian E. Weller and Edward Wolff, *Retirement Security: The Particular Role of Social Security* (Washington, DC: Economic Policy Institute, 2005), for a description of one methodology to convert expected Social Security and DB pension benefits into lump sums.

11. Social Security Administration, "Retirement Benefits," SSA Publication No. 05–10035 (Washington, DC: Social Security Administration, January 2015), 6, http://www.ssa.gov/pubs/EN-05-10035.pdf; *Social Security Amendments of 1983*, H.R. 1900/P.L. 98–21, 98th Congress (1983).

12. Jennifer M. Ortman, Victoria A. Velkoff, and Howard Hogan, "An Aging Nation: The Older Population in the United States. Population Estimates and Projections, Current Population Reports" (Washington, DC: US Census Bureau, 2014), accessed on May 7, 2014, http://www.census.gov/prod/2014pubs/p25-1140.pdf

13. Joseph E. Stiglitz, *The Price of Inequality: How Today's Divided Society Endangers Our Future* (New York, NY: W. W. Norton & Company, Inc., 2013), liv–lv, 45–46, 137.

14. Pension Protection Act of 2006, H.R. 4/P.L. 109–280, 109th Congress (2006).

15. "Regulation Relating to Qualified Default Investment Alternatives in Participant-Directed Account Plans," US Department of Labor, Employee Benefits Security Administration, Fact Sheet (Washington, DC: EBSA, April 2008), accessed October 20, 2014, http://www.dol.gov/ebsa/pdf/fsQDIA.pdf; "Field Assistance Bulletin No. 2008–03" (Washington, DC: EBSA, April 2008), accessed October 20, 2014, http://www.dol.gov/ebsa/pdf/fab2008-3.pdf

16. This is not a question of the size of the welfare, to be clear, but rather a question of the balance between Social Security and private savings. The United States spends similar amounts on offering households basic protections for health, retirement, disability, and unemployment as other advanced economies do. But, a larger share of these expenditures comes in the form of foregone tax revenue to help households get health insurance and retirement savings in the private market, and a smaller share comes in the form of direct government spending. That is, all countries strike a balance between public and private savings, while the balance is tilted more toward private savings than public savings mechanisms in the United States. See Organisation for Economic Cooperation and Development

(OECD), "Social Expenditure Update—Social Spending Is Falling in Some Countries, but in Many Others It Remains at Historically High Levels" (Paris, France: OECD, November 2014), 8.

17. My discussion here only focuses on policy support for households to save not on the policy rationale to support employer interests. Retirement benefits, historically DB pensions, also exist because private and public employers want to recruit and retain the most skilled workers. Public pensions in the United States, for example, date back to 1775 when the Continental Congress offered military pensions to officers in the Revolutionary War as a retention incentive. For an in-depth discussion of the historical development of public pensions in the United States up to the creation of Social Security, see Robert L. Clark, Lee A. Craig, and John Sabelhaus, *State and Local Retirement Plans in the United States* (Northampton, MA: Edward Elgar Publishing, 2011).

18. For the modest levels of benefits paid to beneficiaries, see, for instance, Social Security Administration (SSA), "Benefit Types and Levels, Annual Statistical Supplement, 2014," Tables 2.A20–2.A28 (Washington, DC: SSA, 2014); and for the shares of household incomes of people 65 years and older that come from sources other than Social Security, see SSA, "Income of the Population 55 or Older, 2012," SSA Publication No. 13–11871 (Washington, DC: SSA, 2014).

19. OECD, "Social Expenditure Update."

20. A wide variety of political theories exist that aim to explain the differences in the size of the welfare state as well as the differences of the forms of public policy interventions. For one example, see Nicholas Barr, *The Economics of the Welfare State* (Oxford, UK: Oxford University Press, 2012), Chapters 3 and 4. See also Gøsta Esping-Anderson, *The Three Worlds of Welfare Capitalism* (Princeton, NJ: Princeton University Press, 1990), for a discussion of the foundations of welfare states.

2 Americans' Growing Risk Exposure

1. All quotes taken from *Retirement Security 2015: Roadmap for Policy Makers: Americans' Views of the Retirement Crisis*, a biennial public opinion research conducted by the National Institute on Retirement Security and Greenwald & Associates, March 2015.

2. Dean Baker, J. Bradford De Long, and Paul R. Krugman, "Asset Returns and Economic Growth," *Brookings Papers on Economic Activity* 2005, no. 1 (2005), 289–330, doi: 10.1353/eca.2005.0011; John Y. Campbell and Robert J. Shiller, "Valuation Ratios and the Long-Run Stock Market Outlook," *The Journal of Portfolio Management* 24, no. 2 (1998), 11–26, doi: 10.3905/jpm.24.2.11; Sewin Chan, "Spatial Lock-in: Do Falling House Prices Constrain Residential Mobility?" *Journal of Urban Economics* 49, no. 3 (2001), 567–586, doi:10.1006/juec.2000.2205; Martijn I. Dröes and Wolter H. J. Hassink, "Sale Price Risk of Homeowners" (Utretch, the Netherlands: Utrecht School of Economics, 2009); Peter Englund, Ming Hwang, and John M. Quigley, "Hedging Housing Risk," *Journal of Real Estate Finance and Economics* 24, no. 1/2 (2002), 167–200; Richard Meyer and Kenneth Wieand, "Risk and Return to Housing, Tenure Choice and the Value of Housing in an Asset Pricing Context," *Real Estate Economics* 24, no. 1 (1996), 113–131, doi: 10.1111/1540–6229.00683.

3. Campbell and Shiller, "Valuation Ratios and the Long-Run Stock Market Outlook"; George Akerlof and Robert J. Schiller, *Animal Spirits: How Human Psychology Drives the Economy and Why It Matters for Global Capitalism* (Princeton, NY: Princeton University Press, 2010); Baker et al., "Asset Returns and Economic Growth."

4. Englund et al., "Hedging Housing Risk," 167–200; Meyer and Wieand, "Risk and Return to Housing, Tenure Choice and the Value of Housing in an Asset Pricing Context."

5. David G. Blanchflower and Andrew J. Oswald, "Does High Home-Ownership Impair the Labor Market?" NBER Working Paper No. 19079 (Cambridge, MA: Natural Bureau of Economic Research, 2013), doi: 10.3386/w19079.

6. Benjamin H. Harris, "Tax Reform, Transaction Costs, and Metropolitan Housing in the United States," State and Local Finance Initiative (Washington, DC: Tax Policy Center, Urban Institute and Brookings Institution, 2013).

7. For a discussion of the relevant literature, see Christian Weller and Kate Sabatini, "From Boom to Bust: Did the Financial Fragility of Homeowners Increase in an Era of Greater Financial Deregulation?" *Journal of Economic Issues* 42, no. 3 (2008), 607–632.

8. See, for instance, Jacob S. Hacker, *The Great Risk Shift: The New Economic Insecurity and the Decline of the American Dream* (New York, NY: Oxford University Press, 2008).

9. Jesse Rothstein, "Unemployment Insurance and Job Search in the Great Recession," NBER Working Paper No. 17534 (Cambridge, MA: National Bureau of Economic Research, 2011).

10. Jacob S. Hacker, *The Great Risk Shift*; Karen Dynan, Douglas Elmendorf, and Daniel Sichel, "The Evolution of Household Income Volatility," Working Paper (Washington, DC: Brookings Institution, 2012).

11. Neoclassical economic theory suggests that, based on expansions of the so-called life cycle hypothesis, the existence of labor market uncertainties should translate into households building up precautionary savings that they can rely on when earnings unexpectedly fall. That is, savings should move with earnings to some degree. But, the link between earnings and savings is not necessarily straightforward. Households theoretically should borrow more money if they experience unexpected earnings declines. But, many households may face credit constraints that prevent them from borrowing when they lose their job or see their wages fall. Households may cut their spending and maintain some or all of their saving when they face labor market risks. For reviews of the life cycle, see Martin Browning and Annamaria Lusardi, "Household Saving: Micro Theories and Micro Facts," *Journal of Economic Literature* 34, no. 4 (December 1996), 1797–1855; Martin Browning and Thomas F. Crossley, "The Life-Cycle Model of Consumption and Saving," *Journal of Economic Perspectives* 15, no. 3 (2001), 3–22, doi: 10.1257/jep.15.3.3. More recent theoretical development further suggests that behavioral obstacles may prevent households from optimally saving, possibly exacerbating savings fluctuations when earnings decline. For a review of the relevant literature on psychology and economics, see Stefano DellaVigna, "Psychology and Economics: Evidence from the Field," *Journal of Economic Literature* 47, no. 2 (2009), 315–372, doi: 10.1257/jel.47.2.315.

12. Susan Dynarski, Jonathan Gruber, Robert A. Moffitt, and Gary Burtless, "Can Families Smooth Variable Earnings?" *Brookings Papers on Economic Activity* 1997, no. 1 (1997), 229–303.

13. Both stocks and housing constitute risky assets. This does not mean that renters automatically have less financial market risk exposure than homeowners. Homeowners should have fewer stocks relative to their assets than renters to compensate for their higher housing market risk exposure (João F. Cocco, "Portfolio Choice in the Presence of Housing," *The Review of Financial Studies* 18, no. 2 [2005], 535–567, doi: 10.1093/rfs/hhi006). A selective risk exposure measure that considers only stocks should undercount the risk exposure of homeowners, for instance, and a selective measure that looks only at housing risk ignores, by definition, the risk exposure of renters.

14. Obviously, greater risk exposure also creates more upside potential, which should have led to rising wealth over time. But, that has not been the case, suggesting that the downside risks have outweighed the upside potential for households in large part because policy failed to help households build meaningful risk protections.

15. Harry M. Markowitz, *Portfolio Selection: Efficient Diversification of Investments* 16 (New Haven, CT: Yale University Press, 1970).

16. John Y. Campbell and Robert J. Shiller, "Valuation Ratios and the Long-Run Stock Market Outlook: An Update," NBER Working Paper No. 8221 (Cambridge, MA: Natural Bureau of Economic Research, 2001), doi: 10.3386/w8221; Baker et al., "Asset Returns and Economic Growth."

17. Lower bond rates also imply higher bond prices and thus an inverse relationship between stock and bond prices. Stocks behave in long-term cycles, which is not the case for bonds, so that there is little longer term correlation between stocks and bonds. Campbell and Shiller, "Valuation Ratios and the Long-Run Stock Market Outlook: An Update."

18. Karl E. Case and John M. Quigley, "How Housing Booms Unwind: Income Effects, Wealth Effects, and Feedbacks through Financial Markets," *European Journal of Housing Policy* 8, no. 2 (2008): 161–180; Karl E. Case, John M. Quigley, and Robert J. Shiller, "Home-buyers, Housing and the Macroeconomy," RBA Annual Conference Volume no. acv2003–09, in *Asset Prices and Monetary Policy*, ed. Anthony Richards and Tim Robinson (Sydney, Australia: Reserve Bank of Australia, 2003), 149–188.

19. Shlomo Bernartzi and Richard Thaler, "Heuristics and Biases in Retirement Savings Behavior," *Journal of Economic Perspectives* 21, no. 3 (Summer 2007), 81–104; John Y. Campbell, "Household Finance," *The Journal of Finance* 61, no. 4 (2006), 1553–1604; B. Douglas Bernheim and Antonio Rangel, "Behavioral Public Economics: Welfare and Policy Analysis with Non-Standard Decision Makers," NBER Working Paper No. w11518 (Cambridge, MA: Natural Bureau of Economic Research, 2005).

20. Olivia S. Mitchell, Gary R. Mottola, Stephen P. Utkus, and Takeshi Yamaguchi, "The Inattentive Participant: Portfolio Trading Behavior in 401(k) Plans," Working Paper No. wp115 (Ann Arbor, MI: University of Michigan, Michigan Retirement Research Center, 2006).

21. For summary discussions of the wealth effect, see Congressional Budget Office, "Housing Wealth and Consumer Spending" (Washington, DC: CBO, 2007); James M. Poterba, "Stock Market Wealth and Consumption," *The Journal of Economic Perspectives* 14, no. 2 (2000), 99–118.

22. The logic is the reverse for a stock market bust. Households will need to sell bonds and buy stocks as stock prices are falling and investment opportunities proliferate.

23. For additional details on trends and group differences in financial market risk exposure, see Christian Weller, "Making Sure Money Is Available When We Need It" (Washington, DC: Center for American Progress, March 2013); and Christian Weller and Sara Bernardo, "Aging with Risk: Has Financial Risk Exposure Grown Faster for Older Households since the 1990s?" (forthcoming).

24. For a discussion of alternative explanations, see Weller, "Making Sure Money Is Available When We Need It," and Weller and Bernardo, "Aging with Risk."

25. Alberto Manconi, Massimo Massa, and Ayako Yasuda, "The Role of Institutional Investors in Propagating the Crisis of 2007–2008," *Journal of Financial Economics* 104, no. 3 (June 2012), 491–518.

26. Eugene F. Fama and Kenneth R. French, "Permanent and Temporary Components of Stock Prices," *Journal of Political Economy* 96, no. 2 (1988), 246–273; James M. Poterba and Lawrence H. Summers, "Mean Reversion in Stock Prices: Evidence and Implications," *Journal of Financial Economics* 22, no. 1 (1988), 27–59, doi:10.1016/0304–405X(88)90021–9; Baker et al., "Asset Returns and Economic Growth."

27. Olivia S. Mitchell, Gary R. Mottola, Stephen P. Utkus, and Takeshi Yamaguchi, "The Inattentive Participant: Portfolio Trading Behavior in 401(k) Plans," Working Paper 2006–115 (Ann Arbor, MI: University of Michigan Retirement Research Center, 2006).

28. Weller and Bernardo, "Aging with Risk."

29. Guy Debelle, "Macroeconomic Implications of Rising Household Debt," BIS Working Paper No. 153 (Basel, Switzerland: Bank for International Settlements, 2004), 1–41.

30. Karl E. Case and John M. Quigley, "How Housing Booms Unwind: Income Effects, Wealth Effects, and Feedbacks through Financial Markets," *European Journal of Housing Policy* 8, no. 2 (2008), 161–180; Case et al., "Home-buyers, Housing and the Macroeconomy"; Weller and Bernardo, "Aging with Risk."

31. Rothstein, "Unemployment Insurance and Job Search in the Great Recession"; Bureau of Labor Statistics, US Department of Labor, "Duration of Unemployment, 1994–2010," *The Economics Daily*, updated June 2, 2011, http://www.bls.gov/opub/ted/2011/ted_20110602.htm; Mary C. Daly, Bart Hobijn, Ayşegül Şahin, and Robert G. Valletta, "A Search and Matching Approach to Labor Markets: Did the Natural Rate of Unemployment Rise?" *The Journal of Economic Perspectives* 26, no. 2 (Summer 2012), 3–26.

32. The calculations do not differ much when I separate earnings into thirds rather than fifths.

33. Jacob S. Hacker, *The Great Risk Shift*; Karen Dynan, Douglas Elmendorf, and Daniel Sichel, "The Evolution of Household Income Volatility"; Elise Gould, "2014 Continues a 35-Year Trend of Broad-Based Wage Stagnation," EPI Issue Brief No. 393 (Washington, DC: Economic Policy Institute, 2015); Craig Copeland, "Employment-Based Retirement Plan Participation: Geographic Differences and Trends, 2013," EBRI Issue Brief No. 405 (Washington, DC: Employee Benefits Research Institute, 2014); Melissa Majerol, Vann Newkirk, and Rachel Garfield, "The Uninsured: A Primer—Key Facts about Health Insurance and the Uninsured in America" (Washington, DC: Kaiser Family Foundation, January 2015); Carmen DeNavas-Walt and Bernadette D. Proctor, "Income and Poverty in the United States: 2013," *Current Population Reports* (Washington, DC: US Census Bureau, September 2014).

34. Diane Oakley and Kelly Kenneally, "Retirement Security 2015: Roadmap for Policy Makers" (Washington, DC: National Institute on Retirement Security, March 2015).

3   More Risk, Greater Wealth Inequality

1. All quotes taken from *Retirement Security 2015: Roadmap for Policy Makers: Americans' Views of the Retirement Crisis*, a biennial public opinion research conducted by the National Institute on Retirement Security and Greenwald & Associates, March 2015.

2. I present average wealth instead of median wealth to allow for a meaningful comparison between high-income and low-income families. The median wealth for households in the bottom fifth tends to be very low and highly volatile, creating large and volatile ratios in comparison with the wealth of households in the top fifth. The median wealth gap for households in the top fifth and the middle fifth of income distribution has also grown from a little over 3.1 in 1989 to more than 4.1 in 2013. The slower widening of the wealth gap at the median than in the average suggests that wealth inequality, especially within the top fifth of the income distribution, has also sharply increased. For more details on increasing wealth inequality, see Edward Wolff, "Recent Trends in Household Wealth in the United States: Rising Debt and the Middle-Class Squeeze—an Update to 2007," Working Paper Series No. 159 (Washington, DC: Levy Economics Institute, 2010).

3. I use the *SCF* for my calculations. The *SCF* allows for more detailed analyses of household wealth than is the case for many other data sources, in large part since the *SCF* is the only governmental data set specifically designed to generate a nationally representative survey of household wealth. But, the *SCF* is a cross-sectional data source, which makes it impossible to compare wealth for the same households over time. I hence compare the average wealth for the same group of households, defined by time-invariant characteristics such as birth date, race and ethnicity, and education.

4. See chapter 2 for a detailed discussion of the potentially adverse consequences of wealth volatility.

5. This is the broadest possible definition of emergency savings. Using narrower definitions such as liquid nonretirement financial assets does not change the conclusions of my discussion in this chapter. I use a broader definition since money is somewhat fungible and since a broader definition generates sufficiently large sample sizes to make meaningful comparisons between household groups.

6. For a summary of the basic portfolio theoretical arguments and some evidence, see Luigi Guiso, Tullio Jappelli, and Daniele Terlizzese, "Income Risk, Borrowing Constraints, and Portfolio Choice," *The American Economic Review* 86, no. 1 (1996), 158–172; Jason S. Seligman and Jeffrey B. Wenger, "Asynchronous Risk: Retirement Savings, Equity Markets, and Unemployment," *Journal of Pension Economics and Finance* 5, no. 3 (2006), 237–255, doi: 10.1017/S1474747206002630; Giuseppe Grande and Luigi Ventura, "Labor Income and Risky Assets under Market Incompleteness: Evidence from Italian Data," *Journal of Banking and Finance* 26, no. 2 (2002), 597–620, doi:10.1016/S0378-4266(01)00236-9; Miles S. Kimball, "Standard Risk Aversion," *Econometrica: Journal of the Econometric Society* 61, no. 3 (1993): 589–611. Also models of precautionary savings suggest that higher levels of labor market income uncertainty lead to increased savings (Jim Malley and Thomas Moutos, "Unemployment and Consumption," *Oxford Economic Papers* 48, no. 4 [1996], 584–600; Martha Starr-McCluer, "Health Insurance and Precautionary Savings," *The American Economic Review* 86, no. 1 [1996], 285–295). Models consider income uncertainty generated from both unemployment risk (Eric M. Engen and Jonathan Gruber, "Unemployment Insurance and Precautionary Saving," *Journal of Monetary Economics* 47, no. 3 [2001], 545–579) and earnings volatility (Christopher D. Carroll, Karen E. Dynan, and Spencer D. Krane, "Unemployment Risk and Precautionary Wealth: Evidence from Households' Balance Sheets," *Review of Economics and Statistics* 85, no. 3 [2003], 586–604, doi:10.1162/003465303322369740) and find that households build up a buffer of savings to minimize consumption disruptions during unemployment.

7. See Shlomo Bernartzi and Richard Thaler, "Heuristics and Biases in Retirement Savings Behavior," *Journal of Economic Perspectives* 21, no. 3 (Summer 2007), 81–104 on the heuristics households use to make financial decisions in complex retirement savings.

8. I combine data for all years since the conclusions below are not influenced by any particular year and since there are no discernible trends in the gaps between high and low labor market risk over time.

9. I calculate unemployment rates and relative standard errors—standard error divided by the average—for groups of households. Groups of households for the unemployment risk calculations are circumscribed by time-invariant characteristics, specifically birth date, survey year, race, and education. I add earnings quintiles to these calculations for the earnings risk to control for the level of hourly earnings. To keep the number of observations in each group large enough for robust calculations, I use a white/nonwhite and Hispanic separation for race and ethnicity and at least a college degree/no college degree separation for education.

10. This conclusion does not change when I consider a correlation over time using a synthetic cohort analysis. That is, there is no clear consistent relationship over time from higher labor market risk exposure in the present to lower financial market risk exposure in the future.

11. I define very high financial market risk exposure as having a risky asset concentration greater than 75 percent and a debt to asset ratio of 25 percent. This indicator allows me to combine the two distinct financial market risk measures in a meaningful way.

12. Richard T. Campbell and Cathie Mayes Hudson, "Synthetic Cohorts from Panel Surveys: An Approach to Studying Rare Events," *Research on Aging* 7, no. 1 (March 1985), 81–93.

13. For a review of the relevant literature, see Stefano DellaVigna, "Psychology and Economics: Evidence from the Field," *Journal of Economic Literature* 47, no. 2 (2009), 315–372, doi:

10.1257/jel.47.2.315. For the implications for household savings of systematic behavioral errors, see Bernartzi and Thaler, "Heuristics and Biases in Retirement Savings Behavior."

14. Remember that the underlying argument is that lower liquidity constraints theoretically should have made it easier for households to reallocate their risky and illiquid housing assets. Instead, households increasingly borrowed to finance consumption. Atif R. Mian and Amir Sufi, "House Prices, Home Equity-Based Borrowing, and the U.S. Household Leverage Crisis," *American Economic Review* 101, no. 5 (2011), 2132–2156; David B. Gross and Nicholas S. Souleles, "Do Liquidity Constraints and Interest Rates Matter for Consumer Behavior? Evidence from Credit Card Data," *The Quarterly Journal of Economics* 117, no. 1 (2002), 149–185, doi: 10.1162/003355302753399472.

15. Christian Weller and Derek Douglas, "One Nation Under Debt," *Challenge* 50, no. 1 (February 2007), 54–74; Christian Weller, "Need or Want: What Explains the Run-up in Consumer Debt?" *Journal of Economic Issues* 41, no. 2 (June 2007), 583–591.

16. Households could have theoretically experienced high labor market risk a maximum of eight times since the data are collected every three years, although no group of households had more than five such cumulative episodes of high labor market risk exposure.

4   The Looming Retirement Shipwreck

1. All quotes taken from *Retirement Security 2015: Roadmap for Policy Makers: Americans' Views of the Retirement Crisis*, a biennial public opinion research conducted by the National Institute on Retirement Security and Greenwald & Associates, March 2015.

2. There is no one-size-fits-all transition for American workers into retirement. Rather, people transition in many different ways, depending on their abilities, desires, and socio-economic backgrounds. See Fengyan Tang and Jeffrey A. Burr, "Revisiting the Pathways to Retirement: A Latent Structure Model of the Dynamics of Late-Life Labor Force Behavior," *Ageing and Society* (forthcoming), doi 10.1017/S0144686X14000634.

3. See Ruth Helman, Nevin Adams, and Jack VanDerhei, "The 2014 Retirement Confidence Survey: Confidence Rebounds—for Those with Retirement Plans," EBRI Issue Brief No. 397 (Washington, DC: Employee Benefits Research Institute, 2014), http://www.ebri.org/pdf/briefspdf/EBRI_IB_397_Mar14.RCS.pdf; Mathew Greenwald & Associates, Inc., "2013 Risks and Process of Retirement Survey Report of Findings" (Society of Actuaries, 2013), https://www.soa.org/retirementneedsandrisks; and for data on retirement expectations, see the summary of 2006 survey findings in "The Ariel/Schwab Black Investor Survey: Saving and Investing among Higher Income African-American and White Americans" (Chicago, IL: Ariel Investments, 2008).

4. Christian Weller and David Madland, "Keep Calm and Muddle Through" (Washington, DC: Center for American Progress, 2014).

5. For a recent example, see Charles Ellis, Alicia Munnell, and Andrew Eschtruth, *Falling Short: The Coming Retirement Crisis and What to Do about It* (New York, NY: Oxford University Press, 2014).

6. I explain factors that lead researchers to come to differing conclusions on the level of retirement income adequacy in the appendix to this chapter.

7. The relevant literature comprising both approaches includes John Ameriks and Stephen P. Utkus, "Vanguard Retirement Outlook 2006" (Malvern, PA: Vanguard Center for Retirement Research, 2006); Barbara Butrica, Daniel Murphy, and Sheila Zedlewski, "How Many Struggle to Get by in Retirement?" *The Gerontologist* 50, no. 4 (2010), 482–494, doi: 10.1093/geront/gnp158; Center for Retirement Research at Boston College, "Retirements at Risk: A New National Retirement Risk Index" (Boston:

Center for Retirement Research at Boston College, 2006); Robert Haveman, Karen Holden, Barbara Wolfe, and Andrei Romanov, "Assessing the Maintenance of Savings Sufficiency over the First Decade of Retirement," Working Paper No. 1567 (Munich, Germany: CESIfo, 2005); David Love, Paul Smith, and Lucy McNair, "A New Look at the Wealth Adequacy of Older U.S. Households," *Review of Income and Wealth* 54, no. 4 (2008), 616–642; Annamaria Lusardi and Olivia S. Mitchell, "Financial Literacy and Planning: Implications for Retirement Wellbeing" (Hanover, NH: Dartmouth College, 2006), http://www.dartmouth.edu/-alusardi/Papers/FinancialLiteracy.pdf; John Karl Scholz, Ananth Seshadri, and Surachai Khitatakrun, "Are Americans Saving 'Optimally' for Retirement?" *Journal of Political Economy* 114, no. 4 (2006), 607–643; Mark Warshawsky and John Ameriks, "How Prepared Are Americans for Retirement?" in Olivia S. Mitchell, P. Brett Hammond, and Anna M. Rappaport, eds., *Forecasting Retirement Needs and Retirement Wealth* (Philadelphia, PA: University of Pennsylvania Press, 2000), 33–67; Christian Weller and Edward Wolff, *Retirement Security: The Particular Role of Social Security* (Washington, DC: Economic Policy Institute, 2005).

For a discussion of what it means for households, government, and the economy when a large share of households fall short of meeting their needs in retirement, see Weller and Madland, "Keep Calm and Muddle Through."

8. See, for instance, Butrica et al., "How Many Struggle to Get by in Retirement?"; Center for Retirement Research at Boston College, "Retirements at Risk;" Haveman et al., "Assessing the Maintenance of Savings Sufficiency over the First Decade of Retirement"; Love et al., "A New Look at the Wealth Adequacy of Older U.S. Households"; Weller and Wolff, *Retirement Security: The Particular Role of Social Security.*

9. While commonly used, it is disputed as to how effective the poverty line is as a proxy for the minimum income needed to avoid material hardship in retirement. For an alternative measure of the income needed to meet basic needs in retirement, see Laura H. Russell, Ellen A. Bruce, and Judith Conahan, "A Methodology to Determine Economic Security for Elders" (Boston, MA: Gerontology Institute, University of Massachusetts Boston, and Washington, DC: Wider Opportunities for Women, 2006).

10. Wolff, "Household Wealth Inequality, Retirement Income Security, and Financial Market Swings 1983 to 2010."

11. This approach is anchored in a neoclassical economic theory known as life cycle hypothesis, whereby people smooth their consumption over their life cycle. That implies that they maintain their preretirement consumption in retirement and that their total lifetime consumption relates to their total lifetime income. Recent applications of the life cycle hypothesis to the question of retirement income adequacy include Eric M. Engen, William G. Gale, and Cori E. Uccello, "The Adequacy of Household Saving," *Brookings Papers on Economic Activity* 1999, no. 2 (1999), 65–165, and John Karl Scholz, Ananth Seshadri, and Surachai Khitatakrun, "Are Americans Saving 'Optimally' for Retirement?" *Journal of Political Economy* 114, no. 4 (2006), 607–643.

12. See, for instance, Ameriks and Utkus, "Vanguard Retirement Outlook 2006"; B. Douglas Bernheim, "The Adequacy of Personal Retirement Saving" in David A. Wise, ed., *Facing the Age Wave* (Stanford, CA: Hoover Institute Press, 1997); Ellis et al., *Falling Short*; Alan L. Gustman and Thomas L. Steinmeier, "Effects of Pensions on Savings: Analysis with Data from the Health and Retirement Study," *Carnegie-Rochester Conference Series on Public Policy* 50, no. 1 (1999), 271–324; Peter Henle, "Recent Trends in Retirement Benefits Related to Earnings," *Monthly Labor Review* 95, no. 6 (1972), 12–20; Engen et al., "The Adequacy of Household Saving"; Lusardi and Mitchell, "Financial Literacy and Planning"; James F. Moore and Olivia S. Mitchell, "Projected Retirement Wealth and Saving Adequacy" in Olivia S. Mitchell, P. Brett Hammond, and Anna M. Rappaport, eds., *Forecasting Retirement Needs and Retirement Wealth* (Philadelphia, PA: University of Pennsylvania Press,

2000); Alicia H. Munnell, Francesca Golub-Sass, and Anthony Webb, "What Moves the National Retirement Risk Index? A Look Back and an Update," Issue Brief No. 7–1 (Boston, MA: Center for Retirement Research at Boston College, 2007); RETIRE Project, "2001 RETIRE Project Report" (Atlanta, GA: Georgia State University, 2001); Nari Rhee, "The Retirement Savings Crisis: Is It Worse than We Think?" (Washington, DC: National Institute on Retirement Security, 2013); Warshawsky and Ameriks, "How Prepared Are Americans for Retirement?"; Jack VanDerhei, "Retirement Savings Shortfalls: Evidence from EBRI's Retirement Security Projection Model," EBRI Issue Brief No. 410 (Washington, DC: Employee Benefits Research Institute, 2015); Weller and Wolff, *Retirement Security: The Particular Role of Social Security*." The replacement— retirement income to preretirement income—is less than 100 percent since the income needs of retirees are likely to be lower than those of workers since they no longer need to save for retirement, pay fewer taxes, have no work-related expenses, have smaller families, and do not have a mortgage.

13. For a discussion of a sample of the most influential studies in this debate, see also Keith Miller, David Madland, and Christian Weller, "The Reality of the Retirement Crisis," CAP Issue Brief (Washington, DC: Center for American Progress, 2015).

14. For a summary of the basic theoretical literature on consumption and saving, see Martin Browning and Annamaria Lusardi, "Household Saving: Micro Theories and Macro Facts," *Journal of Economic Literature* 34, no. 4 (1996), 1797–1855.

15. Using wealth to estimate households' future retirement income and thus their retirement income security also has a methodological advantage over using some income statistics to measure how much income retirees have. Income statistics for older households often rely on the Bureau of Labor Statistics' Current Population Survey (CPS)—for instance, the Social Security Administration's Income of the Population 55 and Older. The CPS is nationally representative and has a long track record, so that researchers can compare trends over time. It suffers from some necessary methodological shortcomings, which tend to understate retirement income. The CPS does not count withdrawals from IRAs and 401(k) as income, but it counts regular benefits from DB pensions as income. So, as households increasingly pay for their retirement with withdrawals from their individual accounts and have fewer DB pension benefits than in the past, the CPS tends to miss a growing share of many retirees' income. Wealth measures used in retirement income adequacy studies, however, capture all forms of future income from Social Security, DB pensions, and private savings in housing, DC accounts, and other individual forms of savings. For a discussion of the importance of IRA withdrawals, see Billie Jean Miller and Sylvester J. Schieber, "Employer Plans, IRAs and Retirement Income Provision: Making a Molehill out of a Mountain," *TowersWatson Insider* (New York, NY: Towers Watson, 2013).

16. See our detailed discussion in the appendix on calculating future retirement income.

17. The appendix discusses in great detail my reasons for selecting this particular measure over others in the literature. I should note, though, that all measures find substantial shares of households with insufficient savings and a trend toward worsening retirement income insecurity, where such trend data exist.

18. See Weller and Madland, "Keep Calm and Muddle Through."

19. Rhee, "The Retirement Savings Crisis: Is It Worse than We Think?"

20. Alicia H. Munnell, Anthony Webb, and Francesca Golub-Sass, "The National Retirement Risk Index: An Update," Issue Brief No. 12–20 (Boston, MA: Center for Retirement Research at Boston College, 2012).

21. John Karl Scholz, Ananth Seshadri, and Surachai Khitatakrun, "Are Americans Saving 'Optimally' for Retirement?" *Journal of Political Economy* 114, no. 4 (2006), 607–643.

22. William G. Gale, John Karl Scholz, and Ananth Seshadri, "Are All Americans Saving 'Optimally' for Retirement?" Working Paper (Washington, DC: The Brookings Institution, and Madison, WI: University of Wisconsin-Madison, 2009).

23. Munnell et al., "The National Retirement Risk Index: An Update"; Rhee, "The Retirement Savings Crisis: Is It Worse than We Think?"; Gale et al., "Are All Americans Saving 'Optimally' for Retirement?"; Scholz et al., "Are Americans Saving 'Optimally' for Retirement?"; Barbara A. Butrica, Karen E. Smith, and Howard M. Iams, "This Is Not Your Parents' Retirement: Comparing Retirement Income across Generations," *Social Security Bulletin* 72, no. 1 (2012); VanDerhei, "Retirement Savings Shortfalls." The research by EBRI, another widely cited and somewhat optimistic assessment, specifically finds that the share of GenXers—defined as households between the ages of 40 and 49 in 2014—was comparable to those of Late Boomers—defined as households between the ages of 50 and 59 in 2014, but that the savings shortfalls tend to be larger for younger cohorts, in large part because of higher future health-care costs. See also Jack Vanderhei, "What Causes EBRI Retirement Readiness Ratings™ to Vary: Results from the 2014 Retirement Security Projection Model," EBRI Issue Brief No. 396 (Washington, DC: Employee Benefits Research Institute, 2014).

24. Professor Wolff's research relies on the same data as the CRR, but there are some key methodological differences as we discuss in the appendix.

25. This share is comparable to the 53 percent of households shown as being at risk of not being able to maintain their standard of living in retirement in the NRRI. And both the NRRI and Professor Wolff's research rely on the *SCF*.

26. All data in this paragraph taken from Wolff, "Household Wealth Inequality, Retirement Income Security, and Financial Market Swings 1983 to 2010."

27. See Christian Weller, "How Well Were Retirees Prepared for Retirement before the Great Recession?" *Journal of Aging & Social Policy* 22, no. 2 (2010), 95–98, doi: 10.1080/08959421003621986 for one example of risk-adjusted retirement income calculations for retirees.

28. See, for example, Gale et al., "Are All Americans Saving 'Optimally' for Retirement?" and Scholz et al., "Are Americans Saving 'Optimally' for Retirement?"

29. There is a discussion among researchers on whether to use replacement rates or whether to develop microsimulation models that model future consumption instead of future income. Modeling future consumption has a few practical and policy-relevant disadvantages over modeling future retirement income. First, researchers know too little about consumption in retirement to robustly model households' consumption needs. Second, consumption data are often of lower quality than wealth and income data. And third, researchers forecasting future consumption make strong assumptions about households' ability to access public benefits such as food stamps and housing subsidies. My discussion here focuses on the more established approach of forecasting income rather than consumption. For a good example of the theory behind forecasting future consumption and a thorough application, see Gale et al., "Are All Americans Saving 'Optimally' for Retirement?". And for a critique of forecasting future consumption, see Alicia H. Munnell, Wenliang Hou, and Anthony Webb, "NRRI Update Shows Half Still Falling Short," Issue Brief No. 14–20 (Boston, MA: Center for Retirement Research at Boston College, 2014).

30. The replacement—retirement income to preretirement income—is less than 100 percent since the income needs of retirees are likely to be lower than those of workers. See Miller et al., "The Reality of the Retirement Crisis," for a sample of high, medium, and low replacement rates used in recent studies.

31. Rhee, "The Retirement Savings Crisis: Is It Worse than We Think?"

32. Center for Retirement Research at Boston College, "Retirements at Risk."

33. Butrica et al., "This Is Not Your Parents' Retirement."

34. VanDerhei, "Retirement Savings Shortfalls." Scholz, Gale, and Seshadri similarly calculate individual retirement needs separately for each household, based on their expected expenditures in retirement. Gale et al., "Are All Americans Saving 'Optimally' for Retirement?"

35. For a study that assumes substantial and systematic consumption cuts, see Scholz et al., "Are Americans Saving 'Optimally' for Retirement?" Also Jonathan Skinner, "Are You Sure You're Saving Enough for Retirement?" *The Journal of Economic Perspectives* 21, no. 3 (2007), 59–80, provides a discussion of the factors that determine differences in retirement income adequacy findings, including consumption cuts.

36. For a few additional details, see Miller et al., "The Reality of the Retirement Crisis," and for a summary of the existing evidence on spending behavior in retirement, see Alicia H. Munnell, Matthew S. Rutledge, and Anthony Webb, "Are Retirees Falling Short? Reconciling the Conflicting Evidence," CRR Working Paper 2014–16 (Boston, MA: Center for Retirement Research at Boston College, 2014). See also Ellis et al., *Falling Short*.

37. See, for instance, Center for Retirement Research at Boston College, "Retirements at Risk" and Weller and Wolff, *Retirement Security: The Particular Role of Social Security* for two examples of calculating age–earnings profiles that underlie the calculations of projected future Social Security benefits.

38. Only the *SCF* regularly asks households for the relevant details, while other household surveys such as the University of Michigan's Health and Retirement Survey only ask whether a household is covered under a DB pension. These are household surveys where workers and not employers describe DB pension benefit calculations. This description can be fraught with some error since households may fail to disclose critical details of this calculation or simply do not understand how their DB pension benefits will be calculated in the future. But researchers have shown that people do not make systematic mistakes when describing their pension benefits, that is, for every household that overestimates their DB pension, another one underestimates their future DB pension. Average and median retirement income calculations of future DB pension benefits for the entire population or even subpopulations should consequently not suffer from a bias toward understatement or overstatement of future retirement income. Researchers then typically take the information provided in surveys or from employers on people's DB pensions to calculate expected future pension benefits based on each household's estimated preretirement earnings. See, for instance, Gustman and Steinmeier, "Effects of Pensions on Savings." And for a discussion of the errors associated with self-reported DB pension benefits, see Richard Johnson, Usha Sambamoorthi, and Stephen Crystal, "Pension Wealth at Midlife: Comparing Self-reports with Provider Data," *Review of Income and Wealth* 46, no. 1 (2000), 59–83, doi: 10.1111/j.1475–4991.2000.tb00391.x. Moreover, Scholz et al., "Are Americans Saving 'Optimally" for Retirement?," use a different approach to calculating DB pensions, by extrapolating the probability of having a DB pension and the level of future DB pensions for each household based on current DB pension recipients.

There is some difference in the way CRR and Edward Wolff calculate DB pension benefits. CRR, for instance, uses some approximation of future DB pension benefit coverage and benefit levels even for a small share of households that do not yet have DB pension coverage. Professor Wolff, on the other hand, only calculates the value of future DB pensions only for households that already have a DB pension. This difference stems from the fact that CRR considers younger households as well as older households, so that things can change during their careers and people can still gain a DB pension during their careers, while Edward Wolff includes only older households where career-related changes in benefits are much less likely than among younger households. That is, the methodological difference will have no real effect on retirement income adequacy calculations for the respective populations that are being studied since the same share of households should enter retirement with a DB pension in each calculation.

39. See, for instance, Center for Retirement Research at Boston College, "Retirements at Risk"; Alan Gustman and Thomas Steinmeier, "Effects of Pensions on Savings: Analysis

with Data from the Health and Retirement Study," *Carnegie-Rochester Conference Series on Public Policy* 50, no. 99 (1999), 271–324.

40. Scholz et al., "Are Americans Saving 'Optimally' for Retirement?"
41. See, for instance, Wolff, "Household Wealth Inequality, Retirement Income Security, and Financial Market Swings 1983 to 2010."
42. See, for example, Vanderhei, "What Causes EBRI Retirement Readiness Ratings™ to Vary: Results from the 2014 Retirement Security Projection Model," for a discussion of the effect of excluding future savings in retirement income calculations.
43. See, for example, Center for Retirement Research at Boston College, "Retirements at Risk," for details of their projection of account balances.
44. Ibid.
45. Ibid.
46. See, for example, Wolff, "Household Wealth Inequality, Retirement Income Security, and Financial Market Swings 1983 to 2010."
47. For a discussion of the costs of longevity risk, see Beth Almeida and William B. Fornia, "A Better Bang for the Buck: The Economic Efficiencies of Defined Benefit Pension Plans" (Washington, DC: National Institute on Retirement Security, 2008).
48. Center for Retirement Research at Boston College, "Retirements at Risk"; Wolff, "Household Wealth Inequality, Retirement Income Security, and Financial Market Swings 1983 to 2010."
49. The Center for Retirement Research, for instance, slightly broadens preretirement income beyond just wage and salary earnings to include an assumed rate of return on capital, as long as people have any capital, whereas Edward Wolff, as another example, uses estimated family income near the time of retirement, which excludes capital income in 401(k) plans and IRAs. See Center for Retirement Research at Boston College, "Retirements at Risk," and Wolff, "Household Wealth Inequality, Retirement Income Security, and Financial Market Swings 1983 to 2010."
50. Scholz et al., "Are Americans Saving 'Optimally' for Retirement?"
51. Wage-adjusting preretirement income also means that incomes in different years are truly comparable to each other. The Social Security Administration typically uses wage-adjusted or wage-indexed preretirement income in its replacement rate calculation. For an explanation and some robustness tests—the results do not change much with slightly different indexation methods—see Stephen C. Goss, "Strengthening Social Security to Meet the Needs of Tomorrow's Retirees," testimony before the Subcommittee on Social Security, Pensions, and Family Policy of the Senate Committee on Finance, May 21, 2014.
52. See, for instance, Center for Retirement Research at Boston College, "Retirements at Risk," and Wolff, "Household Wealth Inequality, Retirement Income Security, and Financial Market Swings 1983 to 2010."

5   Social Security: The Leaky *Lifeboat*

1. All quotes taken from *Retirement Security 2015: Roadmap for Policy Makers: Americans' Views of the Retirement Crisis*," a biennial public opinion research conducted by the National Institute on Retirement Security and Greenwald & Associates, March 2015.
2. Social Security Administration, "Program Explainers: Special Minimum Benefit" (Washington, DC: SSA, May 2014).
3. Social Security Administration, "Retirement Benefits," SSA Publication No. 05–10035 (Washington, DC: SSA, January 2015), 6, http://www.ssa.gov/pubs/EN-05-10035.pdf; Social Security Amendments of 1983, H.R. 1900/P.L. 98–21, 98th Congress (1983).

4. Barry Bosworth and Kathleen Burke find that the number of years that women can expect to receive Social Security benefits has in fact fallen in the bottom 40 percent of the earnings distribution from the 1920 to the 1940 birth cohorts. See "Differential Mortality and Retirement Benefits in The Health And Retirement Study" (Washington, DC: Brookings Institution, 2013). And Hilary Waldron concludes that life expectancy for workers born in 1941 in the top half of the earnings distribution increased only by 5.8 more years than for those in the bottom half of the earnings distribution in "Trends in Mortality Differentials and Life Expectancy for Male Social Security–Covered Workers, by Socioeconomic Status," *Social Security Bulletin* 67, no. 3 (2007), 1–28.

5. But the chapter does not address other possible Social Security policy changes that may be necessitated by demographic changes. A number of states, for instance, permit same-sex marriages, but married same-sex partners cannot always receive the same Social Security benefits as heterosexual spouses. It is beyond the scope of this book to address this issue and others that could be addressed in a major Social Security reform. The chapter will hence focus only on the link between Social Security and rising risk exposure.

6. Alicia Munnell and Mauricio Soto, "State and Local Pensions Are Different from Private Plans," State and Local Pension Plans No. 1 (Boston, MA: Center for Retirement Research at Boston College, November 2007). For more details on the basics of public sector benefits, see US Government Accountability Office, "State and Local Government Retiree Benefits: Current Status of Benefit Structures, Protections, and Fiscal Outlook for Funding Future Costs," GAO-07–1156 (Washington, DC: GAO, 2007).

7. Social Security Administration, "Annual Statistical Supplement 2013" (Washington, DC: SSA, 2013). Workers have to work fewer years to qualify for survivorship and disability benefits than to qualify for retirement benefits. Workers who qualify for retirement benefits hence also qualify for survivorship and disability benefits.

8. Social Security Administration, "Monthly Statistical Snapshot—August 2014" (Washington, DC: SSA, 2014).

9. The discussion of spousal benefits also applies to same-sex married couples as long as the couple resides in a state that recognizes same-sex marriage when they receive benefits.

10. Social Security calculates the AIME for a disabled beneficiary or a deceased beneficiary, which is first used as a means to convert lifetime payments into the PIA amount for the beneficiary and the survivors. The main difference is that workers need to have paid into Social Security for shorter periods to qualify for disability and survivorship benefits than is necessary for retirement benefits. The only difference for the AIME calculation in the case of disability or survivorship benefits, compared to retirement benefits, is that the worker's earnings are not averaged over 35 years, as is the case with retirement benefits, but only over the actual number of years up to disability or death. These averaging periods mean that no years with zero earnings are entered into the calculation and the AIME and PIA are consequently much higher than they would have been. The beneficiary receives the PIA if she is disabled, while other beneficiaries receive an additional fraction of the PIA if they are eligible. Spouses, for instance, receive 50 percent of the beneficiary's PIA and each minor child receives 25 percent of the PIA. Survivors receive similar shares of the PIA for as long as they are eligible for benefits.

11. Social Security Administration, "Survivors Benefits," SSA Publication no. 05–10084 (Washington, DC: SSA, July 2013).

12. Social Security Administration, "Early or Late Retirement," *Social Security Online*, accessed September 16, 2014, http://www.socialsecurity.gov/OACT/quickcalc/early_late.html Social Security's specific calculation follows a formula that shows the permanent reduction in retirement benefits for any month that a worker retires before the full-benefit retirement age. Specifically, Social Security reduces the PIA by five-ninth of one percent for each month before the full-benefit retirement age, up to 36 months. The benefit is

further reduced five-twelfth of one percent per month if the number of months exceeds 36, which was not possible when the full-benefit age was 65 years and the earliest retirement age was 65. The benefit is reduced by 30 percent, for instance, if a worker retires at age 62 and the full-benefit age is equal to 67 years. This maximum reduction comes about as 36 months times five-ninth of one percent plus 24 months times five-twelfth of one percent. Similarly, retiring at age 62 when the full-benefit age was 65 reduces benefits by 20 percent, which is just the product of 36 months times five-ninth of one percent.

13. Some employees such as many state and local government employees in 14 states are not covered by Social Security.

14. The self-employed pay both employee and employer share of the payroll tax.

15. Social Security Administration, "Benefit Planner: Maximum Table Earnings, 1937 to 2015," *Social Security Online,* accessed May 18, 2015, http://www.socialsecurity.gov/planners/maxtax.html

16. It is important to note that the shortfall in payroll tax revenue in the years after the Great Recession ended in 2009 through 2012 was in part a result of temporary cuts to the payroll tax, intended to stimulate economic growth. Source for historical trust funds data is Social Security Administration, "The 2014 Annual Report of the Board of Trustees of the Federal Old-Age and Survivors Insurance and Federal Disability Insurance Trust Funds," House Document 113–139, 113th Congress, Second Session (2014).

17. Ibid.

18. Ibid.

19. Ibid.

20. Ibid.

21. Ibid.

22. Social Security Administration, "The 2013 Annual Report of the Board of Trustees, Supplemental Single Years Tables," accessed October 6, 2014, http://www.ssa.gov/oact/tr/2013/lrIndex.html. The exact replacement rate—the ratio of annual Social Security benefits to average lifetime earnings—depends on somebody's age and can vary somewhat. Average earnings are expected to be $46,832 in 2014 and low earnings are equal to 41 percent of average earnings, or $21,074 in Social Security's hypothetical examples.

23. John Schmitt, "Low-Wage Lessons" (Washington, DC: Center for Economic and Policy Research, January, 2012).

24. Social Security Administration, "Annual Statistical Supplement to the Social Security Bulletin, 2013, Tables 4-B1 and 4-B4," SSA 13–11700 (Washington, DC: SSA, February 2014).

25. Rebecca Vallas, Christian Weller, Rachel West, and Jackie Odum, "The Effect of Rising Inequality on Social Security," CAP Issue Brief (Washington, DC: Center for American Progress, February 2015), https://www.americanprogress.org/issues/economy/report/2015/02/10/106373/the-effect-of-rising-inequality-on-social-security/

26. Social Security Administration, "Program Explainers: Special Minimum Benefit" (Washington, DC: SSA May 2014).

27. Craig Feinstein, "Diminishing Effect of the Special Minimum PIA," Actuarial Note No. 154 (Baltimore, MD: Social Security Administration, November 2013).

28. Privatization would also worsen Social Security's financial shortfall. The federal government would incur additional debt under privatization because Social Security would no longer receive all of the funds it currently uses to pay for benefits. The Social Security Administration would have to borrow money immediately or within several years (depending on the privatization plan) from private financial markets or from the US Treasury to cover this additional shortfall. All of the privatization proposals in 2005 would have increased the federal government's debt, although the size of the additional debt created by such proposals varied. Under President Bush's proposal, for instance, the government

would have incurred $17.7 trillion in additional new debt by 2050 in 2005 dollars The proposal introduced by then Sen. John Sununu (R-NH) and Rep. Paul Ryan (R-WI) at the time would have been even worse, increasing the government's debt by $85.8 trillion in 2005 dollars in 2050, because they wanted to divert larger amounts into private accounts in addition to minimum benefit guarantees. Rep. Ryan introduced another version of his privatization proposal in 2010 as part of his "Roadmap for America's Future Act of 2007." This privatization proposal adds to Social Security's long-term deficits but covers those deficits with transfers from general revenue totaling more than $1 trillion. Then there was the proposal made by Sen. Jim DeMint (R-SC), which would have only allowed for the diversion of funds into private accounts as long as Social Security had a cash surplus. This would have increased the federal debt by $3.5 trillion in 2005 dollars in 2050, based on the expectation at the time that the Social Security fund would slip from black to red in 2017. See Jason Furman, "How Would the President's New Social Security Proposal Affect Middle-Class Workers and Social Security Solvency" (Washington, DC: Center for Budget and Policy Priorities, 2005); James Horney and Richard Kogan, "Private Accounts Would Substantially Increase Federal Debt and Interest Payments" (Washington, DC: Center for Budget and Policy Priorities, 2005). All of the estimates are based on calculations made by the Social Security actuaries; and Social Security Administration, "Estimated Financial Effects of Title IV of The Roadmap for America's Future Act of 2010" (Washington, DC: SSA, 2010). See legislation introduced as Title IV of H.R. 4529 (111th Congress) on January 27, 2010, by Rep. Paul Ryan (R-WI) for details on these estimates.

29. Gary Burtless, "Social Security Privatization and Financial Market Risk" (Washington, DC: Center on Social and Economic Dynamics, February 2000), quoted in Christian Weller, *Review of Policy Research* 23, no. 2 (2006), 531–548, doi: 10.1111/j.1541–1338.2006.00214.x

30. This discussion uses a few high-quality and well-respected public opinion polls to illustrate the main arguments, although other polls not cited here support these arguments. Several polls cited in this discussion have been repeated over time with little variation in the findings, unless otherwise stated. The stability of poll findings also suggests that relying on polls from different years should not materially impact the conclusions.

31. Employee Benefit Research Institute (EBRI), "Retirement Confidence Survey" (Washington, DC: EBRI, various years), accessed April 30, 2014, http://www.ebri.org/surveys/rcs/

32. Ibid.

33. Gallup, "Social Security" (Washington, DC: Gallup, Inc., 2014), accessed September 22, 2014, http://www.gallup.com/poll/1693/social-security.aspx. Poll conducted each year since 2001 in the first half of April.

34. Ibid.

35. Ibid.

36. *The Washington Post*, "Results," Washington Post-ABC News Poll (February 23, 2009).

37. Polls find substantial support for leaving survivorship benefits unchanged or for improving them, but there is little evidence on support or opposition to changing survivorship benefits in a specific way.

38. National Academy of Social Insurance (NASI), "Americans Make Hard Choices: A Survey with Trade-off Analysis" (Washington, DC: NASI, 2014), http://www.nasi.org/sites/default/files/research/Americans_Make_Hard_Choices_on_Social_Security.pdf

39. Democracy Corps and Campaign for America's Future and Greenberg Quinlan Rosner, "Polling Results" (Democracy Corps and Campaign for America's Future and Greenberg Quinlan Rosner, 2008).

40. NASI, "Americans Make Hard Choices."

41. Gallup, "Social Security."

42. *Washington Post*, Henry J. Kaiser Family Foundation, and Harvard University, "Social Security Knowledge Poll I" (February 9, 2005).
43. *New York Times* and CBS News, "The New York Times—CBS News Poll" (June 17–19, 2005).
44. American Associations of Retired Persons (AARP), "Retirement Security Survey Report" (Washington, DC: AARP, 2007).
45. Polling Report, Inc., "Social Security," *PollingReport.com* (2014), accessed September 22, 2014, http://www.pollingreport.com/social.htm
46. Jasmine Tucker, Virginia Reno, and Thomas Bethell, "Strengthening Social Security: What Do Americans Want?" (Washington, DC: National Academy of Social Insurance, January, 2013). Greenwald and Associates conducted this poll. It is one of the few polls that specifically asks about the minimum benefit.
47. Gallup, "Social Security."
48. AARP, "Retirement Security Survey Report."
49. *Washington Post*, Henry J. Kaiser Family Foundation, and Harvard University, "Social Security Knowledge Poll I."
50. *New York Times* and CBS News, "The New York Times—CBS News Poll."
51. Tucker et al., "Strengthening Social Security: What Do Americans Want?"
52. Gallup, "Social Security."

6   Sink-or-Swim Retirement Plans

1. All quotes taken from *Retirement Security 2015: Roadmap for Policy Makers: Americans' Views of the Retirement Crisis*, a biennial public opinion research conducted by the National Institute on Retirement Security and Greenwald & Associates, March 2015.
2. Other assets such as bonds and certificates of deposits (CDs) are not completely risk-free. Bond prices can vary before a bond matures and CDs can become worthless if a bank fails. Economists do not consider these assets risky assets since these risks are small compared to the risks associated with investments in stocks and housing. And households have comparatively easy ways to protect themselves from these risks. They can hold bonds to maturity and they can invest money with banks where deposits are backed by federal deposit insurance. Such relatively easy risk protections do not exist with stocks and housing.
3. Christian Weller and Sara Bernardo, "Putting Retirement at Risk: Has Financial Risk Exposure Grown More Quickly for Older Households than Younger Ones?" Paper 102 (Boston, MA: Gerontology Institute, 2014), http://scholarworks.umb.edu/gerontologyinstitute_pubs/102/. Economists consider housing equity a risky asset, akin in many ways to stocks. While owner-occupied housing is technically a nonfinancial asset, economists "treat houses like a standard financial asset"—quoted from Todd Sinai and Nicholas S. Souleles. "Owner-Occupied Housing as a Hedge against Rent Risk," *The Quarterly Journal of Economics* 120, no. 2 (May 2005), 763–789.
4. For a summary of the related literature, see Martin Browning and Annamaria Lusardi, "Household Saving: Micro Theories and Micro Facts," *Journal of Economic Literature* 34, no. 4 (December 1996), 1797–1855.
5. For a review of the relevant literature, see Stefano DellaVigna, "Psychology and Economics: Evidence from the Field," *Journal of Economic Literature* 47, no. 2 (June 2009), 315–372; Shlomo Benartzi and Richard H. Thaler, "Heuristics and Biases in Retirement Savings Behavior," *Journal of Economic Perspectives* 21, no. 3 (2007), 81–104.
6. See, for instance, Christian Weller, "Did Retirees Save Enough to Compensate for the Increase in Individual Risk Exposure?" *Journal of Aging and Social Policy* 22, no. 2 (2010), 152–171.

7. See also Jacob S. Hacker, *The Great Risk Shift: The New Economic Insecurity and the Decline of the American Dream* (New York, NY: Oxford University Press, 2008).

8. See Browning and Lusardi, "Household Saving: Micro Theories and Micro Facts" for a discussion of the evidence on the savings decline in the 1980s.

9. Social Security Administration, "Retirement Benefits," SSA Publication No. 05–10035 (Washington, DC: SSA, January, 2015), 6, http://www.ssa.gov/pubs/EN-05-10035.pdf; Social Security Amendments of 1983, H.R. 1900/P.L. 98–21, 98th Congress (1983).

10. For a discussion of the evidence on the timing and size for a decrease of the personal saving rate in the 1980s, see Browning and Lusardi, "Household Saving: Micro Theories and Micro Facts."

11. There is a less direct connection to changes in labor policy, too. Union members are more likely to have DB pensions than nonunion members as unions negotiate for benefits as well as wages. Some forms of DB pension plans—so-called Taft-Hartley multiemployer DB pension plans—generally can only exist within the context of a collective bargaining agreement. The decline in DB pension coverage has also followed the decline of unionization rates. Labor law changes especially interpretations of existing law through the National Labor Relations Board have made it more difficult for workers to join unions.

12. Other policy changes, particularly new accounting standards, started to introduce similar changes prior to 2006. For a detailed discussion on policies that introduced volatility to DB pension plan funding, see Ilana Boivie, "Who Killed the Private Sector DB Plan?" Issue Brief (Washington, DC: National Institute on Retirement Security, March 2011).

13. Pension funding depends on the employers' assumptions of future interest rates they can earn on their DB pension plans. These interest rates are regulated by PPA. Interest rates tend to fall and thus pension contributions tend to rise during recessions, when companies can least afford the added costs. For a discussion of the link between macroeconomic cycles and interest rates, see Christian Weller and Dean Baker, "Smoothing the Waves of Pension Funding: Could Changes in Funding Rules Help Avoid Cyclical Under-funding?" *The Journal of Policy Reform* 8, no. 2 (June 2005), 131–151.

14. Sarah Holden, Peter Brady, and Michael Hadley, "401(k) Plans: A 25-Year Retrospective," *Investment Company Institute Research Perspective* 12, no. 2 (November 2006), http://www.ici.org/pdf/per12-02.pdf.

15. Ibid.

16. A summary of the many ways by which Fannie Mae and Freddie Mac can offer lower cost mortgages can be found in James H. Carr and Karen Annacker, "The Past and Current Politics of Housing Finance and the Future of Fannie Mae, Freddie Mac, and Homeownership in the United States," *Banking and Financial Services Report* 33, no. 7 (2012), 1–10, https://www.scribd.com/doc/235461123/The-Past-and-Future-of-Fannie-Mae-and-Freddie-Mac-and-Future-of-Homeownerhip.

17. A cursory history of financial innovation from Fannie Mae and Freddie Mac is included in Kelsie Brandlee, "Promoting Homeownership in the United States: The Rise and Fall of Fannie Mae and Freddie Mac" (Iowa City, IA: Center for International Finance and Development, University of Iowa, April 2011), http://www.freerepublic.com/focus/f-news/2915644/posts.

18. See, for example, Robert M. Dunsky and James R. Follain, "Tax-Induced Portfolio Reshuffling: The Case of the Mortgage Interest Deduction," *Real Estate Economics* 28, no. 4 (2000), 683–718; Victor Stango, "The Tax Reform Act of 1986 and the Composition of Consumer Debt," *National Tax Journal* 52, no. 4 (December 1999), 717–739.

19. All private sector DB pension plans are required to give beneficiaries the option of receiving an annuity. Over time, so-called cash balance DB pension plans have become increasingly popular in the private sector. Cash balance DB pension plans tend to offer beneficiaries a choice between taking a lump-sum payment and receiving an annuity. For

details on cash balance DB pension plans, see Christian Weller, "Ensuring Retirement Income Security with Cash Balance Plans" (Washington, DC: Center for American Progress, September 2005).

20. John Y. Campbell and Robert J. Shiller, "Valuation Ratios and the Long-Run Stock Market Outlook," *The Journal of Portfolio Management* 24, no. 2 (Winter 1998), 11–26; John Y. Campbell and Louis M. Viceira, "Long-Horizon Mean-Variance Analysis: A User Guide" (manuscript, Cambridge, MA: Harvard University, 2004).

21. Any form of annuitization will reduce longevity risk. A small longevity risk still remains even with self-annuitization and annuitization through a life insurance company. The employer that sponsors a DB pension plan may go out of business as may the life insurance company, and those business failures could lead to cuts in monthly benefit payments from the DB pension plan or the life insurance company.

22. Jules Lichtenstein and John Turner, "Cash Balance Pension Plans and Older Workers" (Washington, DC: AARP Public Policy Institute, October 2005), http://assets.aarp.org/rgcenter/econ/ib78_pension.pdf; Weller, "Ensuring Retirement Income Security with Cash Balance Plans."

23. Christian Weller and Sam Ungar, "Overhauling Federal Savings Incentives," *Tax Notes Today: Special Report* 42, no. 10 (March 2014). See for a discussion of the evidence on the link between savings plan design complexity and suboptimal savings.

24. Olivia S. Mitchell, Gary R. Mottola, Stephen P. Utkus, and Takeshi Yamaguchi, "The Inattentive Participant: Portfolio Trading Behavior in 401 (k) Plans" (Ann Arbor, MI: Michigan Retirement Research Center, 2006); Christian Weller, "Making Sure the Money Is There When We Need It" (Washington, DC: Center for American Progress, March 2013). For microeconomic evidence on households' failure to reallocate their assets during stock and housing price swings, see Weller and Bernardo, "Putting Retirement at Risk."

25. Hewitt Associates, "Research Highlights: Trends and Experience in 401(k) Plans" (Chicago, IL: Hewitt Associates, Llc, 2009), http://www.aon.com/attachments/thought-leadership/Hewitt_Research_Trends_in_401k_Highlights.pdf

26. US Department of Labor (DOL), Employee Benefits Security Administration (EBSA), "Regulation Relating to Qualified Default Investment Alternatives in Participant-Directed Account Plans" (Washington, DC: DOL, EBSA, April 2008), http://www.dol.gov/ebsa/pdf/fsQDIA.pdf; DOL, EBSA, "Field Assistance Bulletin No. 2008–03" (Washington, DC: DOL, EBSA, April 2008), http://www.dol.gov/ebsa/pdf/fab2008-3.pdf. Due to legal changes enacted with the Pension Protection Act of 2006, DC plans that offer automatic enrollment and meet criteria for a "qualified default investment alternative" ("QDIA") receive "safe harbor" status from the US Department of Labor and are provided with fiduciary relief. QDIA alternatives are mixed investments with both fixed income exposure and equity exposure, such as balanced funds and life cycle funds.

27. VanDerhei et al., "401(k) Plan Asset Allocation, Account Balances, and Loan Activity in 2012." Model portfolios are also referred to as life cycle funds or target date funds. At the end of 2012, 15 percent of assets were invested in this type of fund.

28. Robert J. Shiller, "Historic Turning Points in Real Estate," *Eastern Economic Journal* 34, no 1 (Winter 2008), 1–13. Housing market swings tend to be a little shorter, typically taking about a decade to go through a boom and bust cycle.

29. Regina T. Jefferson, "Rethinking the Risk of Defined Contribution Plans," *Florida Tax Review* 4, no. 9 (2000), 607–683; Marie-Eve Lachance, Olivia S. Mitchell, and Kent Smetters, "Guaranteeing Defined Contribution Pensions: The Option to Buy Back a Defined Benefit Promise," *Journal of Risk and Insurance* 40, no. 1 (2003), 1–16, doi: 10.1111/1539–6975.00044.

30. Shlomo Benartzi, Alessandro Previtero, and Richard H. Thaler, "Annuitization Puzzles," *The Journal of Economic Perspectives* 25, no. 4 (Fall 2011), 149–164; US Government Accountability Office (GAO), "Retirement Income, Ensuring Income throughout

Retirement Requires Difficult Choices," GAO-11–400 (Washington, DC: GAO, June 2011), 7.

31. Leslie Scism, "Insurance Fees, Revealed," *The Wall Street Journal*, updated March 30, 2012, http://online.wsj.com

32. Jeffrey R. Brown, "Rational and Behavioral Perspectives on the Role of Annuities in Retirement Planning," Working Paper No. w13536 (Cambridge, MA: National Bureau of Economic Research, 2007), http://www.nber.org/papers/w13537.pdf

33. Rachel Drew and Christian Weller, "A Safe Investment? Assessing Economic Explanations for the Perceived Risk-Return Trade-off of Owner-Occupied Housing in the United States," paper presented at the Eastern Economic Association Annual Conference, Boston, MA, March 8, 2014.

34. See, for instance, Weller, "Making Sure Money Is Available When We Need It"; Weller and Bernardo, "Putting Retirement at Risk."

35. Christian Weller and Derek Douglas, "One Nation under Debt," *Challenge* 50, no 1 (2007), 54–75.

36. Donald L. Redfoot, Ken Scholen, and S. Kathi Brown, "Reverse Mortgages: Niche Product or Mainstream Solution? Report on the 2006 AARP National Survey of Reverse Mortgage Shoppers" (Washington, DC: AARP Public Policy Institute, 2007), 5–6, http://assets.aarp.org/rgcenter/consume/2007_22_revmortgage.pdf.

7   A Perfect Storm: Labor and Financial Market Risks Feed on Each Other

1. All quotes taken from *Retirement Security 2015: Roadmap for Policy Makers: Americans' Views of the Retirement Crisis*, a biennial public opinion research conducted by the National Institute on Retirement Security and Greenwald & Associates, March 2015.

2. For a discussion of the relevant theoretical and empirical literature that shows the regular co-movements between labor and financial markets over the course of the business cycle, see Christian E. Weller and Jeffrey B. Wenger, "What Happens to Defined Contribution Accounts When Labor Markets and Financial Markets Move Together?" *Journal of Aging & Social Policy* 21, no. 3 (2009), 256–276, doi: 10.1080/08959420902733298.

3. Dean Baker, "The Run-up in Home Prices: A Bubble," *Challenge* 45, no. 6 (2002): 293–319.

4. Dale L. Domian and David A. Louton, "Business Cycle Asymmetry and the Stock Market," *The Quarterly Review of Economics and Finance* 35, no. 4 (Winter 1995): 451–466; Edward E. Leamer, "Housing Is the Business Cycle," NBER Working Paper No. w13428 (Cambridge, MA: National Bureau of Economic Research, September 2007), doi: 10.3386/w13428.

5. Stanley Fischer and Robert C. Merton, "Macroeconomics and Finance: The Role of the Stock Market," Carnegie-Rochester Conference Series on Public Policy 21, North Holland, 1984; Arturo Estrella and Frederic S. Mishkin, "Predicting U.S. Recessions: Financial Variables as Leading Indicators," NBER Working Paper No. 5378 (Cambridge, MA: National Bureau of Economic Research, 1995).

6. Peter Brady and Michael Bogdan, "Who Gets Retirement Plans and Why, 2013," *Investment Company Institute Research Perspective* 20, no. 6 (October 2014), http://www.ici.org/pdf/per20-06.pdf.

7. William M. Rohe and Mark Lindblad, "Reexamining the Social Benefits of Homeownership after the Housing Crisis," Working Paper HBTL-04 (Cambridge, MA: Joint Center for Housing Studies, Harvard University, 2013); Joseph Gyourko and Joseph

Tracy, "Reconciling Theory and Empirics on the Role of Unemployment in Mortgage Default," *Journal of Urban Economics* 80 (March 2014), 87–96.

8. Rajashri Chakrabarti, Donghoon Lee, Wilbert van der Klaauw, and Basit Zafar, "Household Debt and Saving during the 2007 Recession," Staff Reports no. 482 (New York, NY: Federal Reserve Bank of New York, January 2011), http://www.newyorkfed.org/research/staff_reports/sr482.pdf.

9. It may also be possible that employers may cut on their contributions to their employee retirement savings plans when the economy enters a recession. For instance, the following finds that employer contributions fell during the 2001 recession. Alicia Munnell and Annika Sunden, *Coming Up Short: The Challenges of 401(k) Plans* (Washington, DC: Brookings Institution Press, 2004).

10. Josh Bivens and Christian Weller, "The 'Job Loss' Recovery: Not New, Just Worse," *Journal of Economic Issues* 40, no. 3 (2006), 603–628. For example, this report shows that profits recovered substantially faster after the 2001 recession than during previous years.

11. All numbers from David Copeland, "Employment-Based Plan Participation: Geographic Differences and Trends, 2012," EBRI Issue Brief No. 392 (Washington, DC: Employee Benefits Research Institute, 2013), http://www.ebri.org/publications/ib/index.cfm?fa=ibDisp&content_id=5292

12. Contributions to retirement plans tend to decline when workers experience adverse earnings shocks. Those workers who changed jobs and had lower earnings afterwards, for instance, on average contributed 58 percent less after their job change between 2005 and 2007—before the Great Recession. See Irena Dushi and Howard Iams, "The Impact of Employment and Earnings Shocks on Contribution Behavior in Defined Contribution Plans: 2005–2009," *Journal of Retirement* 4, no. 2 (2015), 86–104.

13. For a discussion of the limits of the Saver's Credit for lower income earners and of the benefits of progressive savings matches, see Joe Valenti and Christian Weller, "Creating Economic Security: Using Progressive Savings Matches to Counter Upside-Down Tax Incentives," CAP Issue Brief (Washington, DC: Center for American Progress, 2013).

14. Barbara A. Butrica, Sheila R. Zedlewski, and Philip Issa, "Understanding Early Withdrawals from Retirement Accounts," Discussion Paper 10–02 (Washington, DC: The Urban Institute, May 2010), http://www.urban.org/uploadedpdf/412107-early-withdrawals.pdf

15. Catherine Collinson, "The Retirement Readiness of Three Unique Generations: Baby Boomers, Generation X, and Millennials," TCRS 1171–0514 (Transamerica Center for Retirement Studies, April, 2014), http://www.transamericacenter.org/docs/default-source/resources/center-research/tcrs2014_sr_three_unique_generations.pdf

16. Gary R. Mattola, "Softening the Blow: Income Shocks, Mortgage Payments and Emergency Savings," *Insights: American Financial Capability* (Washington, DC: FIRNA Investor Education Foundation, March 2013); US Department of Housing and Urban Development (HUD), Office of Policy Development and Research, "Report to Congress on the Root Causes of the Foreclosure Crisis" (Washington, DC: HUD, January 2010), http://www.huduser.org/portal/publications/Foreclosure_09.pdf. Slowing mortgage payments also lowers the value of households' home equity below what it otherwise would have been. In extreme cases, households will lose all of their home equity in foreclosures.

17. See Christian E. Weller and Jeffrey B. Wenger, "What Happens to Defined Contribution Accounts When Labor Markets and Financial Markets Move Together?" *Journal of Aging & Social Policy* 21, no. 3 (2009), 256–276, doi: 10.1080/08959420902733298 for a review of some of the key labor market evidence; and Christian Weller and Jaryn Fields, "The Black and White Labor Gap in America," CAP Issue Brief (Washington, DC: Center for American Progress, July 2011) for a summary of some key data.

18. Weller and Wenger, "What Happens to Defined Contribution Accounts When Labor Markets and Financial Markets Move Together?"

19. Ibid.
20. Weller and Fields, "The Black and White Labor Gap in America."
21. Ibid.; Christian Weller and Farah Z. Ahmad, "The State of Communities of Color in the U.S. Economy: Still Feeling the Pain 4 Years into the Recovery" (Washington, DC: Center for American Progress, 2013).
22. For a discussion of the available labor market data on subpopulations of the Asian American community, see Farah Ahmad and Christian Weller, "Reading between the Data: The Incomplete Story of Asian Americans, Native Hawaiians, and Pacific Islanders" (Washington, DC: Center for American Progress, 2014).
23. Debbie Gruenstein Bocian, Wei Li, and Keith S. Ernst, "Foreclosures by Race and Ethnicity: The Demographics of a Crisis," CRL Research Report (Washington, DC: Center for Responsible Lending, June 2010); Rakesh Kochhar, Ana Gonzalez-Barrera, and Daniel Dockterman, "Through the Boom and Bust: Minorities, Immigrants, and Homeownership" (Washington, DC: Pew Hispanic Center, May 2009), http://www.pewhispanic.org/files/reports/109.pdf
24. For similar simulations, see Jason Seligman and Jeffrey B. Wenger, "Asynchronous Risk: Retirement Savings, Equity Markets, and Unemployment," *Journal of Pension Economics and Finance* 5, no. 3 (2006). doi:10.1017/S1474747206002630
25. Theoretically savings and consumption differ from earnings, such that people save more as they get older through their mid-career and they then save less as they near retirement. But empirically consumption and by definition, savings tend to follow earnings more closely than theory predicts. For an in-depth discussion of the data and theory, see Martin Browning and Thomas F. Crossley, "The Life-Cycle Model of Consumption and Saving," *Journal of Economic Perspectives* 15, no. 3 (2001), 3–22, doi:10.1257/jep.15.3.3
26. US Census Bureau, "Income Data, Historical Tables, People, Table P-8, Age—People, All Races, by Median Income and Sex: 1947 to 2013" (Washington, DC: US Census Bureau, 2014). The hypothetical earnings start with $15,000 (in 2013 dollars) at age 30, grow at an annual rate of 2.5 percent in real terms, moderated by a rate of 0.75 percent times the squared difference between the workers age minus 30. The starting salary is close to the median real earnings (in 2013 dollars) recorded for male workers between the ages of 25 and 34, which amounted to $14,672 in 1979.
27. All rates of return are in real terms. The rate of return on stocks is the stock price appreciation plus the dividend yield. Stock prices, dividend yield, long-term government bond rates and consumer price index (CPI-U) are all taken from Robert Shiller, "Irrational Exuberance—IrrationalExuberance.com" (New Haven, CT: Yale University, 2014), accessed November 13, 2014, http://www.irrationalexuberance.com. Corporate bond interest rates are taken from the Board of Governors (BOG), Federal Reserve System, "Release H.15 Selected Interest Rates, Historical Data" (Washington, DC: BOG, 2014), accessed November 10, 2014, http://www.federalreserve.gov/releases/h15/data.htm
28. The alternative scenarios are likely understatements of the actual effects since typical spells of unemployment for those impacted by disproportionately long unemployment spells can be much longer than an extra six months. And it can take years before workers recover to their original savings rate, often for instance, because it takes time before workers reinstate their original matching and nonelective contributions to retirement savings accounts. And finally, a nontrivial share of people with retirement accounts and with home equity will liquidate their savings by borrowing against their assets, thus reducing instead of increasing their assets during a recession.
29. Jack VanDerhei, Sarah Holden, Luis Alonso, and Steven Bass, "401(k) Plan Asset Allocation, Account Balances, and Loan Activity in 2012," EBRI Issue Brief No. 394 (Washington, DC: Employee Benefit Research Institute, 2013), and *Investment Company Institute Research Perspective* 19, no. 12 (December 2013), 1, 14. In 2008, after the Great Recession started,

401(k) loans as a percentage of account balances increased four percentage points over the previous year. In 2009, the share of eligible 401(k) participants with outstanding 401(k) loans increased three percentage points over the previous three years and remained steady at this higher rate following the recession's end. See also Christian E. Weller and Jeffrey Wenger, "Easy Money or Hard Times? Health and 401(k) Loans," *Contemporary Economic Policy* 30, no 1 (January 2012), 29–42, doi:10.1111/j.1465–7287.2011.00251.x for a discussion of pension loan reasons.

30. Barbara A. Butrica, Sheila R. Zedlewski, and Philip Issa, "Understanding Early Withdrawals from Retirement Accounts," Discussion Paper 10–02 (Washington, DC: The Urban Institute, May 2010), http://www.urban.org/uploadedpdf/412107-early-withdrawals.pdf

31. The time adjustment is done by assuming a constant discount rate of three percent in real terms.

8   The Pitfalls of Employer-Sponsored Retirement

1. All quotes taken from *Retirement Security 2015: Roadmap for Policy Makers: Americans' Views of the Retirement Crisis*," a biennial public opinion research conducted by the National Institute on Retirement Security and Greenwald & Associates, March 2015.

2. For a discussion of the US retirement system compared to other countries, see Christian Weller, "The Future of Public Pensions," *Cambridge Journal of Economics* 28, no. 4 (July 2004), 489–504.

3. Organisation for Economic Cooperation and Development (OECD), "Social Expenditure Update—Social Spending Is Falling in Some Countries, but in Many Others It Remains at Historically High Levels" (Paris, France: OECD, November 2014), 8. In 2014, the OECD ranked the United States second for net total social expenditure, which includes direct taxes and social contributions, indirect taxes and net tax breaks for social purposes. It also includes tax incentives for retirement savings. See also Len Burman and Joel Slemrod, "The Hidden Welfare State," in *Taxes in America: What Everyone Needs to Know* (New York, NY: Oxford University Press, 2013) for a description of personal tax expenditures.

4. Some state and local governments as employers are in a somewhat different situation and have to offer retirement benefits that are not part of Social Security to their employees. A number of states including California decided not to participate in Social Security in 1983 during the last major Social Security reform. States that do not participate in Social Security, though, have to offer retirement benefits to their employees that are substantially equivalent to Social Security benefits. That is, some retirement benefits in the public sector are akin to Social Security, while they are comparable to private sector additional savings in states that participate in Social Security, such as Pennsylvania. Alicia Munnell and Mauricio Soto, "State and Local Pensions Are Different from Private Plans," State and Local Pension Plans 1 (Boston, MA: Center for Retirement Research, November 2007); Christian Weller and Ilana Boivie, "The Fiscal Crisis, Public Pensions, and Implications for Labor and Employment Relations," in Daniel Mitchell, ed., *Impact of the Great Recession on Public Sector Employment, Labor and Employment Relations Research* (Ithaca, NY: Cornell University Press, 2011); Internal Revenue Service (IRS), "Government Retirement Plans Toolkit" (Washington, DC: IRS, 2014), accessed January 30, 2014, http://www.irs.gov/Government-Entities/Federal,-State-&-Local-Governments/Government-Retirement-Plans-Toolkit

5. FINRA Investor Education Foundation, "Financial Capability in the United States, Report of Findings from the 2012 National Financial Capability Study" (Washington,

DC: FIRNA Investor Education Foundation, May 2013); Michal Grinstein-Weiss, Michael Sherraden, William Rohe, William Gale, Mark Schreiner, and Clinton Key, "Long-Term Follow-up of Individual Development Accounts: Evidence from the ADD Experiment," CSD Report 12–43 (St. Louis, MO: Center for Social Development, Washington University, 2012).

6. Stefano DellaVigna, "Psychology and Economics: Evidence from the Field," *Journal of Economic Literature* 47, no. 2 (2009), 315–372, doi: 10.1257/jel.47.2.315

7. These are technically tax deferrals. People first get tax breaks while they save for retirement, but then have to pay taxes when they receive income from their retirement savings. Savers still receive a net tax benefit during their lifetime, largely because of tax-free capital income during their savings years and because future tax rates tend to be lower due to lower incomes and greater tax breaks in retirement than during working years.

8. Some DC retirement savings plans, so-called Roth plans, receive contributions after federal income taxes have been paid, but the money withdrawn from these plans are not subject to federal income taxation. But Roth-type plans are not the norm for employer-sponsored retirement plans.

9. My discussion here focuses exclusively on traditional 401(k) plans. So-called Roth 401(k)s also offer tax advantages, but contributions to such retirement savings plans come after federal income taxes have been paid.

10. The dollar limit only applies if it is smaller than 100 percent of an employee's compensation. See Internal Revenue Service (IRS), "COLA Increases for Dollar Limitations on Benefits and Contributions" (Washington, DC: IRS, 2014), accessed December 29, 2014, http://www.irs.gov/Retirement-Plans/COLA-Increases-for-Dollar-Limitations-on-Benefits-and-Contributions; and Internal Revenue Service (IRS), "Retirement Topics—401(k) and Profit-Sharing Plan Contribution Limits" (Washington, DC: IRS, 2014), accessed December 29, 2014, http://www.irs.gov/Retirement-Plans/Plan-Participant,-Employee/Retirement-Topics-401k-and-Profit-Sharing-Plan-Contribution-Limits

11. The dollar limit only applies if it is smaller than 100 percent of an employee's compensation. See IRS, "COLA Increases for Dollar Limitations on Benefits and Contributions" and "Retirement Topics—401(k) and Profit-Sharing Plan Contribution Limits."

12. Janette Kawachi, Karen E. Smith, and Eric J. Toder, "Making Maximum Use of Tax-Deferred Retirement Accounts" (Washington, DC: The Urban Institute, 2005).

13. Employers do not have to pay their share of payroll taxes for Social Security and Medicare for their contributions to a DC retirement account, while employees are typically still responsible for their share of the payroll tax on the contributions they make to a DC account. See Internal Revenue Service (IRS), "Employer 'Pick-Up' Contributions to Benefit Plans," *IRS.gov*, last modified April 1, 2014, http://www.irs.gov/Government-Entities/Federal,-State-&-Local-Governments/Employer-Pick-Up-Contributions-to-Benefit-Plans

Determining the maximum that an employer can contribute on behalf of an employee is a somewhat complicated calculation. The total amount of tax-deferred contributions to DC accounts for 2014, for instance, was $52,000 without catch-up contributions for older employees. Assume that one employee works only for one employer who offered a 401(k) plan in 2014 and contributed the maximum amount for employees—$17,500. The employer could then contribute another $34,500—or almost twice as much—to the employee's account. The employer's contribution limit is smaller if the employee contributes to another employment-based retirement account such as a Self-Employed Plan (SEP). On the other hand, the employer's contribution limit can increase for older employees who are allowed to make additional contributions and if the employee does not make the maximum allowed employee contribution. See IRS, "Retirement Topics—401(k) and Profit-Sharing Plan Contribution Limits."

14. The nondiscrimination test is formula-based. Whether a company is in compliance depends on its share of highly compensated employees. For a discussion, see, for instance, 401(k) Help Center, "Highly Compensated Employee Rules Aim to Make 401k's Fair," *401kHelp-Center.com*, accessed December 30, 2014, http://www.401khelpcenter.com/mpower/feature_030702.html#.VKKqn2cBg. For income limits, see IRS, "COLA Increases for Dollar Limitations on Benefits and Contributions."

15. See IRS, "401(k) Resource Guide—Plan Sponsors—401(k) Plan Overview" (Washington, DC: IRS, 2014), accessed December 30, 2014, http://www.irs.gov/Retirement-Plans/Plan-Sponsor/401k-Resource-Guide-Plan-Sponsors-401k-Plan-Overview. 401(k) Help Center, "Highly Compensated Employee Rules Aim to Make 401k's Fair."

16. See, for example, MBM Advisors, Inc., "FAQ: Automatic Enrollment Safe Harbor 401(k)" (Houston, TX: MBM Advisors, 2014), accessed December 30, 2014, http://www.mbm-inc.com/pdfs/2013%20FAQ%20Automatic%20Enrollment%20Safe%20Harbor%20401%28k%29.pdf

17. The particular data source on which these summary statistics rely does not distinguish between DB pensions and DC plans. Combining both types of employment-based retirement plans into one statistic also has the advantage of creating consistent trends over time.

18. The figure starts in 1975, although data for prior years are available. Data before 1975 are generally not comparable to the data in later years due to the changing requirements for employer contributions that were enacted with the Employee Retirement Income Security Act of 1974.

19. Based on Bureau of Economic Analysis (BEA), "National Income and Product Accounts" (Washington, DC: BEA, 2014).

20. I discuss fees associated with retirement savings in more detail in other chapters. Also see Jennifer Erickson and David Madland, "Fixing the Drain on Retirement Savings: How Retirement Fees Are Straining the Middle Class and What We Can Do about Them" (Washington, DC: Center for American Progress, April, 2014) and Christian Weller and Shana Jenkins, "Building 401(k) Wealth One Percent at a Time: Fees Chip Away at People's Retirement Nest Eggs" (Washington, DC: Center for American Progress, March 2007).

21. All numbers refer to private sector wage and salary workers between the ages of 21 and 64 years. Based on Craig Copeland, "Employment-Based Retirement Plan Participation: Geographic Differences and Trends, 2013," EBRI Issue Brief No. 405 (Washington, DC: Employee Benefits Research Institute, 2014) and Craig Copeland, "Employment-Based Retirement Plan Participation: Geographic Differences and Trends, 2012," EBRI Issue Brief No. 392 (Washington, DC: Employee Benefits Research Institute, 2013).

22. PBGC insurance covers benefits up to a maximum and some benefits are not or only partially covered. The insurance coverage for benefit improvements is phased in over five years.

23. For an easily accessible summary of the relevant literature, see Cass Sunstein and Richard Thaler, *Nudge: Improving Decisions about Health, Wealth, and Happiness* (London, UK: Penguin Books, 2009), 120–133. For a discussion of the rules of thumb that households use in making investment decisions in 401(k) type accounts, see also Shlomo Bernartzi and Richard Thaler, "Heuristics and Biases in Retirement Savings Behavior," *Journal of Economic Perspectives* 21, no. 3 (Summer 2007), 81–104.

24. Christian Weller, "Making Sure Money Is Available When We Need It" (Washington, DC: Center for American Progress, March 2013); Christian Weller, "Protecting Retirement Wealth," *Challenge* 56, no. 4 (2013), 51–88, doi:10.2753/0577–5132560405; Christian Weller and Sara Bernardo, "Putting Retirement at Risk: Has Financial Risk Exposure Grown Faster for Older Households than Younger Ones?" Working Paper (Boston, MA: Gerontology Institute, UMass Boston, 2014).

25. The trends do not change with different thresholds.
26. IDAs can be used to save for a number of different purposes, including retirement. See Michal Grinstein-Weiss, Michael Sherraden, William Gale, William M. Rohe, and Mark Schreiner, "Effects of an Individual Development Account Program on Retirement Saving: Follow-up Evidence from a Randomized Experiment," CSD Working Papers No. 12–54 (St. Louis, MO: Washington University, Center for Social Development, 2012).
27. US Department of the Treasury, "About myRA: Fact Sheet" (Washington, DC: US Department of Treasury, 2014), accessed March 1, 2015, https://myra.treasury.gov/resources/myRA_About.pdf
28. Pension Rights Center, "State-Based Retirement Plans for the Private Sector" (Washington, DC: Pension Rights Center, 2014), accessed January 24, 2014, http://www.pensionrights.org/issues/legislation/state-based-retirement-plans-private-sector; Aleta Sprague, "The California Secure Choice Retirement Savings Program" (Washington, DC: New America Foundation, 2013).
29. American Savings Promotion Act, H.R. 3374/P.L. 113–251, 113th Congress (2014).
30. J. Mark Iwry and David C. John, "Pursuing Universal Retirement Security through Automatic IRAs" (Washington, DC: The Retirement Security Project, 2009); USA Retirement Funds Act, S. 1979, 113th Congress (2013–2014).
31. For a proposal with an explicit government guarantee, see Teresa Ghilarducci, *When I'm Sixty-Four: The Plot against Pensions and the Plan to Save Them* (Princeton, NJ: Princeton University Press, 2008); Teresa Ghilarducci, Robert Hiltonsmith, and Lauren Schmitz, "State Guaranteed Retirement Accounts" Working Paper (New York, NY: Demos, Schwartz Center for Economic Policy Analysis, The New School, 2012). For a proposal with low-risk investment options, see Alicia Munnell, Andrew Eschtruth, and Charles Ellis, *Falling Short: The Coming Retirement Crisis and What to Do about It* (New York, NY: Oxford University Press, 2014), 118–120.
32. For a discussion of savings simplification across a number of nonhousing savings incentives, see Weller and Ungar, "Overhauling Federal Savings Incentives." For a detailed simplification proposal, see The President's Advisory Panel on Federal Tax Reform, *Simple, Fair, and Pro-Growth: Proposals to Fix America's Tax System* (November 2005).

9   Upside-Down Tax Incentives

1. All quotes taken from *Retirement Security 2015: Roadmap for Policy Makers: Americans' Views of the Retirement Crisis*," a biennial public opinion research conducted by the National Institute on Retirement Security and Greenwald & Associates, March 2015.
2. Roth IRAs and Roth 401(k)s receive a different tax advantage. Contributions to these types of retirement savings plans occur after a tax payer has paid income taxes, but investment gains and withdrawals from these savings accounts are tax-free.
3. Pamela Perun and C. Eugene Steuerle, "Reality Testing for Pension Reform" (Philadelphia, PA: Pension Research Council, 2004).
4. Shlomo Bernartzi and Richard Thaler, "Heuristics and Biases in Retirement Savings Behavior," *Journal of Economic Perspectives* 21, no. 3 (Summer 2007), 81–104.
5. Gary R. Mottola and Stephen P. Utkus, "Can There Be Too Much Choice in a Retirement Savings Plan?" (Valley Forge, PA: Vanguard Center for Retirement Research, 2006).
6. Sheena Sethi-Iyengar and others, "How Much Choice Is Too Much? Contributions to 401(k) Retirement Plans," in Olivia S. Mitchell and Stephen P. Utkus, eds., *Pension Design and Structure: New Lessons from Behavioral Finance* (New York, NY: Oxford University Press, 2004).

7. See Internal Revenue Service (IRS), "Topic 558—Additional Tax on Early Distributions from Retirement Plans Other than IRAs," *IRS.gov,* last modified January 29, 2015, http://www.irs.gov/taxtopics/tc558.html for details on potential exceptions to this excise tax.

8. Internal Revenue Service, "Retirement Plans FAQs Regarding Hardship Distributions," *IRS.gov,* last modified March 2, 2015, http://www.irs.gov/Retirement-Plans/Retirement-Plans-FAQs-regarding-Hardship-Distributions#7

9. Internal Revenue Service, "Retirement Plans FAQs Regarding Hardship Distributions."

10. On pension loans, see Christian E. Weller and Jeffrey Wenger, "Easy Money or Hard Times? Health and 401(k) Loans," *Contemporary Economic Policy* 30, no 1 (January 2012), 29–42, doi: 10.1111/j.1465-7287.2011.00251.x. On withdrawals, see Robert Argento, Victoria Bryant, and John Sabelhaus, "Early Withdrawals from Retirement Accounts during the Great Recession," Finance and Economics Discussion Series Working Paper 2013-2 (Washington, DC: Divisions of Research and Statistics and Monetary Affairs, Federal Reserve Board, 2013).

11. See, for instance, Christian E. Weller and Jeffrey Wenger, "Easy Money or Hard Times? Health and 401(k) Loans," *Contemporary Economic Policy* 30, no 1 (January 2012), 29–42, doi: 10.1111/j.1465-7287.2011.00251.x.

12. Joint Center for Housing Studies of Harvard University (JCHS), "The State of the Nation's Housing, 2014" (Cambridge, MA: JCHS, 2014), http://www.jchs.harvard.edu/sites/jchs.harvard.edu/files/sonhr14-color-full.pdf

13. Joe Valenti and Christian E. Weller, "Creating Economic Security: Using Progressive Savings Matches to Counter Upside-Down Tax Incentives" (Washington, DC: Center for American Progress, November, 2013); J. Michael Collins and Leah Gjertson, "Emergency Savings for Low-Income Consumers," Focus 30.1 (Madison, WI: University of Wisconsin–Madison, Institute for Research on Poverty, n.d.), 12–17, http://www.irp.wisc.edu/publications/focus/pdfs/foc301c.pdf

14. Jennifer Brooks, Kasey Wiedrich, Lebaron Sims Jr., and Solana Rice, "Excluded from the Financial Mainstream: How the Economic Recovery Is Bypassing Millions of Americans" (Washington, DC: Corporation for Enterprise Development, 2015).

15. Corporation for Enterprise Development, "Liquid Asset Poverty Rate," *Assets & Opportunity Scorecard,* accessed March 11, 2015, http://scorecard.assetsandopportunity.org/latest/measure/liquid-asset-poverty-rate

16. See also Teresa Ghilarducci, *When I'm Sixty-Four: The Plot against Pensions and the Plan to Save Them* (Princeton, NJ: Princeton University Press, 2008).

17. Internal Revenue Service (IRS), "1040 Tax Tables 2014" (Washington, DC: IRS, 2014), accessed March 11, 2015, http://www.irs.gov/pub/irs-pdf/i1040tt.pdf

18. See Congressional Budget Office (CBO), "The Distribution of Major Tax Expenditures in the Individual Tax System" (Washington, DC: CBO, 2013), http://www.cbo.gov/sites/default/files/43768_DistributionTaxExpenditures.pdf; see also supplemental data for this report (Figure 2), available at http://www.cbo.gov/publication/43768

19. For some illustrative examples and a review of relevant other research, see, for instance, Peter Brady, "The Tax Benefits and Revenue Costs of Tax Deferral" (Washington, DC: Investment Company Institute, September 2012).

20. Peter Brady, "The Tax Benefits and Revenue Costs of Tax Deferral" (Washington, DC: Investment Company Institute, September, 2012).

21. My discussion includes only some of the most important complications, but leaves out additional ones such as the interaction between federal and state income taxes, differential taxes on varying forms of withdrawals such as annuities and self-managed withdrawals, and the potential for differing rates of return by income since higher income earners presumably have more assets and hence often pay lower fees on their investments than is the case for higher income earners.

22. Data from US Bureau of Labor Statistics, *National Compensation Survey* (Washington, DC: US Department of Labor, 2013).

23. Internal Revenue Service (IRS), "Exemptions, Standard Deduction, and Filing Information," Publication 501 (Washington, DC: IRS, 2014), accessed March 12, 2015, http://www.irs.gov/publications/p501/. Those aged 65 or older are able to take a higher standard deduction, specifically $1,550 more individually and up to $2,400 more jointly.

24. Gary R. Mottola, "The Financial Capability of Young Adults—a Generational View" (Washington, DC: FIRNA Investor Education Foundation, March 2014), http://www.usfinancialcapability.org/downloads/FinancialCapabilityofYoungAdults.pdf; Karen Smith, Mauricio Soto, and Rudolph G. Penner, "How Seniors Change Their Asset Holdings during Retirement" (Washington, DC: The Urban Institute, August 10, 2009), http://www.nber.org/2009rrc/3.1%20Smith,%20Soto,%20Penner.pdf; James M. Poterba, Steven F. Venti, and David A. Wise, "401(k) Plans and Future Patterns of Retirement Saving," *The American Economic Review* 88, no. 2, papers and proceedings of the Hundred and Tenth Annual Meeting of the American Economic Association (May 1998), 179–184.

25. Stewart E. Sterk and Melanie B. Leslie, "Accidental Inheritance: Retirement Accounts and the Hidden Law of Succession," *New York University Law Review* 89 (2014), 165–237. The tax code tries to counter this possibility by requiring that households withdraw a minimum share of their savings in IRAs, for instance, no later than the year after they turn seventy-and-a-half years. See Internal Revenue Service (IRS), "Retirement Topic—Required Minimum Distributions," *IRS.gov*, last modified January 26, 2015, http://www.irs.gov/Retirement-Plans/Plan-Participant,-Employee/Retirement-Topics-Required-Minimum-Distributions-%28RMDs%29

26. Higher income households tend to have more assets held in retirement accounts than lower income households and experience a lower rate of decumulation from these accounts, starting at a later age. See, for example, Smith et al., "How Seniors Change Their Asset Holdings during Retirement." See also Congressional Budget Office (CBO), "Will the Demand for Assets Fall When Baby Boomers Retire?" CBO Pub. No. 2843 (Washington, DC: CBO, September 2009), http://www.cbo.gov/sites/default/files/09-08_baby-boomers.pdf

27. The value of these savings incentives as share of after-tax income drops for the top one percent to 2.6 percent. This relative decline at the very top of the income distribution reflects very high incomes and some limits on savings incentives. Counting all itemized deductions, the top earners still receive a larger share of income than lower income earners. See, for instance, Tax Policy Center (TPC), "2013 Table T13–0099 Tax Benefit of All Itemized Deductions; Distribution of Federal Tax Change by Cash Income Percentile" (Washington, DC: TPC, 2015).

28. Eric M. Engen and William G. Gale, "The Effects of 401(k) Plans on Household Wealth" (Washington, DC: National Bureau of Economic Research, 2000); Daniel J. Benjamin, "Does 401(k) Eligibility Increase Saving?" *Journal of Public Economics* 87, no. 5 (2003), 1259–1290.

29. From supplemental data for Congressional Budget Office (CBO), "The Distribution of Major Tax Expenditures in the Individual Income Tax System." The CBO found that the difference in revenues collected from the top quintile of tax payers between the current tax system and a system in which contributions to retirement accounts were taxed as ordinary income and in which investment earnings in retirement accounts were taxed as ordinary investment income was $92 billion.

30. All numbers refer to provisions in the US tax code.

31. The exact length of investment—or tax deferral—does not materially impact the conclusions of my discussion.

32. There is a substantial debate in the literature over the exact discount rate to use for retirement calculations. For a discussion of discount rates for DB pension plans, see Christian Weller and Dean Baker, "Smoothing the Waves of Pension Funding: Could Changes in Funding Rules Help Avoid Cyclical Under-funding," *The Journal of Policy Reform* 8, no. 2 (June 2005), 131–151. I choose six percent here as the discount rate to make my results comparable to others, specifically those generated by the ICI's Peter Brady.

33. The contribution limits are greater than this since the independent contractor can make employer contributions to a SEP IRA, which have higher limits than employee contributions. The employer limit for 2015 is $53,000. See Internal Revenue Service, "SEP Plan FAQs—Contributions," *IRS.gov*, last modified February 23, 2015, http://www.irs.gov/Retirement-Plans/Retirement-Plans-FAQs-regarding-SEPs-Contributions

34. Annamaria Lusardi and Olivia Mitchell, "Financial Literacy and Retirement Preparedness: Evidence and Implications for Financial Education Programs," CFS Working Paper No. 2007/15 (Frankfurt, Germany: Center for Financial Studies, Goethe University Frankfurt, 2007), http://www.econstor.eu/bitstream/10419/25516/1/527633305.pdf

35. Brady, "The Tax Benefits and Revenue Costs of Tax Deferral"; David Love, "What Can the Life Cycle Model Tell Us about 401(k) Contributions and Participation" (Williamstown, MA: Williams College, 2006), http://projects.vassar.edu/lamacro/web/Love.pdf; Geng Li and Paul Smith, "Borrowing From Yourself: 401(k) Loans and Household Balance Sheets," Finance and Economics Discussion Series Working Paper 2008–42 (Washington, DC: Divisions of Research and Statistics and Monetary Affairs, Federal Reserve Board, 2008).

10   Sidelined: The Millions Who Are Left Out

1. All quotes taken from *Retirement Security 2015: Roadmap for Policy Makers: Americans' Views of the Retirement Crisis*, a biennial public opinion research conducted by the National Institute on Retirement Security and Greenwald & Associates, March 2015.

2. Peter Brady, "Who Gets Retirement Plans and Why: An Update," *Investment Company Institute Research Perspective* 17, no. 3 (March 2011).

3. I focus here solely on tax incentives that are intended to get people to save more than they otherwise would, although these incentives are often very inefficient as I argue in chapter 9. The tax code further offers incentives to get people to invest their savings in particular assets such as stocks and municipal bonds, but their primary purpose is not to get people to save more money in the first place.

4. Based on Board of Governors (BOG), Federal Reserve System, *Survey of Consumer Finances—2013*.

5. Calculations of the shares of households self-identifying as nonsavers in the *SCF* in fact show a trend parallel to that of households without any tax-advantaged savings. The share of households identifying as nonsavers, though, is much greater with 52.7 percent in 2013, than the 25.1 percent share of households without any tax-advantaged savings that same year. The difference is in large measure explained by households not being aware that their owner-occupied housing and their DB pensions are in fact ways to save. Calculations based on Board of Governors of the Federal Reserve System, *Survey of Consumer Finances—2013*.

6. Pension loans tend to be a double-edged sword. Some households tend to save more because they have access to their savings through pension loans as would be the case without such loans. But that only holds for households who are otherwise financially savvy. Households that are prone to making financial mistakes because of a desire for instant gratification also do not tend to save more because of access to pension loans. And households often borrow

from their 401(k) loans because they have health problems and need to pay their health-care bills. That is, pension loans likely reduce retirement savings for households that need help in saving for their future the most. See Christian E. Weller and Jeffrey Wenger, "Easy Money or Hard Times? Health and 401(k) Loans," *Contemporary Economic Policy* 30, no 1 (January 2012), 29–42, doi:10.1111/j.1465–7287.2011.00251.x and Christian E. Weller and Jeffrey Wenger, "Boon or Bane: 401(k) Loans and Employee Contributions," *Research on Aging* 36, no 5 (July 2014), 527–556.

7. It is possible that this gap could be explained by the change from DB pensions to 401(k) plans. Assets in 401(k) plans are counted as marketable wealth, while assets in DB pensions are not. That is, household wealth should increase as more households have 401(k) plans and fewer households had DB pensions. And 401(k) plans may have risen faster among households with three or four tax-advantaged savings than among households with one or two tax-advantaged savings. But the data show that the share of households with 401(k) plans has grown faster from 15.9 percent in 1989 to 36.8 percent in 2013 among households with one or two tax-advantaged savings than among households with three or four tax-advantaged savings, who saw an increase in the share with 401(k) plans from 69.2 percent to 82.3 percent during the time period. The relative and absolute change is faster among households with just a few tax-advantaged savings than among those with three or four such assets. Calculations based on Board of Governors of the Federal Reserve System, *Survey of Consumer Finances* (Washington, DC: BOG, various years).

8. The demographic composition of households in each group is very close in the early years, from 1989 to 1998, and in the later years, from 2001 to 2013. Summary data are available from author upon request.

11   Charting a New Course

1. All quotes taken from *Retirement Security 2015: Roadmap for Policy Makers: Americans' Views of the Retirement Crisis*, a biennial public opinion research conducted by the National Institute on Retirement Security and Greenwald & Associates, March 2015.

2. Rebecca Vallas, Christian E. Weller, Rachel West, Jackie Odum, "The Effect of Rising Inequality on Social Security," CAP Issue Brief (Washington, DC: Center for American Progress, February 2015) similarly show that rising inequality has hurt Social Security's finances because increasing earnings inequality has translated into faster benefit growth relative to payroll tax revenue in a progressive benefit structure.

3. This were to be true, too, if part of Social Security's trust funds were invested in the stock market for a long period of time. There is no direct link between the financial performance of the trust funds and benefits that are being paid out. Benefits, for instance, do not go up just because the interest earned on trust funds is greater than expected. This would not change with stock investments in the trust funds. There may be other considerations such as growing uncertainty over the exact trust fund exhaustion date that could prevent such stock market investments, but the relevant bottom line for this chapter is that households are not subject to financial market risk exposure under Social Security, even with the existence of the trust funds. See also Christian E. Weller, "Risky Business? Evaluating Market Risk of Equity Investment Proposals to Reform Social Security," *Journal of Policy Analysis and Management* 19, no. 2 (2000), 263–273, doi: 10.1002/(SICI)1520–6688(200021)19:2<263::AID-PAM5>3.0.CO;2-H

4. Additional examples, not discussed here, include updating divorce benefits, letting college-age children of survivors and disabled workers receive benefits longer. Retirement and Income Security Enhancement (RAISE) Act, S. 2455, 113th Congress (2013–2014).

Another example includes adding a family care-giving benefit, such as the Family Act. Family and Medical Insurance Leave Act of 2013, HR 3712, 113th Cong. (2013–2014); Jane Farrell and Sarah Jane Glynn, "The FAMILY Act: Facts and Frequently Asked Questions" (Washington, DC: Center for American Progress, 2013).

5. Social Security Administration, "Actuarial Publications, Provisions Affecting Level of Monthly Benefits, B5.2," *Social Security Online*, accessed May 5, 2015, http://www.ssa.gov/OACT/solvency/provisions/benefitlevel.html

6. Social Security Administration, "Actuarial Publications, Provisions Affecting Level of Monthly Benefits, B6.2," *Social Security Online*, accessed May 5, 2015, http://www.ssa.gov/OACT/solvency/provisions/benefitlevel.html

7. Social Security Administration, "Actuarial Publications, Provisions Affecting Family Member Benefits, D4," *Social Security Online*, accessed May 5, 2015, http://www.ssa.gov/oact/solvency/provisions/familyMembers.html

8. There is a separate argument in favor of updating survivorship benefits. Currently, a higher income couple with only one earner could also receive $30,000 as a benefit, too. But this benefit would be the combination of an annual benefit of $20,000 for the worker and a spousal benefit of $10,000—the equivalent of 50 percent of the worker's benefit. When one spouse dies, the other one in this example will receive $20,000 in annual benefits or the equivalent of 66 percent of the combined benefit. This unevenness in the treatment of dual-earner couples and single-earner couples is another reason for updating the survivorship benefit. For examples of policy proposals that include this benefit update, see Peter A. Diamond and Peter R. Orszag, *Saving Social Security: A Balanced Approach* (Washington, DC: Brookings Institution Press, 2005) and Christian Weller, "Building it Up, Not Tearing it Down" (Washington, DC: Center for American Progress, 2010).

9. Updating Social Security benefits in such targeted ways also means that these improvements are comparatively easy to pay for. The Social Security actuary estimates that the three provisions discussed here would worsen Social Security's long-term shortfall by 0.42 percent of payroll (Social Security Administration, "Actuarial Publications, Provisions Affecting Level of Monthly Benefits, B5.2 and B6.2"; "Actuarial Publications, Provisions Affecting Family Member Benefits, D4"). That is, an immediate and permanent increase in the payroll tax from 12.4 to 12.82 percent would cover the expected costs for all three updates. Alternatively, applying a two percent tax on earnings above the current cap, above which earnings are not subject to payroll taxes, which was $118,500 in 2015, for the years from 2017 to 2064, followed by a tax of three percent in the subsequent years would generate the revenue necessary to pay for all three updates. Social Security Administration, "Actuarial Publications, Provisions Affecting Payroll Taxes, E2.8," *Social Security Online*, accessed May 5, 2015, http://www.ssa.gov/oact/solvency/provisions/payrolltax.html; Social Security Administration, "Benefits Planner: Maximum Taxable Earnings (1937–2015)," *Social Security Online,* accessed May 5, 2015, www.ssa.gov/planners/maxtax.html

10. For an example of a specific proposal, see Christian E. Weller, "PURE: A Proposal for More Retirement Income Security," *Journal of Aging and Social Policy* 19, no. 1 (2007), 21–38, doi: 10.1300/J031v19n01_02. For a summary of potential state initiatives grouped by household risk exposure, see Christian Weller and Amy Helburn, "States to the Rescue: Policy Options for State Government to Promote Private Sector Retirement Savings," *Journal of Pension Benefits* (2010). See also David E. Morse, "State Initiatives to Expand the Availability and Effectiveness of Private Sector Retirement Plans" (Washington, DC: Center for Retirement Initiatives, Georgetown University, 2014) for a discussion of the legal issues involved in developing state-sponsored savings options. And the Georgetown University Center for Retirement Initiatives also presents a map with summaries of current state-sponsored initiatives. Georgetown University Center for Retirement Initiatives, "Look to the States for Innovation," accessed May 6, 2015, http://cri.georgetown.edu/

states/. Finally, the AARP Public Policy Institute has established a states resource page that highlights state initiatives and discusses some of the policy and legal issues involved in establishing state-sponsored retirement savings options. AARP Public Policy Institute, "State Retirement Savings Resource Center," accessed May 5, 2015, http://www.aarp.org/ppi/state-retirement-plans/

11. Morse, "State Initiatives to Expand the Availability and Effectiveness of Private Sector Retirement Plans"; Robert J. Toth Jr., "Retirement Saving Policy: The Impact of ERISA on State-Sponsored Plan Designs" (Washington, DC: AARP Public Policy Institute, 2014).

12. An Act to Provide Retirement Savings Options for Nonprofit Organizations, H. 3754, 187th General Court of Massachusetts (2011–2012); Pension Rights Center, "State-Based Retirement Plans for the Private Sector," Fact Sheet (Washington, DC: Pension Rights Center, 2014).

13. Weller, "PURE: A Proposal for More Retirement Income Security." The following proposal envisions a five percent contribution, split between employees and employers (2.5 percent each): Teresa Ghilarducci, "Guaranteed Retirement Accounts: Toward Retirement Income Security," EPI Briefing Paper No. 204 (Washington, DC: Economic Policy Institute, 2007) and Teresa Ghilarducci, *When I'm Sixty-Four: The Plot against Pensions and the Plan to Save Them* (Princeton, NJ: Princeton University Press, 2008). For a proposal that envisions starting at a three percent contribution and escalating to around 12 percent, see Rowland Davis and David Madland, "American Retirement Savings Could Be Much Better" (Washington, DC: Center for American Progress, 2013).

14. States would establish a new pooled investment fund administered and managed by public employee pension system, rather than mixing new savings from private sector workers with the funds managed on behalf of public employees such as teachers, firefighters, and police officers.

15. States could, for example, stipulate that money saved through a state-sponsored retirement plan could only be invested in a specific range of low-cost, low-risk mutual funds.

16. For a more detailed discussion of investment options and households' risk exposure with each investment option, see Weller and Helburn, "States to the Rescue: Policy Options for State Government to Promote Private Sector Retirement Savings."

17. Ghilarducci in "Guaranteed Retirement Accounts: Toward Retirement Income Security," for instance, would create a public reserve fund or "balancing fund" that could cover any potential shortfalls between the promised benefits and the actual income to the state-sponsored pooled investment; and Davis and Madland, in "American Retirement Savings Could Be Much Better," would gradually adjust benefits for all current workers and retirees to cover such potential shortfalls, although the risk of shortfalls happening in such pooled investments is minimal and the expected shortfalls, if they happened, are small.

18. For detailed background on turning deductions into one credit, see Christian Weller and Sam Ungar, "The Universal Savings Credit" (Washington, DC: Center for American Progress, 2013). And Christian Weller and Sam Ungar, "Overhauling Federal Savings Incentives. Tax Notes Special Report," *Tax Notes* 142, no. 9 (2014), 1–9, offer a detailed discussion of this proposal and address potential criticisms of it.

19. William Gale, in writing for the Tax Policy Center, argues that an 18 percent matching tax credit is the equivalent of a 15 percent retirement savings deduction. "A Proposal to Restructure Retirement Saving Incentives in a Weak Economy with Long-Term Deficits" (Washington, DC: Urban-Brookings Tax Policy Center, 2011), http://www.brookings.edu/~/media/research/files/papers/2011/9/08%20retirement%20incentives%20gale/0908_retirement_incentives_gale.pdf

20. The exact credit rate depends on a number of factors such as how much revenue policymakers are willing to forego to incentivize savings, the subsequent maximum contribution

amount that could qualify for the credit, as well as on the tax treatment of capital income—interest, dividends, and capital gains in savings accounts. For a detailed discussion of these issues, see Weller and Ungar, "Overhauling Federal Savings Incentives."

21. Roger Altman and others, "Reforming Our Tax System, Reducing Our Deficit" (Washington, DC: Center for American Progress, 2012); National Commission on Fiscal Responsibility and Reform, "The Moment of Truth" (2010); Pete Domenici and Alice Rivlin, "Restoring America's Future: Reviving the Economy, Cutting Spending and Debt, and Creating a Simple, Pro-Growth Tax System" (Washington, DC: Bipartisan Policy Center, 2010); Daniel Baneman and others, "Options to Reform the Deduction for Home Mortgage Interest" (Washington, DC: Urban-Brookings Tax Policy Center, 2011).

22. The streamlining of savings incentives discussed in this chapter could also occur without changing the tax treatment of tax-advantaged savings accounts, although some complexity may remain. The conversion of all deductions into one single credit, on the other hand, already necessitates simplification, and I hence combine tax simplification with other simplification aspects in this chapter.

23. Regulation needs to pay even closer attention to the costs and risks associated with tax-advantaged savings than is currently the case. The Consumer Financial Protection Bureau will play a crucial role in ensuring that savers will save and invest their money in appropriate vehicles, regardless of whether the existing system of tax deductions stays in play or whether a newly created tax credit replaces it.

24. These withdrawal reasons are default reasons—that is, savers can withdraw money for these reasons—unless they contractually agree to a smaller set of withdrawal reasons. Savers could, for instance, agree to invest their money in life insurance annuities that pay a lifetime income upon retirement in exchange for giving up the opportunity to use their savings for medical expenses, education, and other specified reasons. These choices also include the choice to restrict one's options if savers value the associated benefits of the restrictions more than the restrictions.

25. Evidence from rules guiding 401(k) loans—an example of giving savers access to their money before retirement with some restrictions—suggests that some savers value having access to their savings before retirement and thus save more than they otherwise would have. But the evidence also indicates that policymakers may want to put in place some restrictions on such withdrawals to prevent financially less sophisticated households from saving too little. See Jeffrey Wenger and Christian Weller, "Boon or Bane: Loans and Employee Contributions," *Research on Aging* 36, no. 5 (July, 2014), 527–556.

26. Christian Weller, "Fun with Numbers: Disclosing Risk to Individual Investors," *Journal of Pension Benefits* (Spring 2011).

27. Ibid.

28. US Department of Labor, Employee Benefits Security Administration (EBSA), "Regulation Relating to Qualified Default Investment Alternatives in Participant-Directed Account Plans" (Washington, DC: EBSA, April 2008), http://www.dol.gov/ebsa/pdf/fsQDIA.pdf; US Department of Labor, Employee Benefits Security Administration (EBSA), "Field Assistance Bulletin No. 2008–03" (Washington, DC: EBSA, April 2008), http://www.dol.gov/ebsa/pdf/fab2008-3.pdf

29. For some discussion on default annuities in 401(k) plans, see William G. Gale, J. Mark Iwry, David C. John, and Lina Walker, "Increasing Annuitization in 401(k) Plans with Automatic Trial Income," RSP Paper No. 2008–2 (Washington, DC: The Retirement Security Project, 2008); J. Mark Iwry and John A. Turner, "Automatic Annuitization: New Behavioral Strategies for Expanding Lifetime Incomes in 401(k)s," RSP Paper No. 2009–2 (Washington, DC: The Retirement Security Project, 2009). For a discussion of the cognitive limitations individuals face when valuing annuities, which points to the role policy can play in encouraging annuitization, see Jeffrey R. Brown, Arie Kapteyn,

Erzo F. P. Luttmer, and Olivia S. Mitchell, "Are Cognitive Constraints a Barrier to Annuitization," Issue Brief No. 15–6 (Boston, MA: Center for Retirement Research at Boston College, 2015).

30. Christian E. Weller, "Making Sure Money Is Available When We Need It" (Washington, DC: Center for American Progress, 2013); Christian Weller and Kate Sabatini, "From Boom to Bust: Did the Financial Fragility of Homeowners Increase in an Era of Greater Financial Deregulation?" *Journal of Economic Issues* 42, no. 3 (2008), 607–632; Christian Weller and Sara Bernardo, "Aging with Risk: Has Financial Risk Exposure Grown Faster for Older Households Since the 1990s?" *Journal of Aging and Social Policy* (forthcoming).

31. Weller, "Making Sure Money Is Available When We Need It"; Weller and Sabatini, "From Boom to Bust"; Weller and Bernardo, "Aging with Risk."

32. See Will Fischer and Chye-Ching Huang, "Mortgage Interest Deduction Is Ripe for Reform: Conversion to Tax Credit Could Raise Revenue and Make Subsidy More Effective and Fairer" (Washington, DC: Center on Budget and Policy Priorities, 2013), http://www.cbpp.org/cms/?fa=view&id=3948; Altman et al., "Reforming Our Tax System, Reducing Our Deficit."

33. The exact credit rates would again depend on maximum credit amounts and whether the new system of credits for homeowners is supposed to be revenue-neutral relative to the current system of mortgage interest deductions.

34. Considering what we know about heuristics in financial decisions, most households will choose to make the minimum amount to get the higher credit, so that the minimum share of the credit that goes into a savings account has to be reasonably large to build substantial savings over time. For a discussion of heuristics in financial decisions, see Shlomo Bernartzi and Richard Thaler, "Heuristics and Biases in Retirement Savings Behavior," *Journal of Economic Perspectives* 21, no. 3 (Summer 2007), 81–104. For a summary of the evidence on so-called anchoring of complex financial decisions that inform some of the relevant heuristics, see Cass Sunstein and Richard Thaler, *Nudge: Improving Decisions about Health, Wealth, and Happiness* (London, UK: Penguin Books, 2009), 120–133.

BIBLIOGRAPHY

401(k) Help Center. "Highly Compensated Employee Rules Aim to Make 401k's Fair." Accessed December 30, 2014. http://www.401khelpcenter.com/mpower/feature_030702. html#.VKKqn2cBg

AARP Public Policy Institute. "State Retirement Savings Resource Center." Accessed May 5, 2015. http://www.aarp.org/ppi/state-retirement-plans/

Ahmad, Farah, and Christian Weller. "Reading between the Data: The Incomplete Story of Asian Americans, Native Hawaiians, and Pacific Islanders." Washington, DC: Center for American Progress, 2014.

Akerlof, George, and Robert J. Schiller. *Animal Spirits: How Human Psychology Drives the Economy and Why It Matters for Global Capitalism.* Princeton, NJ: Princeton University Press, 2010.

Almeida, Beth, and William B. Fornia. "A Better Bang for the Buck: The Economic Efficiencies of Defined Benefit Pension Plans." Washington, DC: National Institute on Retirement Security, 2008.

Altman, Rober, William Daley, John Podesta, Robert Rubin, Leslie Samuels, Lawrence Summers, Neera Tanden, and Antonio Weiss with Michael Ettlinger, Seth Hanlon, and Michael Linden. "Reforming Our Tax System, Reducing Our Deficit." Washington, DC: Center for American Progress, 2012.

American Associations of Retired Persons (AARP). "Retirement Security Survey Report." Washington, DC: AARP, 2007.

American Savings Promotion Act. H.R. 3374/P.L. 113–251, 113th Congress (2014).

Ameriks, John, and Stephen P. Utkus. "Vanguard Retirement Outlook 2006." Malvern, PA: Vanguard Center for Retirement Research, 2006.

An Act to Provide Retirement Savings Options for Nonprofit Organizations. H. 3754, 187th General Court of Massachusetts (2011–2012).

Argento, Robert, Victoria Bryant, and John Sabelhaus. "Early Withdrawals from Retirement Accounts during the Great Recession." Finance and Economics Discussion Series Working Paper 2013–2, Divisions of Research and Statistics and Monetary Affairs, Federal Reserve Board, 2013.

Ariel Investments. "The Ariel/Schwab Black Investor Survey: Saving and Investing among Higher Income African-American and White Americans." Chicago, IL: Ariel Investments, 2008.

Baker, Dean. "The Run-up in Home Prices: A Bubble." *Challenge* 45, no. 6 (2002): 93–119.

Baker, Dean, De Long J. Bradford, and Paul Krugman. "Asset Returns and Economic Growth." *Brookings Papers on Economic Activity* 2005, no. 1 (2005): 289–330. doi:10.1353/ eca.2005.0011

Baneman, Daniel, Hang Nguyen, Jeffrey Rohaly, and Eric Toder. "Options to Reform the Deduction for Home Mortgage Interest." Washington, DC: Urban-Brookings Tax Policy Center, 2011.

Barr, Nicholas. *The Economics of the Welfare State*. Oxford, UK: Oxford University Press, 2012.

Benartzi, Shlomo, Alessandro Previtero, and Richard Thaler. "Annuitization Puzzles." *The Journal of Economic Perspectives* 25, no. 4 (Fall 2011): 143–164.

Benartzi, Shlomo, and Richard Thaler. "Heuristics and Biases in Retirement Savings Behavior." *Journal of Economic Perspectives* 21, no. 3 (2007): 81–104.

Benjamin, Daniel J. "Does 401(k) Eligibility Increase Saving?" *Journal of Public Economics* 87, no. 5 (2003): 1259–1290.

Bernheim, B. Douglas. "The Adequacy of Personal Retirement Saving: Issues and Options." In *Facing the Age Wave*, edited by David A. Wise. Stanford, CA: Hoover Institute Press, 1997.

Bernheim, B. Douglas, and Antonio Rangel. "Behavioral Public Economics: Welfare and Policy Analysis with Non-Standard Decision Makers," NBER Working Paper No. 11518. Washington, DC: National Bureau of Economic Research, 2005.

Blanchflower, David G., and Andrew J. Oswald. "Does High Home-Ownership Impair the Labor Market?" NBER Working Paper No. 19079. Washington, DC: National Bureau of Economic Research, 2013.

Board of Governors (BOG), Federal Reserve System. "Release H.15 Selected Interest Rates, Historical Data." Washington, DC: BOG, 2014. http://www.federalreserve.gov/releases/h15/data.htm.

———. *Survey of Consumer Finances*. Washington, DC: BOG, various years.

———. *Survey of Consumer Finances—2013*. Washington, DC: BOG, 2014.

Boivie, Ilana. "Who Killed the Private Sector DB Plan?" Issue Brief. Washington, DC: National Institute on Retirement Security, March 2011.

Bosworth, Barry, and Kathleen Burke. "Differential Mortality and Retirement Benefits in The Health And Retirement Study." Washington, DC: Brookings Institution, 2013.

Brady, Peter. "The Tax Benefits and Revenue Costs of Tax Deferral." Washington, DC: Investment Company Institute, September 2012.

———. "Who Gets Retirement Plans and Why: An Update." *Investment Company Institute Research Perspective* 17, no. 3 (March 2011).

Brady, Peter, and Michael Bogdan. "Who Gets Retirement Plans and Why, 2013." *Investment Company Institute Research Perspective* 20, no. 6 (October 2014). http://www.ici.org/pdf/per20-06.pdf

Brandlee, Kelsie. "Promoting Homeownership in the United States: The Rise and Fall of Fannie Mae and Freddie Mac." Iowa City, IA: Center for International Finance and Development, University of Iowa, April 2011. http://www.freerepublic.com/focus/f-news/2915644/posts

Brooks, Jennifer, Kasey Wiedrich, Lebaron Sims Jr., and Solana Rice. "Excluded from the Financial Mainstream: How the Economic Recovery Is Bypassing Millions of Americans." Washington, DC: Corporation for Enterprise Development, 2015.

Browning, Martin, and Thomas F. Crossley. "The Life-Cycle Model of Consumption and Saving." *Journal of Economic Perspectives* 15, no. 3 (2001): 3–22. doi:10.1257/jep.15.3.3.

Browning, Martin, and Annamaria Lusardi. "Household Saving: Micro Theories and Macro Facts." *Journal of Economic Literature* 34, no. 4 (1996): 1797–1855.

Brown, Jeffrey R. "Rational and Behavioral Perspectives on the Role of Annuities in Retirement Planning." Working Paper No. w13536. Washington, DC: National Bureau of Economic Research, 2007. http://www.nber.org/papers/w13537.pdf

Brown, Jeffrey R., Arie Kapteyn, Erzo F.P. Luttmer, and Olivia S. Mitchell. "Are Cognitive Constraints a Barrier to Annuitization." Issue Brief No. 15–6. Boston, MA: Center for Retirement Research at Boston College, 2015.

Bureau of Economic Analysis (BEA). "National Income and Product Accounts." Washington, DC: BEA, 2014.

———. "National Income and Product Accounts (NIPA)." Washington, DC: BEA, 2014.

Bureau of Labor Statistics (BLS), Department of Labor. "Employee Cost Index (ECI)." Washington, DC: BLS, 2014.

———. "Duration of Unemployment, 1994–2010." *The Economics Daily*, June 2, 2011. http://www.bls.gov/opub/ted/2011/ted_20110602.htm

Burman, Len, and Joel Slemrod. "The Hidden Welfare State." In *Taxes in America: What Everyone Needs to Know*. New York, NY: Oxford University Press, 2013.

Burtless, Gary. "Social Security Privatization and Financial Market Risk." Washington, DC: Center on Social and Economic Dynamics, February 2000, quoted in Christian Weller, *Review of Policy Research* 23, no. 2 (2006): 531–548. doi:10.1111/j.1541–1338.2006.00214.x

Butrica, Barbara A., Sheila R. Zedlewski, and Philip Issa. "Understanding Early Withdrawals from Retirement Accounts." Discussion Paper 10–02. Washington, DC: The Urban Institute, 2010. http://www.urban.org/uploadedpdf/412107-early-withdrawals.pdf

Butrica, Barbara, Daniel Murphy, and Sheila Zedlewski. "How Many Struggle to Get by in Retirement?" *The Gerontologist* 50, no. 4 (2010): 482–494. doi:10.1093/geront/gnp158

Butrica, Barbara, Karen E. Smith, and Howard M. Iams. "This Is Not Your Parents' Retirement: Comparing Retirement Income across Generations." *Social Security Bulletin* 72, no. 1 (2012).

Campbell, John Y. "Household Finance." *The Journal of Finance* 61, no. 4 (2006): 1553–1604.

Campbell, John Y., and Robert J. Shiller. "Valuation Ratios and the Long-Run Stock Market Outlook." *The Journal of Portfolio Management* 24, no. 2 (1998): 11–26. doi:10.3905/jpm.24.2.11

———. "Valuation Ratios and the Long-Run Stock Market Outlook: An Update." NBER Working Paper No. 8221. Washington, DC: National Bureau of Economic Research, 2001.

Campbell, John Y., and Louis M. Viceira. "Long-Horizon Mean-Variance Analysis: A User Guide." Manuscript. Cambridge, MA: Harvard University, 2004.

Campbell, Richard T., and Cathie Mayes Hudson. "Synthetic Cohorts from Panel Surveys: An Approach to Studying Rare Events." *Research on Aging* 7, no. 1 (March 1985): 81–93.

Carr, James H., and Karen Annacker. "The Past and Current Politics of Housing Finance and the Future of Fannie Mae, Freddie Mac, and Homeownership in the United States." *Banking and Financial Services Report* 33, no. 7 (2012): 1–10.

Carroll, Christopher D., Karen E. Dynan, and Spencer D. Krane. "Unemployment Risk and Precautionary Wealth: Evidence from Households' Balance Sheets." *Review of Economics and Statistics* 85, no. 3 (2003): 586–604. doi:10.1162/003465303322369740

Case, Karl E., and John M. Quigley. "How Housing Booms Unwind: Income Effects, Wealth Effects, and Feedbacks through Financial Markets." *European Journal of Housing Policy* 8, no. 2 (2008): 161–180.

Case, Karl E., John M. Quigley, and Robert J. Shiller. "Home-Buyers, Housing and the Macroeconomy." In *Asset Prices and Monetary Policy*, edited by Anthony Richards and Tim Robinson, 149–188. Sydney, Australia: Reserve Bank of Australia, 2003.

Center for Retirement Research at Boston College. "Retirements at Risk: A New National Retirement Risk Index." Boston, MA: Center for Retirement Research at Boston College, 2006.

Chakrabarti, Rajashri, Donghoon Lee, Wilbert van der Klaauw, and Basit Zafar. "Household Debt and Saving during the 2007 Recession." Staff Reports. New York, NY: Federal Reserve Bank of New York, January 2011. http://www.newyorkfed.org/research/staff_reports/sr482.pdf

Chan, Sewin. "Spatial Lock-in: Do Falling House Prices Constrain Residential Mobility?" *Journal of Urban Economics* 49, no. 3 (2001): 567–586. doi:10.1006/juec.2000.2205

Clark, Robert L., Lee A. Craig, and John Sabelhaus. *State and Local Retirement Plans in the United States.* Northampton, MA: Edward Elgar Publishing, 2011.

Cocco, João F. "Portfolio Choice in the Presence of Housing." *The Review of Financial Studies* 18, no. 2 (2005): 535–567. doi:10.1093/rfs/hhi006

Collins, J. Michael, and Leah Gjertson. "Emergency Savings for Low-Income Consumers." Focus 30.1. Madison, WI: University of Wisconsin–Madison, Institute for Research on Poverty, n.d.

Collison, Catherine. "The Retirement Readiness of Three Unique Generations: Baby Boomers, Generation X, and Millennials." Transamerica Center for Retirement Studies, April 2014. http://www.transamericacenter.org/docs/default-source/resources/center-research/tcrs2014_sr_three_unique_generations.pdf

Congressional Budget Office (CBO). "Housing Wealth and Consumer Spending." Washington, DC: CBO, 2007.

———. "The Distribution of Major Tax Expenditures in the Individual Tax System." Washington, DC: CBO, 2013. http://www.cbo.gov/sites/default/files/43768_Distribution-TaxExpenditures.pdf

———. "Will the Demand for Assets Fall When Baby Boomers Retire?" Washington, DC: CBO, September 2009. http://www.cbo.gov/sites/default/files/09-08_baby-boomers.pdf

Copeland, Craig. "Employment-Based Plan Participation: Geographic Differences and Trends, 2012." EBRI Issue Brief No. 392. Washington, DC: Employee Benefits Research Institute, 2013. http://www.ebri.org/publications/ib/index.cfm?fa=ibDisp&content_id=5292

———. "Employment-Based Plan Participation: Geographic Differences and Trends, 2013." EBRI Issue Brief No. 405. Washington, DC: Employee Benefits Research Institute, 2014. http://www.ebri.org/publications/ib/index.cfm?fa=ibDisp&content_id=5292

———. "Employment-Based Retirement Plan Participation: Geographic Differences and Trends, 2013." EBRI Issue Brief. Washington, DC: Employee Benefits Research Institute, 2014.

Corporation for Enterprise Development. "Liquid Asset Poverty Rate." *Assets & Opportunity Scorecard.* Accessed March 11, 2015. http://scorecard.assetsandopportunity.org/latest/measure/liquid-asset-poverty-rate

Daly, Mary C., Bart Hobijn, Ayşcegül Sahin, and Robert G. Valletta. "A Search and Matching Approach to Labor Markets: Did the Natural Rate of Unemployment Rise?" *The Journal of Economic Perspectives* 26, no. 2 (2012): 3–26.

Davis, Rowland, and David Madland. "American Retirement Savings Could Be Much Better." Washington, DC: Center for American Progress, 2013.

Debelle, Guy. "Macroeconomic Implications of Rising Household Debt." BIS Working Paper No. 153. Basel, Switzerland: Bank for International Settlements, 2004.

DellaVigna, Stafano. "Psychology and Economics: Evidence from the Field." *Journal of Economic Literature* 47, no. 2 (2009): 315–372. doi:10.1257/jel.47.2.315

Democracy Corps and Campaign for America's Future and Greenberg Quinlan Rosner Research. "Polling Results." 2008.

Diamond, Peter A., and Peter R. Orszag. *Saving Social Security: A Balanced Approach.* Washington, DC: Brookings Institution Press, 2005.

Domenici, Pete, and Alice Rivlin. "Restoring America's Future: Reviving the Economy, Cutting Spending and Debt, and Creating a Simple, Pro-Growth Tax System." Washington, DC: Bipartisan Policy Center, 2011.

Domian, Dale L., and David A. Louton. "Business Cycle Asymmetry and the Stock Market." *The Quarterly Review of Economics and Finance* 35, no. 4 (Winter 1995): 451–466.

Drew, Rachel, and Christian Weller. "A Safe Investment? Assessing Economic Explanations for the Perceived Risk-Return Trade-off of Owner-Occupied Housing in the United States." Paper presented at the Eastern Economic Association Annual Conference, 2014.

Dröes, Martijn I., and Wolter H. J. Hassink. "Sale Price Risk of Homeowners." Utretch, the Netherlands: Utrecht School of Economics, 2009.

Dunsky, Robert M., and James R. Follain. "Tax-Induced Portfolio Reshuffling: The Case of the Mortgage Interest Deduction." *Real Estate Economics* 28, no. 4 (2000): 683–718.

Dushi, Irena, and Howard Iams. "The Impact of Employment and Earnings Shocks on Contribution Behavior in Defined Contribution Plans: 2005–2009." *Journal of Retirement* 4, no. 2 (2015): 86–104.

Dynan, Karen, Douglas Elmendorf, and Daniel Sichel. "The Evolution of Household Income Volatility." Working Paper, Washington, DC: Brookings Institution, 2012.

Dynarski, Susan, Jonathan Gruber, Robert A. Moffitt, and Gary Burtless. "Can Families Smooth Variable Earnings?" *Brookings Papers on Economic Activity* 1997, no. 1 (2009): 229–303.

Ellis, Charles, Alicia Munnell, and Andrew Eschtruth. *Falling Short: The Coming Retirement Crisis and What to Do about It.* New York, NY: Oxford University Press, 2014.

Employee Benefit Security Administration (EBSA), Department of Labor. "Private Pension Bulletin, Abstract of Form 5500—Historical Tables." Washington, DC: EBSA, 2014.

Employee Benefits Research Institute (EBRI). "Retirement Confidence Survey." Washington, DC: EBRI, various years. http://www.ebri.org/surveys/rcs/

Engen, Eric M., and William G. Gale. "The Effects of 401(k) Plans on Household Wealth." Washington, DC: National Bureau of Economic Research, 2000.

Engen, Eric M., William Gale, and Cori E. Uccello. "The Adequacy of Household Saving." *Brookings Papers on Economic Activity* 1999, no. 2 (1999): 65–165.

Engen, Eric M., and Jonathan Gruber. "Unemployment Insurance and Precautionary Saving." *Journal of Monetary Economics* 47, no. 3 (2001): 545–579.

Englund, Peter, Ming Hwang, and John M. Quigley. "Hedging Housing Risk." *Journal of Real Estate Finance and Economics* 24, no. 1/2 (2002): 167–200.

Epsing-Anderson, Gøsta. *The Three Worlds of Welfare Capitalism.* Princeton, NJ: Princeton University Press, 1990.

Erickson, Jennifer, and David Madland. "Fixing the Drain on Retirement Savings: How Retirement Fees Are Straining the Middle Class and What We Can Do about Them." Washington, DC: Center for American Progress, April 2014.

Fama, Eugene, and Kenneth R. French. "Permanent and Temporary Components of Stock Prices." *Journal of Political Economy* 96, no. 2 (1988): 246–73.

Family and Medical Insurance Leave Act of 2013. HR 3712, 113th Cong. (2013–2014).

Farrell, Jane, and Sarah Jane Glynn. "The FAMILY Act: Facts and Frequently Asked Questions." Washington, DC: Center for American Progress, 2013.

Feinstein, Craig. "Diminishing Effect of the Special Minimum PIA." Actuarial Note No. 154. Baltimore. MD: Social Security Administration, November 2013.

Fidelity Brokerage Services. "How Much Do You Need to Retire?" Fidelity Viewpoints. Smithfield, RI: Fidelity Brokerage Services, January 30, 2014. https://www.fidelity.com/viewpoints/retirement/8X-retirement-savings

FINRA Investor Education Foundation. "Financial Capability in the United States, Report of Findings from the 2012 National Financial Capability Study." Washington, DC: FIRNA Investor Education Foundation, May 2013.

Fischer, Stanley, and Robert C. Merton. "Macroeconomics and Finance: The Role of the Stock Market." Carnegie-Rochester Conference Series on Public Policy 21, 1984.

Fischer, Will, and Chye-Ching Huang. "Mortgage Interest Deduction Is Ripe for Reform: Conversion to Tax Credit Could Raise Revenue and Make Subsidy More Effective and Fairer." Washington, DC: Center on Budget and Policy Priorities, 2013. http://www.cbpp.org/cms/?fa=view&id=3948

Furman, Jason. "How Would the President's New Social Security Proposal Affect Middle-Class Workers and Social Security Solvency." Washington, DC: Center for Budget and Policy Priorities, 2005.

Gale, William G. "A Proposal to Restructure Retirement Saving Incentives in a Weak Economy with Long-Term Deficits." Washington, DC: Urban-Brookings Tax Policy Center, 2011. http://www.brookings.edu/~/media/research/files/papers/2011/9/08 retirement incentives gale/0908_retirement_incentives_gale.pdf

Gale, William G., J. Mark Iwry, David C. John, and Lina Walker. "Increasing Annuitization in 401(k) Plans with Automatic Trial Income." RSP Paper No. 2008–2. Washington, DC: The Retirement Security Project, 2008.

Gale, William G., John Carl Scholz, and Ananth Seshadri. "Are All Americans Saving 'Optimally' for Retirement?" Working Paper. Washington, DC: Brookings Institution, 2009.

Gallup. "Social Security." Washington, DC: Gallup, Inc., 2014. http://www.gallup.com/poll/1693/social-security.aspx

Georgetown University Center for Retirement Initiatives. "Look to the States for Innovation." Accessed May 6, 2015. http://cri.georgetown.edu/states/

Ghilarducci, Teresa. "Guaranteed Retirement Accounts: Toward Retirement Income Security." EPI Briefing Paper. Washington, DC: Economic Policy Institute, 2007.

———. *When I'm Sixty-Four: The Plot against Pensions and the Plan to Save Them.* Princeton, NJ: Princeton University Press, 2008.

Ghilarducci, Teresa, Robert Hiltonsmith, and Lauren Schmitz. "State Guaranteed Retirement Accounts." Working Paper. New York, NY: Demos, Schwartz Center for Economic Policy Analysis, The New School, 2012.

Goss, Stephen C. "Strengthening Social Security to Meet the Needs of Tomorrow's Retirees." Testimony before the Subcommittee on Social Security, Pensions, and Family Policy of the Senate Committee on Finance, May 21, 2014.

Gould, Elise. "2014 Continues a 35-Year Trend of Broad-Based Wage Stagnation." EPI Issue Brief. Washington, DC: Economic Policy Institute, 2015.

Grande, Giuseppe, and Luigi Ventura. "Labor Income and Risky Assets under Market Incompleteness: Evidence from Italian Data." *Journal of Banking and Finance* 26, no. 2 (2002): 597–620. doi:10.1016/S0378-4266(01)00236-9

Grinstein-Weiss, Michal, Michael Sherraden, William Gale, William Rohe, and Mark Schreiner. "Effects of an Individual Development Account Program on Retirement Saving: Follow-up Evidence from a Randomized Experiment." CSD Working Papers No. 12–54. St. Louis, MO: Center for Social Development, Washington University, 2012.

Grinstein-Weiss, Michal, Michael Sherraden, William Rohe, William Gale, Mark Schreiner, and Clinton Key. "Long-Term Follow-up of Individual Development Accounts: Evidence from the ADD Experiment." CSD Report 12–43. St. Louis, MO: Center for Social Development, Washington University, 2012.

Gross, David B., and Nicholas Souleles. "Do Liquidity Constraints and Interest Rates Matter for Consumer Behavior? Evidence from Credit Card Data." *The Quarterly Journal of Economics* 117, no. 1 (2002): 149–185. doi:10.1162/003355302753399472

Gruenstein Bocian, Debbie, Wei Li, and Keith S. Ernst. "Foreclosures by Race and Ethnicity: The Demographics of a Crisis." CRL Research Report. Washington, DC: Center for Responsible Lending, June 2010.

Guiso, Luigi, Tullio Jappelli, and Daniele Terlizzese. "Income Risk, Borrowing Constraints, and Portfolio Choice." *The American Economic Review* 86, no. 1 (1996): 158–172.

Gustman, Alan L., and Thomas L. Steinmeier. "Effects of Pensions on Savings: Analysis with Data from the Health and Retirement Study." *Carnegie-Rochester Conference Series on Public Policy* 50, no. 1 (1999): 271–324.

Gyourko, Joseph, and Joseph Tracy. "Reconciling Theory and Empirics on the Role of Unemployment in Mortgage Default." *Journal of Urban Economics* 80 (March 2014): 87–96.

Hacker, Jacob S. *The Great Risk Shift: The New Economic Insecurity and the Decline of the American Dream*. New York, NY: Oxford University Press, 2008.

Harris, Benjamin H. "Tax Reform, Transaction Costs, and Metropolitan Housing in the United States." State and Local Finance Initiative. Washington, DC: Tax Policy Center, Urban Institute and Brookings Institution, 2013.

Haveman, Robert, Karen Holden, Barbara Wolfe, and Andrei Romanov. "Assessing the Maintenance of Savings Sufficiency over the First Decade of Retirement." Working Paper No. 1567. München, Germany: CESIfo, 2005.

Heidkamp, Maria, William Mabe, and Barbara DeGraaf. "The Public Workforce System: Serving Older Job Seekers and the Disability Implications of an Aging Workforce." NTAR Leadership Center Report. New Brunswick, NJ: John J. Heldrich Center for Workforce Development, 2012.

Helman, Ruth, Nevin Adams, and Jack VanDerhei. "The 2014 Retirement Confidence Survey: Confidence Rebounds—for Those with Retirement Plans." EBRI Issue Brief No. 397. Washington, DC: Employee Benefits Research Institute, 2014.

Henle, Peter. "Recent Trends in Retirement Benefits Related to Earnings." *Monthly Labor Review* 95, no. 6 (1972): 12–20.

Hewitt Associates. "Research Highlights: Trends and Experience in 401(k) Plans." Lincolnshire, IL: Hewitt Associates, LLC, 2009. http://www.aon.com/attachments/thought-leadership/Hewitt_Research_Trends_in_401k_Highlights.pdf

Holden, Sarah, Peter Brady, and Michael Hadley. "401(k) Plans: A 25-Year Retrospective." *Investment Company Institute Research Perspective* 12, no. 2 (November 2006).

Horney, James, and Richard Kogan. "Private Accounts Would Substantially Increase Federal Debt and Interest Payments." Washington, DC: Center for Budget and Policy Priorities, 2005.

Internal Revenue Service (IRS). "401(k) Resource Guide—Plan Sponsors—401(k) Plan Overview." Washington, DC: IRS, 2014. http://www.irs.gov/Retirement-Plans/Plan-Sponsor/401k-Resource-Guide-Plan-Sponsors-401k-Plan-Overview

———. "1040 Tax Tables 2014." Washington, DC: IRS, 2014. http://www.irs.gov/pub/irs-pdf/i1040tt.pdf

———. "COLA Increases for Dollar Limitations on Benefits and Contributions." Washington, DC: IRS, 2014. http://www.irs.gov/Retirement-Plans/COLA-Increases-for-Dollar-Limitations-on-Benefits-and-Contributions

———. "Employer 'Pick-Up' Contributions to Benefit Plans." *IRS.gov*, April 1, 2014. http://www.irs.gov/Government-Entities/Federal,-State-&-Local-Governments/Employer-Pick-Up-Contributions-to-Benefit-Plans

———. "Exemptions, Standard Deduction, and Filing Information." Washington, DC: IRS, 2014. http://www.irs.gov/publications/p501/

———. "Government Retirement Plans Toolkit." Washington, DC: IRS, 2014. http://www.irs.gov/Government-Entities/Federal,-State-&-Local-Governments/Government-Retirement-Plans-Toolkit

———. "Retirement Plans FAQs Regarding Hardship Distributions." *IRS.gov*, March 2, 2015. http://www.irs.gov/Retirement-Plans/Retirement-Plans-FAQs-regarding-Hardship-Distributions#7

———. "Retirement Topic—Required Minimum Distributions." *IRS.gov*, January 26, 2015. http://www.irs.gov/Retirement-Plans/Plan-Participant,-Employee/Retirement-Topics-Required-Minimum-Distributions-%28RMDs%29

———. "Retirement Topics—401(k) and Profit-Sharing Plan Contribution Limits." Washington, DC: IRS, 2014. http://www.irs.gov/Retirement-Plans/Plan-Participant,-Employee/Retirement-Topics-401k-and-Profit-Sharing-Plan-Contribution-Limits

———. "Topic 558—Additional Tax on Early Distributions from Retirement Plans Other than IRAs." *IRS.gov*, January 29, 2015. http://www.irs.gov/taxtopics/tc558.html

Iwry, J. Mark, and David C. John. "Pursuing Universal Retirement Security through Automatic IRAs." Washington, DC: The Retirement Security Project, 2009.

Iwry, J. Mark, and John A. Turner. "Automatic Annuitization: New Behavioral Strategies for Expanding Lifetime Incomes in 401(k)s." RSP Paper No. 20092. Washington, DC: The Retirement Security Project, 2009.

Jefferson, Regina T. "Rethinking the Risk of Defined Contribution Plans." *Florida Tax Review* 4, no. 9 (2000): 607–683.

Johnson, Richard, Usha Sambamoorthi, and Stephen Crystal. "Pension Wealth at Midlife: Comparing Self-Reports with Provider Data." *Review of Income and Wealth* 46, no. 1 (2000): 59–83. doi:10.1111/j.1475–4991.2000.tb00391.x

Joint Center for Housing Studies of Harvard University (JCHS). "The State of the Nation's Housing, 2014." Cambridge, MA: JCHS, 2014. http://www.jchs.harvard.edu/sites/jchs.harvard.edu/files/sonhr14-color-full.pdf

Kawachi, Janette, Karen E. Smith, and Eric J. Toder. "Making Maximum Use of Tax-Deferred Retirement Accounts." Washington, DC: The Urban Institute, 2005.

Kimball, Miles S. "Standard Risk Aversion." *Econometrica: Journal of the Econometric Society* 61, no. 3 (1993): 589–611.

Kochhar, Rakesh, Ana Gonzalez-Barrera, and Daniel Dockterman. "Through the Boom and Bust: Minorities, Immigrants, and Homeownership." Washington, DC: Pew Hispanic Center, May 2009. www.pewhispanic.org/files/reports/109.pdf

Lachance, Marie-Eve, Olivia S. Mitchell, and Kent Smetters. "Guaranteeing Defined Contribution Pensions: The Option to Buy Back a Defined Benefit Promise." *Journal of Risk and Insurance* 40, no. 1 (2003): 1–16. doi:10.1111/1539–6975.00044

Lazonick, William. "Labor in the Twenty-First Century: The Top 0.1% and the Disappearing Middle Class." In *Inequality, Uncertainty and Opportunity: The Varied and Growing Role of Finance in Labor Relations*, edited by Christian E. Weller. Ithaca, NY: Cornell University Press, 2015.

Leamer, Edward E. "Housing in the Business Cycle." NBER Working Paper No. w13428, Washington, DC: National Bureau of Economic Research, 2007.

Lichtenstein, Jules, and John Turner. "Cash Balance Pension Plans and Older Workers." Washington, DC: AARP Public Policy Institute, October 2005. http://assets.aarp.org/rgcenter/econ/ib78_pension.pdf

Li, Geng, and Paul Smith. "Borrowing from Yourself: 401(k) Loans and Household Balance Sheets." Finance and Economics Discussion Series Working Paper 2008–42. Washington,

DC: Divisions of Research and Statistics and Monetary Affairs, Federal Reserve Board, 2008.

Love, David. "What Can the Life Cycle Model Tell Us about 401(k) Contributions and Participation." Williamstown, MA: Williams College, 2006. http://projects.vassar.edu/lamacro/web/Love.pdf

Love, David, Paul Smith, and Lucy McNair. "A New Look at the Wealth Adequacy of Older U.S. Households." *Review of Income and Wealth* 54, no. 4 (2008): 616–642.

Lusardi, Annamaria, and Olivia Mitchell. "Financial Literacy and Retirement Preparedness: Evidence and Implications for Financial Education Programs." CFS Working Paper No. 2007/15. Frankfurt, Germany: Center for Financial Studies, Goethe University Frankfurt, 2007. http://www.econstor.eu/bitstream/10419/2551 6/1/527633305.pdf

Lusardi, Annamaria, and Olivia S. Mitchell. "Financial Literacy and Planning: Implications for Retirement Wellbeing." Hanover, NH: Dartmouth College, 2006.

Majerol, Melissa, Vann Newkirk, and Rachel Garfield. "The Uninsured: A Primer—Key Facts about Health Insurance and the Uninsured in America." Washington, DC: Kaiser Family Foundation, January 2015.

Malley, Jim, and Thomas Moutos. "Unemployment and Consumption." *Oxford Economic Papers* 48, no. 4 (1996): 584–600.

Manconi, Alberto, Massimo Massa, and Ayako Yasuda. "The Role of Institutional Investors in Propagating the Crisis of 2007–2008." *Journal of Financial Economics* 104, no. 3 (June 2012): 491–518.

Markowitz, Harry M. *Portfolio Selection: Efficient Diversification of Investments.* Vol. 16. New Haven, CT: Yale University Press, 1970.

Matthew Greenwald & Associates, Inc. "2013 Risks and Process of Retirement Survey Report of Findings." Schaumburg, IL: Society of Actuaries, 2013. https://www.soa.org/retirementneedsandrisks/

Mattola, Gary R. "Softening the Blow: Income Shocks, Mortgage Payments and Emergency Saving." Insights: American Financial Capability. Washington, DC: FIRNA Investor Education Foundation, March 2013.

Mattola, Gary R., and Stephen P. Utkus. "Can There Be Too Much Choice in a Retirement Savings Plan?" Valley Forge, PA: Vanguard Center for Retirement Research, 2006.

MBM Advisors, Inc. "FAQ: Automatic Enrollment Safe Harbor 401(k)." Houston, TX: MBM Advisors, 2014. http://www.mbm-inc.com/pdfs/2013%20FAQ%20Automatic%20 Enrollment%20Safe%20Harbor%20401%28k%29.pdf

Meyer, Richard, and Kenneth Wieand. "Risk and Return to Housing, Tenure Choice and the Value of Housing in an Asset Pricing Context." *Real Estate Economics* 24, no. 1 (2002): 113–131. doi:10.1111/1540–6229.00683

Mian, Atif R., and Amir Sufi. "House Prices, Home Equity-Based Borrowing, and the U.S. Household Leverage Crisis." *American Economic Review* 101, no. 5 (2011): 2132–2156.

Miller, Billie Jean, and Sylvester J. Schieber. "Employer Plans, IRAs and Retirement Income Provision: Making a Molehill out of a Mountain." Towers Watson Insider. New York, NY: Towers Watson, 2013.

Miller, Keith, David Madland, and Christian Weller. "The Reality of the Retirement Crisis." CAP Issue Brief. Washington, DC: Center for American Progress, 2015.

Mishkin, Frederic S., and Atruro Estrella. "Predicting U.S. Recessions: Financial Variables as Leading Indicators." NBER Working Paper No. 5378, Washington, DC: National Bureau of Economic Research, 1995.

Mitchell, Olivia S., Gary Mottola, Stephen P. Utkus, and Takeshi Yamaguchi. "The Inattentive Participant: Portfolio Trading Behavior in 401(k) Plans." Working Paper 115. Ann Arbor, MI: University of Michigan, Retirement Research Center, 2006.

Mondragon-Velez, Camilo. "How Does Middle-Class Financial Health Affect Entrepreneurship in America?" Washington, DC: Center for American Progress, May 2015.

Moore, James F., and Olivia S. Mitchell. "Projected Retirement Wealth and Saving Adequacy." In *Forecasting Retirement Needs and Retirement Wealth*, edited by Olivia S. Mitchell, P. Brett Hammond, and Anna M. Rappaport. Philadelphia, PA: University of Pennsylvania Press, 2000.

Morrissey, Monique. "Beyond 'Normal' Raising the Retirement Age Is the Wrong Approach for Social Security." EPI Briefing Paper. Washington, DC: Economic Policy Institute, 2011.

Morse, David E. "Retirement Saving Policy: The Impact of ERISA on State-Sponsored Plan Designs." Washington, DC: AARP Public Policy Institute, 2014.

———. "State Initiatives to Expand the Availability and Effectiveness of Private Sector Retirement Plans." Washington, DC: Center for Retirement Initiatives, Georgetown University, 2014.

Mottola, Gary R. "The Financial Capability of Young Adults—A Generational View." Washington, DC: FIRNA Investor Education Foundation, March 2014. http://www.usfinancialcapability.org/downloads/FinancialCapabilityofYoungAdults.pdf

Munnell, Alicia, Francesca Golub-Sass, and Anthony Webb. "What Moves the National Retirement Risk Index? A Look Back and an Update." Issue Brief No. 7-1. Boston, MA: Center for Retirement Research at Boston College, 2007.

Munnell, Alicia H., and Matthew S. Rutledge. "Are Retirees Falling Short? Reconciling the Conflicting Evidence." CRR Working Paper 2014–16. Boston, MA: Center for Retirement Research at Boston College, 2014.

Munnell, Alicia, Wenliang Hu, and Anthony Webb. "NRRI Update Shows Half Still Falling Short." Boston, MA: Center for Retirement Research at Boston College, 2014.

Munnell, Alicia, and Mauricio Soto. "State and Local Pensions Are Different from Private Plans." State and Local Pension Plans. Boston, MA: Center for Retirement Research at Boston College, 2007.

Munnell, Alicia, and Annika Sunden. *Coming Up Short: The Challenges of 401(k) Plans.* Washington, DC: Brookings Institution Press, 2004.

National Academy of Social Insurance (NASI). "Americans Make Hard Choices: A Survey with Trade-off Analysis." Washington, DC: NASI, 2014. http://www.nasi.org/sites/default/files/research/Americans_Make_Hard_Choices_on_Social_Security.pdf

National Bureau of Economic Research (NBER). "Business Cycle Dates." Washington, DC: NBER, 2014. http://www.nber.org/cycles.html

National Commission on Fiscal Responsibility and Reform. "The Moment of Truth." 2010.

National Institute on Retirement Security. *Retirement Security 2015: Roadmap for Policy Makers: Americans' Views of the Retirement Crisis.* Biennial public opinion research conducted by the National Institute on Retirement Security and Greenwald & Associates, March 2015.

New York Times and *CBS News.* "The New York Times—CBS News Poll," June 17, 2005.

Oakley, Diane, and Kelly Kenneally. "Retirement Security 2015: Roadmap for Policy Makers." Washington, DC: National Institute on Retirement Security, March 2015.

Organisation for Economic Cooperation and Development (OECD). "Social Expenditure Update—Social Spending Is Falling in Some Countries, but in Many Others It Remains at Historically High Levels." Paris, France: OECD, November 2014.

Ortman, Jennifer M., Victoria A. Velkoff, and Howard Hogan. "An Aging Nation: The Older Population in the United States. Population Estimates and Projections." Current Population Reports. Washington, DC: US Census Bureau, 2014. http://www.census.gov/prod/2014pubs/p25-1140.pdf

Pension Protection Act of 2006. H.R. 4/P.L. 109–280, 109th Congress (2006).

Pension Rights Center. "State-Based Retirement Plans for the Private Sector." Fact Sheet. Washington, DC: Pension Rights Center, 2014. http://www.pensionrights.org/issues/legislation/state-based-retirement-plans-private-sector

Perun, Pamela, and C. Eugene Steuerle. "Reality Testing for Pension Reform." Philadelphia, PA: Pension Research Council, 2004.

Polling Reports Inc. "Social Security." *PollingReport.com.* Accessed September 22, 2014. http://www.pollingreport.com/social.htm

Porter, Katherine. "The Damage of Debt." *Washington and Lee Law Review* 69, no. 2 (2012): 979–1022.

Poterba, James M. "Stock Market Wealth and Consumption." *The Journal of Economic Perspectives* 14, no. 2 (2000): 99–118.

Poterba, James M., and Lawrence H. Summers. "Mean Reversion in Stock Prices: Evidence and Implications." *Journal of Financial Economics* 22, no. 1 (1988): 27–59. doi:10.1016/0304–405X(88)90021–9.

Poterba, James M., Steven F. Venti, and David A. Wise. "401(k) Plans and Future Patterns of Retirement Saving." *The American Economic Review.* Papers and proceedings of the Hundred and Tenth Annual Meeting of the American Economic Association, 88, no. 2 (May 1998): 179–184.

Proctor, Bernadette D., and Carmen DeNavas-Walt. "Income and Poverty in the United States: 2013." Current Population Reports. Washington, DC: US Census Bureau, September 2014.

Redfoot, Donald L., Ken Scholen, and S. Kathi Brown. "Reverse Mortgages: Niche Product or Mainstream Solution? Report on the 2006 AARP National Survey of Reverse Mortgage Shoppers." Washington, DC: AARP Public Policy Institute, 2007. http://assets.aarp.org/rgcenter/consume/2007_22_revmortgage.pdf

Renzetti, Claire M. "Economic Stress and Domestic Violence." Harrisburg, PA: VAWnet, a project of the National Resource Center on Domestic Violence, September 2009.

RETIRE Project. "2001 RETIRE Project Report." Atlanta, GA: Georgia State University, 2001.

Retirement and Income Security Enhancement (RAISE) Act. S. 2455, 113th Congress (2013–2014).

"Retirement Security 2015: Roadmap for Policy Makers | Americans' Views of the Retirement Crisis." Biennial public opinion research conducted by the National Institute on Retirement Security and Greenwald & Associates, March 2015.

Rhee, Nari. "The Retirement Savings Crisis: Is It Worse than We Think?" Washington, DC: National Institute on Retirement Security, 2013.

Rohe, William M., and Mark Lindblad. "Reexamining the Social Benefits of Homeownership after the Housing Crisis." Working Paper HBTL-04. Cambridge, MA: Joint Center for Housing Studies, Harvard University, 2013.

Rothstein, Jesse. "Unemployment Insurance and Job Search in the Great Recession." NBER Working Paper No. 17534. Washington, DC: National Bureau of Economic Research, 2011.

Russell, Laura H., Ellen A. Bruce, and Judith Conahan. "A Methodology to Determine Economic Security for Elders." Boston, MA: University of Massachusetts, 2006, and Washington, DC: Wider Opportunities for Women, 2006.

Schmitt, John. "Low-Wage Lessons." Washington, DC: Center for Economic and Policy Research, January 2012.

Scholz, John Carl, Ananth Seshadri, and Surachai Khitatakrun. "Are Americans Saving 'Optimally' for Retirement?" *Journal of Political Economy* 114, no. 4 (2006): 607–643.

Scism, Leslie. "Insurance Fees, Revealed." *The Wall Street Journal*, March 30, 2012. http://online.wsj.com

Seligman, Jason S., and Jeffrey B. Wenger. "Asynchronous Risk: Retirement Savings, Equity Markets, and Unemployment." *Journal of Pension Economics and Finance* 5, no. 3 (2006): 237–255. doi:10.1017/S1474747206002630

Sethi-Iyengar, Sheena, Gur Huberman, and Wei Jiang. "How Much Choice Is Too Much? Contributions to 401(k) Retirement Plans." In *Pension Design and Structure: New Lessons from Behavioral Finance*, edited by Olivia S. Mitchell and Stephen P. Utkus. New York, NY: Oxford University Press, 2004.

Shiller, Robert J. "Historic Turning Points in Real Estate." *Eastern Economic Journal* 34, no. 1 (Winter 2008): 1–13.

Shiller, Robert J. "Irrational Exuberance—IrrationalExuberance.com." New Haven, CT: Yale University, 2014. Accessed November 6, 2014. http://www.irrationalexuberance.com

Sinai, Todd, and Nicholas Souleles. "Owner-Occupied Housing as a Hedge against Rent Risk." *The Quarterly Journal of Economics* 120, no. 2 (May 2005): 763–789.

Skinner, Jonathan. "Are You Sure You're Saving Enough for Retirement." *The Journal of Economic Perspectives* 21, no. 3 (2007): 59–80.

Smith, Karen, Mauricio Soto, and Rudolph G. Penner. "How Seniors Change Their Asset Holdings During Retirement." Washington, DC: The Urban Institute, August 10, 2009. http://www.nber.org/2009rrc/3.1 Smith, Soto, Penner.pdf

Social Security Administration (SSA). "Actuarial Publications, Provisions Affecting Family Member Benefits, D4." *Social Security Online.* Accessed May 5, 2015. http://www.ssa.gov/oact/solvency/provisions/familyMembers.html

———. "Actuarial Publications, Provisions Affecting Level of Monthly Benefits, B5.2." *Social Security Online.* Accessed May 5, 2015. http://www.ssa.gov/OACT/solvency/provisions/benefitlevel.html

———. "Actuarial Publications, Provisions Affecting Level of Monthly Benefits, B6.2." *Social Security Online.* Accessed May 5, 2015. http://www.ssa.gov/OACT/solvency/provisions/benefitlevel.html

———. "Actuarial Publications, Provisions Affecting Payroll Taxes, E2.8." *Social Security Online.* Accessed May 5, 2015. http://www.ssa.gov/oact/solvency/provisions/payrolltax.html

———. "Annual Statistical Supplement 2013." Washington, DC: SSA, 2013.

———. "Annual Statistical Supplement to the Social Security Bulletin, 2013, Tables 4-B1 and 4-B4." Washington, DC: SSA, February 2014.

———. "Benefit Planner: Maximum Table Earnings, 1937 to 2015." *Social Security Online.* Accessed May 18, 2015. http://www.socialsecurity.gov/planners/maxtax.html

———. "Benefits Planner: Maximum Taxable Earnings (1937–2015)." *Social Security Online.* Accessed May 5, 2015. http://www.ssa.gov/planners/maxtax.html

———. "Benefit Types and Levels, Annual Statistical Supplement, 2014, Tables 2.A20–2.A28." Washington, DC: SSA, 2014.

———. "Early or Late Retirement." *Social Security Online.* Accessed September 16, 2014. http://www.socialsecurity.gov/OACT/quickcalc/early_late.html

———. "Estimated Financial Effects of Title IV of The Roadmap for America's Future Act of 2010." Washington, DC: SSA, 2010.

———. "Income of the Population 55 or Older, 2012." Washington, DC: SSA, 2014.

———. "Monthly Statistical Snapshot—August 2014." Washington, DC: SSA, 2014.

———. "Program Explainers: Special Minimum Benefit." Washington, DC: SSA, May 2014.

———. "Retirement Benefits." Washington, DC: SSA, January 2015. http://www.ssa.gov/pubs/EN-05-10035.pdf

———. "Survivors Benefits." Washington, DC: SSA, July 2013.

———. "The 2014 Annual Report of the Board of Trustees of the Federal Old-Age and Survivors Insurance and Federal Disability Insurance Trust Funds." House Document 113–139, 113th Congress, Second Session, 2014.

———. "The 2013 Annual Report of the Board of Trustees of the Federal Old-Age and Survivors Insurance and Federal Disability Insurance Trust Funds, Supplemental Single Years Tables." Accessed October 6, 2014, http://www.ssa.gov/oact/tr/2013/lrIndex.html

Social Security Amendments of 1983. H.R. 1900/P.L. 98–21, 98th Congress (1983).

Sprague, Aleta. "The California Secure Choice Retirement Savings Program." Washington, DC: New America Foundation, 2013.

Starr-McCluer, Martha. "Health Insurance and Precautionary Savings." *The American Economic Review* 86, no. 1 (1996): 285–295.

Sterk, Stewart E., and Melanie B. Leslie. "Accidental Inheritance: Retirement Accounts and the Hidden Law of Succession." *New York University Law Review* 89 (2014): 165–237.

Stiglitz, Joseph. *The Price of Inequality: How Today's Divided Society Endangers Our Future*. New York, NY: W.W. Norton & Company Inc., 2013.

Strango, Victor. "The Tax Reform Act of 1986 and the Composition of Consumer Debt." *National Tax Journal* 52, no. 4 (1999): 717–739.

Sunstein, Cass, and Richard Thaler. *Nudge: Improving Decisions about Health, Wealth, and Happiness*. London, UK: Penguin Books, 2009.

Tang, Fengyan, and Jeffrey A. Burr. "Revisiting the Pathways to Retirement: A Latent Structure Model of the Dynamics of Late-Life Labor Force Behavior." *Ageing and Society* (forthcoming). doi:10.1017/S0144686X14000634

Tax Policy Center (TPC). "2013 Table T13–0099 Tax Benefit of All Itemized Deductions; Distribution of Federal Tax Change by Cash Income Percentile." Washington, DC: TPC, 2015.

The President's Advisory Panel on Federal Tax Reform. *Simple, Fair, and Pro-Growth: Proposals to Fix America's Tax System*, 2005.

The Washington Post. "Results." Washington Post–ABC News Poll, February 23, 2009.

The Washington Post, Henry J. Kaiser Family Foundation, and Harvard University. "Social Security Knowledge Poll I," February 9, 2005.

Tucker, Jasmine, Virginia Reno, and Thomas Bethell. "Strengthening Social Security: What Do Americans Want?" Washington, DC: National Academy of Social Insurance, January 2013.

USA Retirement Funds Act. S. 1979, 113th Congress (2013–2014).

US Bureau of Labor Statistics. *National Compensation Survey*. Washington, DC: US Department of Labor, 2013.

U.S. Census Bureau. "Income Data, Historical Tables, People, Table P-8, Age—People, All Races, by Median Income and Sex: 1947 to 2013." Washington, DC: US Census Bureau, 2014.

US Department of Housing and Urban Development (HUD), Office of Policy Development and Research. "Report to Congress on the Root Causes of the Foreclosure Crisis." Washington, DC: HUD, January 2010. http://www.huduser.org/portal/publications/Foreclosure_09.pdf

US Department of Labor, Employee Benefits Security Administration (EBSA). "Field Assistance Bulletin No. 2008–03." Washington, DC: EBSA, April 2008. http://www.dol.gov/ebsa/pdf/fab2008-3.pdf

———. "Regulation Relating to Qualified Default Investment Alternatives in Participant-Directed Account Plans." Fact Sheet. Washington, DC: EBSA, April 2008. http://www.dol.gov/ebsa/pdf/fsQDIA.pdf

US Department of the Treasury. "About myRA: Fact Sheet." Washington, DC: US Department of the Treasury, 2014. https://myra.treasury.gov/resources/myRA_About.pdf

US Government Accountability Office. "State and Local Government Retiree Benefits: Current Status of Benefit Structures, Protections, and Fiscal Outlook for Funding Future Costs." Washington, DC: GAO, 2007.

———. "Retirement Income, Ensuring Income throughout Retirement Requires Difficult Choices." Washington, DC: GAO, June 2011.

Valenti, Joe, and Christian Weller. "Creating Economic Security: Using Progressive Savings Matches to Counter Upside-Down Tax Incentives." CAP Issue Brief. Washington, DC: Center for American Progress, November 2013.

Vallas, Rebecca, Christian Weller, and Jackie Odum. "The Effect of Rising Inequality on Social Security." CAP Issue Brief. Washington, DC: Center for American Progress, February 2015. https://www.americanprogress.org/issues/economy/report/2015/02/10/106373/the-effect-of-rising-inequality-on-social-security/

VanDerhei, Jack. "Retirement Savings Shortfalls: Evidence from EBRI's Retirement Security Projection Model." EBRI Issue Brief No. 410. Washington, DC: Employee Benefits Research Institute, 2015.

———. "What Causes EBRI Retirement Readiness™ Ratings to Vary: Results from the 2014 Retirement Security Projection Model." EBRI Issue Brief No. 396. Washington, DC: Employee Benefits Research Institute, 2014.

VanDerhei, Jack, Sarah Holden, Luis Alonso, and Steven Bass. "401(k) Plan Asset Allocation, Account Balances, and Loan Activity in 2012." EBRI Issue Brief No. 394. Washington, DC: Employee Benefits Research Institute, 2013, and *Investment Company Institute Research Perspective* 19, no. 12 (December 2013). http://www.ebri.org/pdf/briefspdf/EBRI_IB_012-13.No394.401k-Update-2012.pdf

Waldron, Hilary. "Trends in Mortality Differentials and Life Expectancy for Male Social Security–Covered Workers, by Socioeconomic Status." *Social Security Bulletin* 67, no. 3 (2007): 1–28.

Warshawsky, Mark, and John Ameriks. "How Prepared Are Americans for Retirement?" In *Forecasting Retirement Needs and Retirement Wealth*, edited by Olivia S. Mitchell, P. Brett Hammond, and Anna M. Rappaport, 33–67. Philadelphia, PA: University of Pennsylvania Press, 2000.

Weller, Christian, E. "Building It Up, Not Tearing It Down." Washington, DC: Center for American Progress, 2010.

———. "Did Retirees Save Enough to Compensate for the Increase in Individual Risk Exposure." *Journal of Aging and Social Policy* 22, no. 2 (2010): 152–171.

———. "Ensuring Retirement Income Security with Cash Balance Plans." Washington, DC: Center for American Progress, September 2005.

———. "How Well Were Retirees Prepared for Retirement before the Great Recession?" *Journal of Aging and Social Policy* 22, no. 2 (2010): 95–98. doi:10.1080/08959421003621986

———. "Making Sure Money Is Available When We Need It." Washington, DC: Center for American Progress, March 2013.

———. "Need or Want: What Explains the Run-up in Consumer Debt?" *Journal of Economic Issues* 41, no. 2 (June 2007): 583–591.

———. "Protecting Retirement Wealth." *Challenge* 56, no. 4 (2013): 51–88. doi:10.2753/0577-5132560405

———. "PURE: A Proposal for More Retirement Income Security." *Journal of Aging and Social Policy* 19, no. 1 (2007): 21–38. doi:10.1300/J031v19n01_02

———. "Raising the Retirement Age for Social Security: Implications for Low Wage, Minority, and Female Workers." Washington, DC: Center for American Progress, 2005.

———. "Risky Business? Evaluating Market Risk of Equity Investment Proposals to Reform Social Security." *Journal of Policy Analysis and Management* 19, no. 2 (2000): 263–273. doi:10.1002/(SICI)1520–6688(200021)19:2<263::AID-PAM5>3.0.CO;2-H

———. "The Future of Public Pensions." *Cambridge Journal of Economics* 28, no. 4 (July 2004): 489–504.

Weller, Christian E., and Farah Z. Ahmad. "The Black and White Labor Gap in America." Christian Weller and Farah Z Ahmad, "The State of Communities of Color in the U.S. Economy: Still Feeling the Pain 4 Years into the Recovery." Washington, DC: Center for American Progress, 2013.

Weller, Christian E., and Dean Baker. "Smoothing the Waves of Pension Funding: Could Changes in Funding Rules Help Avoid Cyclical Under-Funding?" *The Journal of Policy Reform* 8, no. 2 (June 2005): 131–151.

Weller, Christian E., and Sara Bernardo. "Putting Retirement at Risk: Has Financial Risk Exposure Grown More Quickly for Older Households than Younger Ones?" Paper 102. Boston, MA: Gerontology Institute, University of Massachusetts–Boston, 2014.

Weller, Christian E., and Sara Bernardo. "Aging with Risk: Has Financial Risk Exposure Grown Faster for Older Households Since the 1990s?" *Journal of Aging and Social Policy*, forthcoming.

Weller, Christian E., and Ilana Boivie. "The Fiscal Crisis, Public Pensions, and Implications for Labor and Employment Relations." In *Impact of the Great Recession on Public Sector Employment, Labor and Employment Relations Research*, edited by Daniel Mitchell. Ithaca, NY: Cornell University Press, 2011.

Weller, Christian E., and Derek Douglas. "One Nation under Debt." *Challenge* 50, no. 1 (February 2007): 54–74.

Weller, Christian E., and Jaryn Fields. "The Black and White Labor Gap in America." CAP Issue Brief. Washington, DC: Center for American Progress, July 2011.

Weller, Christian E., and Amy Helburn. "States to the Rescue: Policy Options for State Government to Promote Private Sector Retirement Savings." *Journal of Pension Benefits* 18, no. 1 (2010): 37–47.

Weller, Christian E., and Shana Jenkins. "Building 401(k) Wealth One Percent at a Time: Fees Chip Away at People's Retirement Nest Eggs." Washington, DC: Center for American Progress, 2007.

Weller, Christian E., and Jessica Lynch. "Wealth in Freefall." Washington, DC: Center for American Progress, April 2009.

Weller, Christian E., and David Madland. "Keep Calm and Muddle Through." Washington, DC: Center for American Progress, 2014.

Weller, Christian E., and Kate Sabatini. "From Boom to Bust: Did the Financial Fragility of Homeowners Increase in an Era of Greater Financial Deregulation?" *Journal of Economic Issues* 42, no. 3 (2008): 607–632.

Weller, Christian E., and Sam Ungar. "Overhauling Federal Savings Incentives." *Tax Notes Today: Special Report* 42, no. 10 (March 2014).

———. "The Universal Savings Credit." Washington, DC: Center for American Progress, 2013.

Weller, Christian E., and Jeffrey Wenger. "Boon or Bane: 401(k) Loans and Employee Contributions." *Research on Aging* 36, no. 5 (July 2014): 527–556.

————. "Easy Money or Hard Times? Health and 401(k) Loans." *Contemporary Economic Policy* 30, no. 1 (January 2012): 29–42.

————. "What Happens to Defined Contribution Accounts When Labor Markets and Financial Markets Move Together?" *Journal of Aging and Social Policy* 21, no. 3 (2009): 256–276. doi:10.1080/08959420902733298

Weller, Christian E., and Edward Wolff. *Retirement Security: The Particular Role of Social Security.* Washington, DC: Economic Policy Institute, 2005.

Wenger, Jeffrey, and Christian E. Weller. "Fun with Numbers: Disclosing Risk to Individual Investors." *Research on Aging* 36, no. 5 (Spring 2011).

Wolff, Edward. "Household Wealth Inequality, Retirement Income Security, and Financial Market Swings 1983 to 2010." In *Inequality, Uncertainty and Opportunity: The Varied and Growing Role of Finance in Labor Relations*, edited by Christian E. Weller. Ithaca, NY: Cornell University Press, 2015.

————. "Recent Trends in Household Wealth in the United States: Rising Debt and the Middle-Class Squeeze—an Update to 2007." Working Paper Series No. 159. Annandale-on-Hudson, NY: Levy Economics Institute, 2010.

INDEX

401(k) plans
  auto-enrollment in
    (*see* auto-enrollment)
  emergence of, 2, 44, 78
  hardship withdrawal from, 122–3
  loans from, 123, 142–4
  safe-harbor plans, 105
  tax advantages of, 92, 103–5, 139
  value compared to Social Security, 48
  see also defined contribution plans;
    savings, forms of

annuities
  as counter to longevity risk, 53–4, 75,
    82–3, 156, 161, 183n21
  Social Security privatization
    proposals involving, 65–6 (*see*
    also Social Security, pitfalls of
    privatization)
  see also defined benefit pensions,
    self-annuitization
assets
  risky, 16, 21, 37, 168n13, 181n2
  risky asset concentration, 16–18,
    19–22, 30, 32–5, 36–7, 85–7
    (*see also* financial market risk
    exposure; risk exposure,
    demographic differences in)
  tax-advantaged (*see* tax-advantaged
    savings)
  see also debt to assets ratio

auto-enrollment, 10, 81, 102, 105,
  112, 116
  auto-IRA, 116 (*see also*
    Individual Retirement
    Accounts (IRAs))
  in defined benefit pensions vs.
    defined contribution plans, 102
  in state-sponsored retirement
    plans, 155
auto-escalation, 81, 105
auto-IRA, 116. *See also*
  Individual Retirement
  Accounts (IRAs)

behavioral economics, insights into
  savings behavior, 76–7, 122. *See*
  also diversification, psychological
  obstacles to; risk (actual),
  psychological obstacles to
  managing; savings, behavioral
  obstacles to
Brookings Institution, 47
business cycle, 90, 91–2, 96

Center for Retirement Research at
  Boston College (CRR), 45–7,
  50, 53
Coverdell Education Savings Account
  (ESA), 122, 124–5, 127, 139, 149.
  See also education, expense of
  children's

CPSIA information can be obtained
at www.ICGtesting.com
Printed in the USA
LVOW03*2129100316

478687LV00012B/52/P